THE HERITAGE OF AFRICAN POETRY

An anthology of oral
and written poetry

edited with an introduction
and notes by

ISIDORE OKPEWHO

Longman

Longman Group UK Limited,
Longman House, Burnt Mill, Harlow,
Essex CM20 2JE, England
and Associated Companies throughout the world.

First published 1985
Reprinted 1988

British Library Cataloguing in Publication Data

The Heritage of African poetry.
   1. African poetry—Translations into English
   2. English poetry—Translations from
African languages
   I. Okpewho, Isidore
   808.81′0096   PL8013.E5
   ISBN 0-582-72704-9

Library of Congress Cataloging in Publication Data

The Heritage of African poetry.
   Bibliography: p.
   Includes index.
   I. African poetry.   I. Okpewho, Isidore.
PL8011.H4   1985   808.81′0096   84-19360
ISBN 0-582-72704-9

Set in Lasercomp Spectrum

Illustrations by Henry Iles

Produced by Longman Group (FE) Ltd
Printed in Hong Kong

Acknowledgements

This anthology was completed during my year (1982–83) as a Woodrow Wilson Fellow at the Smithsonian Institution, Washington D.C. I wish to acknowledge my gratitude to the Board of Trustees of the Woodrow Wilson International Center for scholars for the unique opportunity and services offered me by the fellowship. I would particularly like to thank Amy Worden, my research assistant, for her professional diligence and good humour; and Bill Dunn, the Assistant Director for Administration, for the promptness of his secretarial staff.

We are grateful to the following for permission to reproduce copyright material:

Associated Book Publishers for the poems 'Post Mortem' and 'I Think it Rains' by Wole Soyinka, pp.31, 430 *Idandre and Other Poems* (Methuen, London); the author's agents and the author, Kofi Awoonor for the poems 'Kodzo the Imbecile' and 'Zanu's Death' pp.83–4, 59–60 *Guardians of the Sacred World* (New York, 1979), 'Songs of Abuse: i. to Stanislaus the Renegade' p.20 *Ride Me Memory*, 'Stop the Death Cry' p.62 *Night of my Blood*; Ernest Benn Ltd. for extracts from the songs 'A Mother to her First Born' and 'Rain Making Litany' from *The Lango: A Nilotic Tribe of Uganda* by J.H. Driberg; the author, Kwesi Brew for his poem 'A Plea for Mercy'; Cambridge University Press for the poems 'Love Song', 'The Sky' and 'The Well' pp.51, 64, 69 *African Poetry* ed. Ulli Beier(1966); the author, J.P. Clark Bekederemo for his poems 'Agbor Dancer', 'Ibadan', 'Streamside Exchange' and 'The Casualties'; The College Press (Pvt.) Ltd. for the extract 'Take up arms and Liberate Yourselves' pp.26–7 *Songs that Won the Liberation War* ed. A.J.C. Fongweni (1982); Rex Collings Ltd. for the poems 'I Anoint My Flesh (Tenth day of Fast)' by Wole Soyinka, p.19 *A Shuttle in the Crypt*; Dr C.G. Darah for the poem 'Independence' trans. in his Thesis, Ibadan Univ. 1982; East African Publishing House for the extract 'I am Ignorant of the Good World in the Clean Book' by Okot p'Bitek, pp.111–4 *Song of Lawino* (Nairobi, 1966), and the poems 'The People Went to War' by Antonio Jacinto and 'Militant's Poem' by Jorge Rebelo, pp. 93, 108 *When Bullets begin to Flower* ed. Margaret Dickinson (Nairobi, 1972); the author's agents for the poem 'Distanced' by J.C. Echeruo, p.13 *Distanced*, copyright Michael Echeruo; Editions Robert Laffont for the poem 'Dry Your Tears, Africa' by Bernard Dadié; Ghana Publishing Corporation for an extract from 'Elavanyo Concerto' by Atukwei Okai in *Lorgorligi Logarithms*; Heinemann Educational Books Ltd. for the poems 'Autumn Burns Me' by Lenrie Peters p.4 *Satellites*, 'Nightsong: Country', 'Abolish Laughter First' and 'Their Behaviour' by Dennis Brutus p.44, 128 *Letters to Martha* (1968), 'Where has my Love Blown his Horn?', 'If Death were not There' and 'Coward, Crawl Back' pp.40, 143, 103 *Horn of My Love* ed. Okot p'Bitek, 'Dear God' by Dennis Brutus p.67 *Stubborn Hope* (1979), 'Peasants' by Syl Cheyney-Coker in *The Graveyard has Teeth*, 'Issatou Died' by Lenrie Peters in *Selected Poetry*, 'When the Carnival Finally Closes' and 'The Sweet Brew at Chitakale' by Jack Mapanje pp.61, 23 *Of Chameleons and Gods*, 'With Purity hath Nothing been Won' by Taban lo Liyong p.12 *Another Nigger Dead* (1972), 'Yes, Mandela, we shall be moved' and 'For Melba' by Keorapetse Kgositsile p.95, 87 *Seven South African Poets* ed. C. Pieterse (1971), 'Martin Luther King' by Amin Kassam p.73 *Poems from East Africa* ed. Cook and Rubadiri (1971); Heinemann Educational Books Ltd and Editions du Seuil for the poem 'I Came With You ('For Khalam')' by Leopold Sedar Senghor, trans. in *Nocturnes* by Reed and Wake (1969); Heinemann Educational Books and Nwamife Publishers Ltd. for the poem 'The Odo-Masquerade' and an extract from the poem 'If we should all die' pp.39, 154 *Poetic Heritage: Igbo Traditional Verse* ed. R. Egudu and D. Nwoga (Nwanko-Ifijika, 1971); Indiana University Press for the poem 'Loser of Everything' by David Diop p.39 *David Diop, Hammer Blows and Other Writings* ed. Smpondo & Jones (Bloomington, 1973); International African Institute for the poem 'Nyagumbie!, Nyagumbie!' in the article 'A Chopi Love-Song and a Story in Ki-Lenge' by E. Dora Earthy, pp.475–7 *Africa 4.4* (1931); the author, Jonathan Kariara for his poem 'Vietnam' copyright J. Kariara; Kenya Literature Bureau for the poem 'Daybreak' by Susan Iwanga from *Pulsations*, and an extract from the poem 'Without You' by Oda Ofeimun; the authors, I.M. Lewis and B.W. Andrzejewski for the poem 'Poet's Lament on the Death of his Wife' pp.64–6 *Somali Poetry* (OUP); Longman Group Ltd. for the poems 'Armanda' and 'An Evening Libretto' by Jared Angira in *Cascades*

(Drumbeat), 'Easter Penitance' by Michael J.C. Echeruo, p.12 *Mortality*, 'The Stone Speaks' and 'Look at this Globe' by M.B. Zimunya *Thought Tracks* (Drumbeat); the author, Professor J.H. Kwabena Nketia for the poems 'Lament' pp.69–70 *Funeral Dirges of the Akan People* (Univ. College, Achimote 1955) and 'Drum Appeal' trans. by J.H.K. Nketia p.30 *Introduction to African Literature* (Longman); NOK Publishers International for extracts from 'Afa' and 'Evacuation' by Pol Ndu *Songs for Seers*; Dr Femi Osofisan for the author, Odia Ofeimun for the poem 'How Can I Sing' in *Opon Ifa vol 2, 1* (Oct., 1976); Oxford University Press for the extract 'Beginning of the White Bagre' pp. 121–2 *The Myth of the Bagre* by Jack Goody, copyright OUP 1972, and the poems 'Shaka' p.88f *Izibongo: Zulu Praise-Poems* ed. Trevor Cope, copyright OUP 1968, 'In Praise of the Ironsmith' from *Shona Praise Poetry* compiled by Aaron C. Hodza ed. and trans. by George Fortune, copyright OUP 1979, 'Relentlessly she drives me', 'Prayer to Masks', 'Taga for Mbaye Dyop' and 'Camp 1940' by Leopold Sedar, pp. 59, 9, 42, 39–40 *Selected Poems of Leopold Sedar Senghor* trans. John Reed and Clive Wake, copyright OUP 1964, 'A Warrior Sings His Praises' p.42f *The Heroic Recitations of the Bahima of Ankole* by H.F. Morris, copyright OUP 1964, 'Moshoeshoe' pp.71–2 *Lithoko: Sotho Praise-Poems* ed. and trans. M. Damane and P.B. Sanders, copyright OUP 1974, 'The Birth of Shaka' and 'Sunset' in *Sounds of a Cowhide Drum* by Oswald Mbuyiseni Mtshali, copyright M.O. Mtshali (1971), 'The Train' by B.M. Khaketha pp.150–1 *Heroic Poetry of the Basotho* by D.P. Kunene, copyright OUP 1971, 'On Companionship' p.185 *Swahili Poetry* by Lyndon Harries, copyright OUP 1962, 'Salute to Fabuni', 'The Baboon' and 'To Ogun' pp.210f, 172–4 *The Current and Form of Yoruba Ijala* by S.A. Babalola, copyright OUP 1966; Presence Africaine for the poem 'On Variety' from the article 'The Total Structure of Yoruba Poetry' *Presence Africaine 8–10* (1956); the author, Flavian Renaivo for his poem 'Choice'; Routledge & Kegan Paul plc for the poem 'The Army is Going to War' from *Social Institutions of the Kipsigis* by J.C. Peristiany (1964); the author, David Rubadiri for his poem 'An African Thunderstorm'; School of Oriental and African Studies for the extract 'Sunjata Summons His Generals' pp.63–71 *Sunjata: Three Mandinka Versions* by G. Innes (London, 1974) and the poems 'Fall of Kaabu' p.55f *Kaabu and Fuladu: Historical Narratives of the Gambian Mandinka* by G. Innes (London 1976), 'The Ballad of Aliyu' by C.G.B. Gidley from *Mantanfas: A Study in Oral Tradition*; Sidgewick and Jackson Ltd for an extract from *Ethiopia* by Sylvia Pankhurst; Arthur H. Stockwell Ltd for extract from the poem 'Young Africa's Plea' by Dennis Chukwude Osadebay from *Africa Sings*; Tanzania Publishing House for the poems 'I will Cling to your Garment' and 'What is Death Like?' by Eric S. Ng'maryo pp.147, 149 *Summons: Poems for Tanzania* ed. R.S. Mbala (1980), 'Bamako' in *Sacred Hope* trans. Marga Holness 1974; Andrew Tracey, International Library of African Music and the International African Institute for the poem 'Katini's Complaint' by Hugh Tracey, p.12 *Chopi Musicians* (London, 1948); University of Ife and the author, Professor Wande Abimbola for the poem 'The Lion Refused to Perform Sacrifice' pp.103–5 *Ifa Divination Poetry* (New York, 1977); University of Texas Press for the poem 'But for Death' in 'Iwi Chants – an Introduction' p.170 *Forms of Folklore in Africa* ed. Bernth Lindform, copyright 1977 The University of Texas Press (Austin); University of Zambia and the author Professor Mitchell for the poem 'The Cases' from *The Kalela Dance*; Dr Theo Vincent on behalf of *Black Orpheus* for the poems 'To the Anxious Mother' by Valente Malagatana & 'Love Apart' by Christopher Okigbo; Witwatersrand University Press for the poem 'The Earth does not get Fat' in the article 'Songs of the Ngoni People' by Margaret Read pp.14–5 *Bantu Studies 11* (1937) copyright Witwatersrand Univ. Press; Witwatersrand Univ. Press and the author Dr Sam Uzochukwu for the poem 'The Widow's Lament' in the article 'Igbo Elegiac Poetry' p.294 *African Studies 37,2* (1978), copyright Witwatersrand Univ. Press, Johannesburg.

We have unfortunately been unable to trace the copyright owners of 'Gbassey – Blades in Regiment' by Mukstarr Mustapha from *A Selection of African Poetry* ed. Senanu and Vincent (1976), 'On Truth' from *Kanuri Songs* by J.R. Patterson, Lagos (1926), 'Pedestrian to Passing Benz-Man' by Albert Ojuka from p.103 *Uhuru's Fire* by Adrian Roscoe (CUP, 1977), 'Heavensgate' by Christopher Okigbo from pp.3–4 *Labyrinths* (London, 1971), or the authors Amin Kassam and Keorapetse Kgoositsile, and would appreciate any information that would enable us to do so.

Contents

Acknowledgements

PART ONE **Introduction**

The nature of African oral poetry	3
The development of modern African poetry	11
Relationships between the oral and written poetry	20
On the selection and arrangement of poems	30
How to use the anthology	32

PART TWO **The anthology**

LOVE   37

1	Where has my love blown his horn? (*Acholi, Uganda*)	39
2	What a fool he is! (*Amhara, Ethiopia*)	39
3	I will satisfy my desire (*Bagirmi, Nigeria*)	40
4	Nyagumbe! Nyagumbe! (*Chopi, Mozambique*)	41
5	A mother to her first-born (*Lango, Uganda*)	43
6	Nightsong: Country *Dennis Brutus*	46
7	Dry your tears, Africa! *Bernard Dadié*	46
8	For Melba *Keorapetse Kgositsile*	47
9	To the anxious mother *Valente Malangatana*	48
10	I will cling to your garment *Eric S. Ng'maryo*	49
11	Without you *Odia Ofeimun*	49
12	Love apart *Christopher Okigbo*	50
13	Choice *Flavien Ranaivo*	50
14	I came with you *Léopold Sédar Senghor*	51
15	Relentlessly she drives me *Léopold Sédar Senghor*	52

PRAISE   53

16	A warrior sings his praises (*Bahima, Uganda*)	55
17	Ali, Lion of the World! (*Hausa, Nigeria*)	56
18	The odo-masquerade (*Igbo, Nigeria*)	58
19	In praise of the blacksmith (*Shona, Zimbabwe*)	60
20	Moshoeshoe (*Sotho, Lesotho*)	61
21	Salute to Fabunmi (*Yoruba, Nigeria*)	62
22	Shaka (*Zulu, South Africa*)	64
23	Agbor dancer *John Pepper Clark*	66
24	Martin Luther King *Amin Kassam*	67
25	The birth of Shaka *Oswald Mbuyiseni Mtshali*	68
26	Bamako *Agostinho Neto*	69
27	Elavanyo concerto *Atukwei Okai*	70
28	Taga for Mbaye Dyob *Léopold Sédar Senghor*	73

CRITICISM   75

29	Katini's complaint (*Chopi, Mozambique*)	77
30	Kodzo the imbecile (*Ewe, Ghana*)	78
31	Attack traders (*Igbo, Nigeria*)	79

32	Lamba courts (*Kelela, Zambia*)	80
33	The woes of independence (*Urhobo, Nigeria*)	81
34	Armanda *Jared Angira*	83
35	Songs of abuse: (i) To Stanislaus the renegade *Kofi Awoonor*	85
36	I am ignorant of the Good Word in the Clean Book *Okot p'Bitek*	86
37	Abolish laughter first, I say *Dennis Brutus*	89
38	Peasants *Syl Cheyney-Coker*	90
39	Loser of everything *David Diop*	91
40	Easter penitence *Michael J.C. Echeruo*	92
41	Yes, Mandela, we shall be moved *Keorapetse Kgositsile*	93
42	When this carnival finally closes *Jack Mapanje*	94
43	How can I sing? *Odia Ofeimun*	94
44	Pedestrian, to passing Benz-man *Albert Ojuka*	95
45	I anoint my flesh *Wole Soyinka*	96

THE ENVIRONMENT | | 97 |

46	The sky (*Ewe, Ghana*)	99
47	The train (*Sotho, Lesotho*)	99
48	The baboon (*Yoruba, Nigeria*)	100
49	Ibadan *John Pepper Clark*	102
50	Daybreak *Susan Lwanga*	102
51	The sweet brew at Chitakale *Jack Mapanje*	103
52	Sunset *Oswald Mbuyiseni Mtshali*	104
53	Autumn burns me *Lenrie Peters*	104
54	An African thunderstorm *David Rubadiri*	105
55	I think it rains *Wole Soyinka*	107
56	The stone speaks *M.B. Zimunya*	108

REFLECTION | | 109 |

57	On truth (*Kanuri, Nigeria*)	111
58	The well (*Susu, Guinea*)	111
59	On companionship (*Swahili, Kenya*)	112
60	Life's variety (*Yoruba, Nigeria*)	113
61	The lion refused to perform sacrifice (*Yoruba, Nigeria*)	113
62	An evening libretto *Jared Angira*	115
63	Their behaviour *Dennis Brutus*	116
64	Streamside exchange *John Pepper Clark*	117
65	With purity hath nothing been won *Taban lo Liyong*	118
66	Look at this globe *M.B. Zimunya*	118

APPEAL | | 119 |

67	Drum appeal (*Akan, Ghana*)	121
68	Rain-making litany (*Lango, Uganda*)	122
69	The White Bagre (*LoDagaa, Ghana*)	123
70	To Ogun (*Yoruba, Nigeria*)	127
71	A plea for mercy *Kwesi Brew*	129
72	Dear God *Dennis Brutus*	130
73	Afa (before Chukwu at dusk) *Pol Ndu*	131
74	Heavensgate: (i) the passage *Christopher Okigbo*	132
75	Young Africa's plea *Dennis Chukwude Osadebay*	133
76	Prayer to masks *Léopold Sédar Senghor*	134

WAR   135
77 Coward, crawl back! (*Acholi, Uganda*)   137
78 The army is going to war (*Kipsigis, Kenya*)   137
79 Sunjata summons his generals (*Mandinka, Gambia*)   139
80 The fall of Kaabu (*Mandinka, Gambia*)   144
81 Take up arms and liberate yourselves (*Shona, Zimbabwe*)   147
82 The casualties *John Pepper Clark*   148
83 The people went to war *Antonio Jacinto*   150
84 Vietnam *Jonathan Kariara*   151
85 Evacuation *Pol Ndu*   153
86 A militant's poem *Jorge Rebelo*   154
87 Camp 1940 *Léopold Sédar Senghor*   155

DEATH   157
88 If death were not there (*Acholi, Uganda*)   159
89 Mother! Mother! (*Akan, Ghana*)   160
90 Zanu's death (*Ewe, Ghana*)   161
91 Widow's lament (*Igbo, Nigeria*)   162
92 The earth does not get fat (*Ngoni, Malawi*)   162
93 Poet's lament on the death of his wife (*Somali, Somalia*)   164
94 But for death (*Yoruba, Nigeria*)   165
95 Stop the death-cry *Kofi Awoonor*   166
96 Distanced *Michael J. C. Echeruo*   167
97 Gbassay – blades in regiment *Mukhtarr Mustapha*   167
98 What is death like? *Eric S. Ng'maryo*   168
99 Isatou died *Lenrie Peters*   169
100 Post mortem *Wole Soyinka*   170

PART THREE **Notes and questions**   171

PART FOUR **About the poets**   269

Index of first lines   277

For Ngozi, B. O. C., Stanley, T. O. T.,
Kodit, Godfrey and George

PART ONE
Introduction

This anthology has two principal aims. The first is to introduce students of African poetry to the major topics which have occupied the attention of African poets whatever their medium of expression. Consequently, every poem in this anthology is accompanied by detailed explanations designed to bring out not only *what* the poet is trying to say but *how* he is doing so. In expressing himself, every poet endeavours to borrow ideas not only from the common human experience but also from the environment that he is familiar with. Since Africa is a very diverse continent ethnically, historically and geographically, it is necessary to provide notes that will help the student understand how this variety of factors is reflected in the major topics or issues that the poets have constantly addressed themselves to.

The second and perhaps more important aim of this anthology is to give the oral traditional poetry of Africa its deserved place both in the literature curriculum and in our general understanding of what poetry tries to do. A good deal of interest has been shown in this poetry within the last few decades. It has been collected and translated by many scholars, some with greater skill and understanding than others; a few modern African poets, anxious to return to their culture and show the world that they come from a respectable cultural background, have used ideas and techniques from the oral tradition in writing their works; and in more recent times this form of literature has received nearly as much serious study as the written one in institutions of higher learning not only in Africa but outside it. The time has therefore come for us to stop treating oral poetry as something unfamiliar or inferior to the written variety. One way to correct the situation is to examine how poets in both traditions have handled the same issues in their various ways. But, first, let us try to understand how oral poetry works so as to appreciate the basis of the modern poet's relationship to it.

The nature of African oral poetry

There used to be a widely-held view – especially among European anthropologists who studied African societies in the nineteenth and early twentieth centuries – that there was nothing of true poetic merit in African oral literature. Poetry, these scholars argued, is a mark of an advanced culture or civilisation and the business of men of specialised skill and training who devote their time to observing and commenting on life with beauty and seriousness. Traditional African societies were, in their view, still groping in the dark with elementary problems of existence and had not yet attained the level of achievement whereby men could indulge in the pursuit of poetic excellence; besides, their languages were not yet sufficiently developed to cope with the complex techniques of poetic expression. For a long time, the study of traditional African literature was done by these foreign scholars who had very little feeling for the languages and customs that they met. Some of them did, of course, try to understand the basic grammatical systems of the languages and even learnt some patterns of speech; but their understanding of these languages could not be compared to that of native speakers for whom the words have meanings and implications that go far beyond the ordinary patterns of sound. Within the past three decades, African scholars have undertaken to collect and present samples of their people's poetry to the outside world. Because these native scholars have a much better feeling for the languages in which this poetry has been composed, their publications have succeeded in revealing to us the high poetic skill of the composers of the poetry.

Who are these traditional African poets? There are many situations in which poetry was, and still is, spoken or sung in traditional African society, and it would be better for us to see the poets within the contexts in which they operate. Some of these situations are somewhat restricted in the sense that the poet is charged with chanting a specific type of poetry and would need to have undergone a formal training for the purpose. Poets in this category could be found in the royal courts of communities ruled by kings, or else attached to wealthy or powerful men in societies dominated by privileged men. Among the Mandinka of western Africa, the *griot* was traditionally a court poet attached to the king for the purpose of singing the king's glories and recording in his songs important historical events surrounding the ruling family. The same duty was performed among the Ashanti of Ghana by the court poet known as *kwadwumfo*; among the Rwanda of central Africa such a poet was called an *umusizi*; among the Zulu of southern Africa, the *imbongi* (praise-singer) traditionally played that role; and so forth. Another kind of restricted context in which we find poets of a highly specialised nature is the ritual. Notable examples of such poets (some of whose poetry is represented in this anthology under *Appeal*) are the *bo netuuri* (speakers) at the Bagre initiation ceremony among the LoDagaa of northern Ghana, and the *babalawo* (diviners) among the Yoruba of Nigeria.

One of the distinguishing marks of poets in this restricted category is that in most cases they attain their position after a rather long period of formal training. Some of this training takes place within the family which has traditionally played the artistic role and in which it is understood that a son would succeed his father in the task; in such a situation the young man attends his father very closely from early youth and is instructed as often as necessary on the appropriate idioms of the art as well as the strict processes. This was the case with the *griots* in the old monarchical days, and is still very much the case with the *babalawo* today. Indeed, the training was sometimes so well organised that there was a specific school or association set up for the purpose of training young men in the skills of the specialised poetry: in Rwanda the *umutwe w'abasizi* (association of court poets) was made up of families officially recognised for the task of singing court poetry, with a president (*intebe*) at its head.

Among other things, these poets are trained to handle some of the rather delicate tasks peculiar to their profession. The king is glorified with exaggerated images appropriately chosen to swell his pride and give him a high sense of his ancestry. If, however, he suffers any failure in war or commits an unwise act of leadership, the court poet takes care to choose words of caution or blame that would not earn him the anger of the king. In the case of the diviner, he requires some imaginative skill to manipulate the recognised verses of his chant around the special problems brought to him by various clients. It used to be assumed that because these forms of poetry were handed down from father to son or from one generation to another, there were no changes or differences between one version of a chant and another. But more recent study has shown that even in these more restricted forms of traditional poetry the poet still has to depend on his imagination as he is called upon to perform the same texts in a variety of occasions.

A second and more widely-spread category of oral poet is the freelance entertainer, whose work is not tied to such narrow situations as the king's court or the diviner's consultation room. This is the kind of poet who relies on his skill at singing or chanting traditional poems to earn him some material rewards wherever possible. Such a performer usually has other kinds of work that he does on a more or less steady basis, and only uses his poetic art to supplement his living. Even if he does his open performances on a

5

more regular basis, he is nevertheless a free agent whose work is not tied to a king or a cult.

One situation in which such a freelance poet may be commonly found is at a place where there is some form of merrymaking. The performer may or may not be invited to the ceremony; in many cases he has heard that there is a party somewhere (a wedding, a child-naming ceremony, a house-warming party, etc.), and he simply picks up his instruments and goes there, alone or with a group. Among the Yoruba of Nigeria this sort of situation is quite common: you would be dancing or drinking with your friends at a party, when suddenly a drummer turns up at your side to sing your praises and wish you blessings with his music. Another situation where the freelance poet operates is at a funeral ceremony. In many traditional African communities a professional or skilled mourner is often welcome (again, he or she may or may not be specifically invited) because his well-chosen songs of sorrow enhance the solemnity of the occasion. Quite often the singer celebrates the ancestors of the aggrieved person in his songs, so that the latter feels a considerable sense of pride compensating his loss in no small way. The Gambian poet Lenrie Peters makes a reference to such paid mourners in his poem *Isatou died* (no. 99 in this anthology); another good example of such a professional mourner is the *nyatiti* (harp) singer among the Luo of Kenya. Perhaps a final kind of freelance poet is the wayside musician — whether a handicapped person or an able-bodied opportunist. Since his entire livelihood depends on his art, the wayside musician has to summon his imagination so as to affect the passer-by with sufficient sympathy or delight.

Understandably, the training and preparation of the free-lance poet is not as formal or regulated as that of the poet in the more restricted environments treated above. In most cases the individual simply attaches himself to an accomplished poet — who may be a relative or a family friend — becoming a member of his household and doing odd jobs for him while he gradually picks up the skill in singing songs and playing the musical instrument that accompanies them. Alternatively, a naturally talented person may just watch an experienced performer over a long period, listening closely to his skilful control of words and rhythms as well as his handling of the instrument; he could then construct his own instrument and practise quietly that skilful combination of words and music. In whatever way he learns the art of oral poetry, the freelance performer is perhaps much freer in his use of the text of his songs than the performer in a restricted context. Take the mourner or the praise-singer at the party. He already has a set of phrases which he regularly uses either for praising or for mourning people. He simply needs to fit the names, the status, the career or the attributes of the new subject in the proper places, and that will serve him well for the occasion. This is not to say that the job is easy. It takes a considerable effort as well as skill to master the technique of adjustment; this is the skill that he picks up during the period of informal training.

Why do we use the word *poets* to describe these performers in the oral tradition — what is so poetic about their work? To understand this, we must abandon the false assumption that poetry necessarily has to do with words or the order in which they are arranged. A group of measured lines which describes a situation is simply *verse*, and may have very little that is poetic about it. On the other hand, it is possible for a combination of music and movement (dance) in a performance that has no words at all to be described as very *poetic*, due to the sheer force that we feel while observing it. The essence of true poetry therefore lies in its power to appeal strongly to our appreciation and, in a sense, lift us up. There are basically two ways in which a piece of poetry can appeal to us. One is by touching us emotionally, so that we feel either pleasure or pain; the other is by stirring our minds deeply so that we reflect on some aspect of life or some significant idea. To understand how poetry can achieve this power, however, we have to examine the situation or process within which it is created.

As far as the oral tradition is concerned, we cannot properly understand the songs (such as we have in this anthology) unless we can direct our minds toward the actual performance of them. These songs are not written to be read but are chanted openly for an audience (whether limited or large) to appreciate with their eyes and their ears. In many ways, an oral poetry performance may be usefully compared to a modern stage play, in which a performer has to support his words with the right movement of his body or control of his voice so as to make an effective impression. Take the Igbo poem *Attack traders* (no. 31), which condemns the behaviour of some married women towards their husbands during the Nigerian civil war. In the last line of the song, we are told how at the end of the war these irresponsible women become so powerless that they are forced to come begging before the same husbands they had been treating with contempt. The change of attitude here — from arrogance to submission — is so striking that the performer

7

necessarily adopts an appropriate tone of singing as well as facial expression so as to bring out the humiliation contained in that last line. Add to all this the fact that the music at this point may be either softened or stopped completely so as to emphasise the statement, and you can see what a striking difference there is between reading the words on the printed page and seeing them actually performed by a dance group.

This is poetry which affects us with delight: we are impressed by the performer's effective imitation of the humiliated wife in these words, and we end up laughing. We can see a parallel effect when we consider the poetry that conveys sorrow. Take the Ewe poem *Zanu's death* (no. 90). The poem is sufficiently touching and impressive as it stands, with the images of the ram, the boat that crosses the final river, death as a plunderer of the field of life, and the various other symbols with which the poet paints the picture of the finality of death. But watch the old man as he intones those lines, his face drawn and his head shaking at the appropriate moments, and you can appreciate how much more moving the poem is in performance than on the printed page.

Oral poetry achieves its forcefulness not only at the hands of the performer himself. Part of this forcefulness comes from the participation of various persons (present at the scene of perform-ance) in the creative act taking place. Albert B. Lord has said in his significant book *The Singer of Tales* that 'an oral poem is not composed *for* but *in* performance.' Part of what Lord means is that a piece of song achieves its true poetic life not in the text which the singer has in his mind before he begins his performance, but in the version of it which he is made to present by the circumstances surrounding his performance. One of these factors which helps the creative act at the scene of performance may be the performer's colleague − his apprentice perhaps − who accompanies him and probably plays a musical instrument for him. Take the Gambian Mandinka piece here entitled *Sunjata summons his generals* (no. 79), which is part of a long narrative poem about the exploits of the legendary Mandinka ruler, Sunjata. In line 100 the narrator's accompanist, Amadu, persuades him to enumerate some of the descendants of one of Sunjata's generals, Tira Makhang. Since many families in the Gambia apparently trace their descent from Tira Makhang, there are likely to be some members of the singer's audience (in an open performance of this poem) who would feel *lifted up* at the mention of their family. Although many of us as readers have no direct connection with that society, we would have a better view of the poetic merit of that poem if we understood this background to the inclusion of many lines there.

Another interesting example may be seen in the Igbo self-praising poem *The odo-masquerade* (no. 18). Part of the appeal of this tradition of masquerade poetry is that the words are chanted at considerable speed and that the self-praising performer makes as many claims as possible. In this particular poem, there would seem to be someone copying down the words of the performer at some speed. When the performer tells us, toward the end of the poem, that 'The copyist cannot pick up/All that flows from my mouth, what I am singing,' it is obvious that the presence of the copyist has made him all the more conscious of the demand on him to show how fast he can chant. The atmosphere of competition creates a certain excitement among the observing audience, which is a credit to the poetic quality of such a performance.

Some of the emotional delight that we get from oral poetry comes from the musical quality that is contained in the song or chant. There are two kinds of music which we generally hear in the performance of oral poetry. One of these is the instrumental music – of drums, strings, wooden gongs, rattles, even hand-clapping or foot-stamping – that accompanies the songs. The value of this accompaniment is not only that it helps to regulate the words of the song into measured movement, but also that it inspires in both singer and audience a general enjoyment which results in several lines of passages being sung over and over again. Many repetitions (of whole lines or parts of them) that we find in the printed texts of oral poetry look redundant or ridiculous, but their usefulness may become clear to us if we enquire carefully into the circumstances from which they come. Examples of such repetition in this anthology may be found in the Acholi love song (no. 1), the Akan drum appeal (no. 67), the Kipsigi war chant (no. 78), and several others. Repetition is also used for emphasising a very significant point or a pressing need, as in the Lango rain chant (no. 68); but it is basically the product of the sort of emotional excitement that music inspires.

The other kind of music we hear in oral poetry is vocal or tonal. This vocal music may be seen in many respects, and I think we can go to Yoruba oral poetry for two rather useful examples. For instance, in the performance of Yoruba hunters' poetry, *ijala* (examples of which we have in numbers 21, 48, 70), the chanter usually adopts a high trembling tone, the effect of which is to provide the right pace and level of excitement for the words which

9

are chanted at some speed. An even more effective use of vocal music can be seen in the technique whereby the poet makes tonal changes on a word. There is an interesting example of this in a piece of Yoruba divination poetry (*ifa*) collected by the expert in this field, Professor Wande Abimbola of the University of Ife. This is a story about a soothsayer who, on his visit to a town, is confronted by a mob of merrymakers at a wedding and asked to explain his mission in the town. The soothsayer, anxious to win the favour of the crowd, begins his explanation by showering blessings on the citizens of the town and especially on the bride:

> She will deliver many children.
> The wife will live to be old like Oluyẹyẹntuyẹ.
> The wife will be as old as Oluyẹyẹntuyẹ.

Oluyeyentuye, as Abimbola explains, is a Methuselah of Yoruba oral tradition; the soothsayer (as, of course, the performer) in varying the accents on that name has succeeded in emphasising the long life which he wishes for the bride. In the end he is released by the mob; likewise, the performer has given a good account of himself as a poet. This effective poetic use of vocal music is possible because Yoruba, like many African languages, is a highly tonal language, and this quality works to the advantage of the oral poet in performance.

In these various ways, therefore, African oral poetry satisfies one of the basic requirements of all poetry, which is to touch us emotionally so that we feel either delight or pain. Some elements of the actual performance — i.e. the way in which others, such as the accompanist, or audience, participate in the creation of poetry — have been emphasised, not because there is no poetic value in the words themselves, but because in this tradition 'the bare words,' as Ruth Finnegan has said in her book, *Oral Literature in Africa*, 'can *not* be left to speak for themselves.' Otherwise, if we look closely enough at what the oral poet is saying, we will find numerous examples of the kind of imaginative quality which we have been taught to recognise in modern poetry. Take the Sotho poet's praise to King Moshoeshoe (no. 20): so desperate is his enemy Tyopho to escape the plundering 'hyena' (Moshoeshoe) that he tries to defend himself 'with a baby's cradle-skin'! Or take the Yoruba poet's description of the baboon (no. 48): the hunter's crouching to take aim at the animal is seen in the light of a man prostrating before his father-in-law. Or the Mandinka poet's description of the bloody fighting around the walls of Kaabu (no. 80):

You would plunge into human blood up to your knees;
Blood was soaking the walls and they were collapsing.

All these suggest that, quite apart from the peculiar techniques that he employs in the oral performance, the African oral poet is just as capable as his modern counterpart of painting powerful mental pictures by his use of words.

This appeal to our imagination brings us finally to the second major business of poetry: that of stirring our minds deeply so that we think intelligently on some concept or aspect of life. Again, there are various ways in which this can happen. The section on *Reflection* includes some oral poems which discuss, with seriousness and depth, some of the fundamental problems of life. The Susu poem entitled *The well* (no. 58) is a deceptively simple piece which analyses the contents of the human head more from a psychological than from a biological point of view. No. 61 is an *ifa* divination chant which – somewhat in the style of a parable – uses a myth to treat a philosophical issue: the conflict between human will and chance. Even poems that do not treat directly philosophical issues sometimes demand that we make an effort to find the connection between the various images used: this, in a sense, is what happens when we hear the Igbo masquerade poet (no. 18) describe himself variously as a bird, a tripod, a gong, a thorny weed, etc. We should bear in mind that poetry like this helps the traditional society to teach its youth to acquire a sharpness of wit – by reciting a variety of ideas all centred on the same theme. Although the poem comes in the form of a high-spirited performance, the ideas that it carries will remain in the minds of the audience long after the performance is over.

The development of modern African poetry

The coming of Europeans and other foreigners to Africa drastically reduced the importance of the traditional African poet in the communication of ideas in the society. Both in the royal households and among the general population, the story was the same. In the royal courts of the ancient Mandinka kingdoms, the *griot* not only recounted heroic deeds of the olden days so as to persuade the ruling king not to fall short of expectations, but he also instructed the prince on the culture and traditions of his society so that when the time came for him to rule he would be properly equipped. But when the old African kingdoms became subject to European colonial power, many kings sent their princes to the white man's country to learn, partly because it seemed such a prestigious thing to do and partly because the future seemed to belong to those trained in the white man's culture. Among the general population, the youths drifted steadily away from entertainments where they used to derive much of their cultural education. They were taught in some mission schools that following masquerades was pagan worship, and even they gradually began to look upon masquerades as dirty and unfashionable.

Traditional culture – and those like the oral poet who sustained it for a long time – no longer appealed to the younger generation. What attracted them now was European education and culture. And it was not enough to receive all this in Africa: for the African youth in the colonial period, the highest mark of achievement was to secure a passage overseas (whether through a legitimate scholarship or by 'stowing away' in a ship) to study in England, France, or the United States of America. It was from among these African students in Europe and America that many of the first or 'pioneer' African poets emerged.

They were not, of course, the first such talented Africans to set foot on foreign soil. Some had been taken away in previous centuries as slaves at a tender age and were later to astonish their white audiences with their literary skill, writing everything from poetry and drama to autobiography and anti-slavery propaganda. Since these writers, at the time of enslavement, were too young to appreciate the virtues of their African culture, their relationship to this culture was fundamentally weak and at best romantic; many saw the European culture into which they had been forced as naturally superior and were apologetic about their race.

Let us take three examples, all of them from West Africa. Juan Latino (1516–94) was taken away at the age of twelve to Spain and spent his life mostly in the service of noble families. His poems, which were written in Latin (the educated language of that period), were mostly in praise of the king of Spain (Philip II) and the reigning pope Pius V, and filled with Christian sentiments. The image of Africa in Latino's poetry is not very strong; in fact, one of his poems praising Philip he prays that 'The barbarous people will be converted both in body and mind and will obey Christ.' Phillis Wheatley was taken to America at the age of seven or eight, and made a deep impression on her American readers as a marvellous genius. The following unfortunate poem is the only place where she mentions Africa in her entire volume of poetry:

> 'Twas mercy brought me from my pagan land,
> Taught my benighted soul to understand
> That there's a God, that there's a Saviour too:
> Once I redemption neither sought nor knew,
> Some view our sable race with scornful eye,
> 'Their colour is a diabolic dye.'
> Remember, Christians, Negroes, black as Cain,
> May be refin'd, and join th' angelic train.

Olaudah Equiano (born in Nigeria in 1745) was taken away when he was aged twelve, first to America and the West Indies and later to England where he achieved prominence as an advocate of the abolition of slavery. He was one of the few slaves to retain a loyal memory of his African origins, vividly recounted in his autobiographical works. But his picture of the African homeland was mostly romantic and, as with the other writers, filled with religious sentiments. His long poem, reflecting on his life since

> When taken from my native land,
> by an unjust and cruel band

is appropriately titled *Miscellaneous Verses or Reflections on the State of my mind during my first Convictions: of the Necessity of believing the Truth and experiencing the inestimable Benefits of Christianity.*

The real beginnings of modern (i.e., written) African poetry may be traced to the 'pioneer' verse written during the colonial period. To understand the background to that verse we must look briefly at the cultural situation in the colonies ruled by Britain and France, the two principal colonial powers. The British taught their language and their culture in schools run by them. Although the missionaries in the British colonies discouraged certain indigenous African customs as 'pagan,' the colonial government did not force their culture on the Africans and certainly did not formally tamper with the cultural identity of the Africans. The situation was somewhat different in the French colonies. In addition to teaching their language and culture in the schools, the French tended to degrade the African cultural identity by upholding French culture as the highest level of human attainment. This attitude was institutionalised in the policy of *assimilation* that was pursued by them in Senegal, their first West African colony. Here the French effectively divided the citizenship in two: those who were born in a few select towns (Dakar, St. Louis, Gorée, and Rufisque) were automatically considered French citizens, while those born anywhere else in the country were classed as *indigènes* with inferior rights. For a long time many francophone Africans bitterly resented, and opposed, this ugly distinction between Africans in their homeland.

Two kinds of poetry were written by Africans during the colonial period. Those who were educated at home by colonial teachers took advantage of their newly acquired skills and tried their hands at verse-making. In Madagascar, for instance, Jean-Joseph Rabearivelo wrote a considerable amount of French verse and created a literary circle around himself. In Nigeria some newspapers like *The African Messenger, The Nigerian Advocate, The Yoruba News,* and *The Dawn* encouraged the new poetry by featuring various pieces in their columns. There were also literary circles like the Onitsha Literary Club, formed by Nnamdi Azikiwe and his colleagues and supported by a British poet-trader by the name of John Murray Stuart-Young, in which a good deal of verse was written. This home-grown African poetry was on the whole inconsequential. The writers cherished their newly acquired medium of expression and were mostly satisfied with imitating the European poets (many of them obsolete) that they had been exposed to. Their poetry was mostly immature and politically 'safe', as may be seen in Azikiwe's *Third Class Clerk* (1925) in which the poet reflects

> Tomorrow is our pay day,
> But I am not concerned;
> The greedy sharks will be at bay
> To grab what I had earned —
> With ten per cent along!

Rabearivelo himself devoted much of his early verse to imitating French models; indeed his love of French culture was so strong that in 1937 he committed suicide when the colonial officials persistently blocked his attempts to go to France.

The poetry written by Africans who had gone to study in the white man's land (or had returned home thereafter) was, however, considerably different. Here we begin to encounter a real objection to the colonial presence and the consequent insult to the dignity of the black man. Whatever injustice the young African may have suffered at home under the colonial administration was nothing compared to what he found in the white man's land; here he was blatantly treated as an inferior being, long after slavery was declared officially illegal. Of the 'pioneer' anglophone poets, it is true that some were not very hostile to Britain in their work; for instance, the Nigerian Dennis Osadebay, although he had nationalist feelings, wrote certain embarrassing pieces of verse like *Africa Speaks to England* which begins 'England,/I love you and I fight for you,' and others like the Ghanaian Gladys Casely-Hayford and Michael Dei-Anang wrote a good deal of romantic verse idealising Africa. But some of these were at least meant to present Africa in a positive light, as against the low esteem in which the white man held it. Other anglophone poets, however, did not hesitate to use strong language. The racial issue was very pronounced in the poetry of the Ghanaian Raphael E.G. Armattoe, as may be seen in the following lines from his volume entitled *Deep Down the Black Man's Mind* (1950):

> Our God is black:
> Shout it from the forests
> from the hills to the woodlands
> Let the woodlands re-echo
> Our God is black.

And even Azikiwe, generally driven by a sense of justice, shows his fierceness in the following lines from a poem titled *Lynching* (1930):

> The beast cares not
> What harm he does,
> So long in passion, blind,
> He's satisfied.
>
> What does he care
> So long he's white?
> The action of the mob
> Approves his crime.

The level of hostility to white culture was nevertheless higher in francophone African poetry. The French had long upheld the equality (*egalité*) and brotherhood (*fraternité*) of man as the ideals on which their nation was founded since their revolution (1789); they had also advertised French culture as the highest mark of excellence and brought their colonies to look up to it. Unfortunately, the Africans who went to study in France saw for themselves the emptiness of the deliberate colonial policy to make Frenchmen out of them and of the dream of enjoying a cultural brotherhood with fellow intellectuals among the Europeans.

Paris, the French capital, had a particular significance. London was a political and cultural metropolis only for those who went to the United Kingdom. But for many centuries Paris has been the cultural capital of the entire European world and here one could find a colony of writers and intellectuals from Britain, the United States of America, Germany and other European nations. There were also a handful of black writers and intellectuals from various French colonies in both Africa and the West Indies. In Paris these blacks discovered that their European colleagues were not quite prepared to consider them as equals whether socially or intellectually. They therefore found themselves united by a common feeling of being Negro 'exiles' in Paris. Prominent among this group were Leon Gontran Damas of French Guyana, Aimé Césaire of Martinique, and Léopold Sédar Senghor of Senegal. Of the three, Damas was perhaps the most vehement in his condemnation of the violence done by France to the ancestral African culture and in his projection of the black personality, as may be seen in his volume *Pigments* (Paris, 1937). In 1939 Césaire coined the term *négritude* as an ideology for those committed to project the black personality and culture. But it is Senghor who in several volumes of poetry and essays has done most to give this ideology a solid foundation and set the tone for francophone poetry generally.

The principal themes and images of negritude are all present in Senghor's poetry. One of these is the glorification of African customs, African traditions, and the African landscape. Where the Europeans spoke of these with contempt, the negritude poet turned the tables and saw them as beautiful: like the ancestral masks and the rhythmic quality of African music in *Prayer to masks* (no. 76), the evocative picture of grain-huts in the twilight in *I came with you* (no. 14), the moonlit darkness of the African night in *Relentlessly she drives me* (no. 15), or the imagined 'white savannahs and unending sands' of *Camp 1940* (no. 87). Another theme in negritude is the intense admiration of the colour black. In numerous poems by Senghor the word *black* is mentioned either in its own terms or in the context of other colours, especially white, with the deliberate aim of emphasising its beauty; in many cases this beauty is conveyed by the image of a black woman, so much so that in Senghor's poetry a beautiful black woman is invariably a symbol of the African race and culture. But perhaps the most striking note in negritude poetry is its condemnation of the damage and injustice done by the white race to the black, and also its exposure of the decline of white civilisation. The former theme is present to some extent in *Camp 1940* while the latter may be seen in *Prayer to masks*. All these issues and images were intended as contributions to the defence of black culture and the African continent in its struggle, during the first half of this century, for liberation from European dominance.

However, despite his challenge to white culture, Senghor was ultimately in favour of peace and conciliation. He conceived of a world in which black and white would live in harmony; as we can see in *Prayer to masks*, he was anxious that African culture (with its spiritual qualities) should join hands with European culture to save human civilisation from total collapse. Although his colleague Léon Damas opposed the enlistment of black soldiers in the 1939–45 war against Hitler, Senghor felt it was a just cause in which the black race had a stake (see his heroic treatment of black soldiers in *Camp 1940*). Not all negritude African poets, however, took such a polite view of the relationship between white and black. In the poetry of David Diop, a Senegalese poet who died rather early, there is a much stronger feeling of confrontation between Africa and Europe: his contribution here, *Loser of everything* (no. 39), which exposes the crime of colonisation, is mild compared with some of his other poems.

The situation in other African nations ruled by European powers like Spain and Portugal was much worse – people were treated far more inhumanly and the traditional culture was more severely suppressed – and the little amount of poetry that managed to get published shows evidence of the seriousness of this situation. Jorge Rebelo's *A militant's poem* (no. 86) reveals the desperate and defiant attitude of the average young man to the colonial authority in Portuguese-held Mozambique. And part of the reason that Agostinho Neto uses the images of life and growth so persistently in his poem *Bamako* (no. 26) is that the Portuguese colonial system was equally persistent in suppressing those privileges in his native country.

However, between 1957 and 1967 a large number of African nations won political independence from Britain and France, and it is interesting to see what kind of poetry has been written in the continent since Africans took control of their own affairs. One significant development in post-independence African poetry has been that the anglophone and francophone writers, who seemed earlier on to have adopted slightly different attitudes and techniques, are now united in just about everything but the language used. For instance, very few of the pre-independence anglophone poets studied literature at a level serious enough for them to be acquainted with the modern trends and techniques in poetry: Osadebay studied law, Azikiwe graduated in the social sciences,

Raphael Armattoe of Ghana and Abioseh Nicol of Sierra Leone studied medicine, and so on. The result was that some of these poets used forms and idioms of the English language – such as 'thou cometh', or 'what ails thee' – that were no longer current in the best poetry written at the time. On the contrary, since the French policy of assimilation aimed consciously to make Frenchmen out of Africans, there was an emphasis on cultural education; consequently, the pre-independence francophone poets were already in touch with the best and latest that French poetry had to offer. Senghor himself studied literature and culture (and taught in French schools), and other poets like Jean-Joseph Rabearivelo of Madagascar and Felix Tchicaya U Tam'si of Congo-Brazzaville were as deeply influenced as Senghor was by the modern techniques that were to be found in French poetry.

But many of today's anglophone poets – such as Cheyney-Coker of Sierra Leone; Awoonor and Okai of Ghana; Clark, Soyinka, Okigbo, Echeruo and Ndu of Nigeria; Rubadiri of Malawi: p'Bitek of Uganda; Brutus of South Africa – have not only studied literature but taught it at higher levels, and have therefore written poetry that matches the francophone one in technical quality. Whereas the work of pre-independence writers was published mostly in newspapers like *The Yoruba News*, the improvement in technique of the post-independence poetry was helped in no small way by magazines edited by specialists in literature – like *The Horn*, published at Ibadan University, Nigeria; *Black Orpheus*, published by the Mbari Club, a cultural circle based at Ibadan and closely connected to the university; East African journals like *Zuka*; and so on.

Perhaps a more important area of agreement between post-independence anglophone and francophone poetry is in subject-matter as well as tone. There are two major reasons for this. One, it has become clear that the British colonial policy of leaving Africans to themselves has not done any better for African culture and traditions than the French programme of assimilation: the clash of cultures which resulted has had a more damaging effect on African culture than anyone had at first realised. Consequently, anglophone African poetry today shows the same vigorous assertion of the African way of life – belief, music, even speech, as well as condemnation of European culture – that was already present in negritude poetry. Perhaps the best example of this is Okot p'Bitek's *Song of Lawino* (from which no. 36 comes).

The second reason has to do with political developments

within various African nations in recent times, which have made today's poets sad and angry critics of their governments and societies as well as of the European powers. To start with, most African nations are made up of communities separated by ethnic and religious differences. Before independence these communities joined hands in fighting colonialism; but after independence the rivalries between them became emphasised and in some cases led to cruel civil wars such as in the Congo, Nigeria, and more recently Chad. A good deal of modern African poetry reflects bitterly on this sad, bloody and terrifying decline of relationships. In some of his poems, notably *Viaticum* (not included here), U Tam'si has tried to convey some of the torment in the Congolese experience; from the anglophone side poems in this anthology by Clark (no. 82) and Ndu (no. 85) give an equally painful picture of the Nigerian civil war.

But even more of the anger in contemporary African poetry is directed at the continuing presence of the white man in African society and politics. When Syl Cheyney-Coker in *Peasants* (no. 38) laments 'the agony of those who study meaningless 'isms in incomprehensible languages,' he is condemning the way in which the language and ideas of the white man have continued to create divisions between elements of the African society. This foreign presence has perhaps been more bitterly condemned in poetry dealing with the situation in southern Africa. In addition to poems from Angola (nos. 26 and 83) and Mozambique (no. 86), which in their various ways reflect the pain of living under the Portuguese colonial regime, this collection also includes poems by Dennis Brutus (nos. 37, 63) and Oswald Mbuyiseni Mtshali (nos. 25, 52) which expose some of the unfeeling horror of *apartheid*. One of the angriest statements on the southern African situation has indeed been made by the Nigerian Wole Soyinka in a more recent volume, *Ogun Abibiman*. When Samora Machel of Mozambique declared a state of war against South Africa in 1976, Soyinka published that volume in support of Machel's position. In the following passage from the book, declaring that it was now time for war and no more for talking, he reveals his impatience with the dishonesty and intrigue of the European powers:

> For Dialogue
> Dried up in the home of Protestations [*i.e. the United Nations*]
> Sanctions
> Fell to seductive ploys of Interests
> Twin to dry-eyed arts of Expediency.

Diplomacy
Ran aground on Southern Reefs.

This statement, from a prominent anglophone poet who had once ridiculed negritude as unnecessary propaganda, indicates that both in subject-matter (i.e. the defence of black culture) and in tone (i.e. a touch of criticism) anglophone and francophone poetry are today very close to one another. On the whole the poets are sad about the state of affairs not only in their countries and in Africa but in the world generally, and this sadness causes them to be critical. This does not mean that they do not write about topics that involve a certain amount of cheerfulness, as shown in the *Praise* section here. But even in these we can detect some criticism underneath the general tone of celebration: see, for example, nos. 23, 25, and 27. And because most African poets reject the influence of the colonial experience on African culture, there is a greater tendency among them now than ever before to go back to that culture so as to rediscover and cultivate some of its traditional qualities.

Relationships between the oral and written poetry

We can see these relationships in terms of similarities and differences. With regard to similarities, these could in turn be examined on two planes. First, there is no doubt that since the oral poet and the writer-poet are both human, they are liable to respond to situations and experiences in largely the same way; such similarities could be very easily dismissed. Indeed, this anthology has been organised on the basis of the themes or topics which have constantly occurred in both oral and written African poetry; part of the justification for this is that poets in the two traditions are motivated by very much the same factors and issues even though they have developed in different backgrounds. Take the theme of death. It is a very significant factor of human experience and inevitably attracts the imagination of the oral poet as much as of the writer-poet: each of them reacts to the idea or the fact of death either with submission or with courage, depending on his inclinations as a man. Or take the theme of criticism. It may be said that poetry in any form is some kind of comment on life or the ideas surrounding it. But one of the most useful duties performed by the poet (like other kinds of artists) is to comment sensitively on the evils prevailing in the social or political life of his people; we can see both the oral and modern poet doing this here. In terms of technique, what makes the poet unique is that he is far more skilled than most members of his community in the imaginative use of language and in influencing us thereby. As we read the poems we see how the oral poet and his writer counterpart make the best use of the resources available in their respective media to influence the feelings and the minds of other people.

The second and perhaps more important way of understanding the similarities between the modern African poet and his forerunner in the oral tradition is by examining the indebtedness of one to the other. As we saw above, one of the major elements in modern African poetry is a reaction against the harmful influence of the colonial experience on African culture. Many African poets today believe it is their duty as Africans to reach back at their ancestral poetic traditions and give them a new lease of life, and they have done so in a variety of ways. One way has been to make age-old African customs, beliefs and ideas — which Western civilisation had taught us to regard as primitive and ignorant, and even some pioneer African poets like Osadebay had dismissed as 'child-like faith' — the subjects of modern poetry. Thus Kofi Awoonor follows the tradition of most Ghanaian (especially his native Ewe) communities in composing dirges which accept that there is a line of communication between the living and the dead (see no. 95). In *Prayer to masks* (no. 76) Senghor recognises and enshrines in modern poetry the traditional African custom of appealing to ancestors through mask-figures. In *Gbassay* (no. 97) Mukhtarr Mustapha transfers the ritual of initiation from the traditional Sierra Leonean cult to modern poetry. The Yoruba concept of *abiku* — a child that dies and is reborn many times over — has been treated in poetry by J.P. Clark and Wole Soyinka. Soyinka himself has done more than any other African writer to make the symbols of traditional African mythology the basis of his creative work: in various plays, novels and poems, especially his poem *Idanre* (not included here), he had made the Yoruba god of iron, Ogun (see no. 70), his ideal of the revolutionary artist constantly involved in the struggle to correct society.

Modern African poetry has also looked to traditional culture for the flavour of its language. In the 1960s and 1970s many African writers and scholars, anxious to come as close as possible to their oral traditions, debated rather sharply whether the language of poetry should be simple or complex; the debate was particularly encouraged by the practice of some poets in writing pieces (very much in the style of modern European poets who have influenced them) that their own countrymen had found hard to understand. Some people felt that poetry makes its greatest impact when it is easily understood, and that the charm of most traditional poetry lies in an easy flow of meaning which the audience can readily grasp and respond to. Okot p'Bitek's *Song of Lawino* was very widely received when it was published in 1966, and gave a great inspiration to those who felt that simplicity was the true mark of African poetry: as we can see from the extract here (no. 36), the audience of such a satirical poem would not need to rack their brains to get a laugh. However, there were some people (like Wole Soyinka) who argued that not all traditional poetry is simple; that there are some forms like divination or cult poetry which come in a secret, coded language and in complex idioms not easily understood by common men; and that many of the pieces of traditional poetry which have been published in 'simple' versions are only the products of poor translation. Certainly the translation of Yoruba *ifa* (divination) poetry which appears as no. 61 in this anthology does not come close to reflecting the complexity of idiom for which that tradition is known. Pol Ndu's poem *Afa* (no. 73), which echoes the same tradition of divination poetry (among the Igbo), is a good model for those modern African poets who want to combine the best of the African oral tradition with the techniques of modern European poetry in their attempt to deal with the complex issues of today.

The modern poets have been so anxious to return to the flavour of the indigenous language that they make conscious efforts to echo the rhythm of speech of their people and even borrow some indigenous words and sounds. If we read Awoonor's *To Stanislaus the renegade* (no. 35) aloud properly, and with the right African accent, we can feel the impact of someone abusing another — very much as in the Ewe tradition (see no. 30) which Awoonor tries to echo. And anyone who listened to the late Okot p'Bitek recite his poems (as well as tell stories) can tell that *Lawino's complaint* is intended to be read with a native tone of mockery.

Even more revealing is the practice of using actual African words in poetry written in English or French. The Zaïrean poet Antoine-Roger Bolamba begins his poem *Portrait* thus:

> I have my gri-gri
> > gri-gri
> > gri-gri

my calm bounding awake
clings to the wavy limbs of the Congo.

In *Elavanyo concerto* (no. 27) Okai uses an indigenous exclamation 'Hei' to lament Galileo's plight; and although he gives us the English translation for 'Elavanyo' once (line 52) he uses the word nevertheless, four times, obviously because he feels that its peculiarly African sound works better for his kind of poetry (Okai enjoys reading his poetry aloud before audiences) than the English. Even the very 'modern' Soyinka, in an abuse poem called *Malediction*, uses Yoruba words quite happily; although he uses English to shower curses on his adversary in most of the poem, at one point he breaks into Yoruba to give his abuse greater sauciness and bite.

Some other modern poets have followed this practice. The idea is that, although they accept that they will continue to use the European language to reach a wider audience even within Africa, they would wish to hear the rhythms of the native speech within the texture of their work. In fact the desire to be closer to the language has driven certain Western-educated poets to try their hands at writing poetry in their indigenous languages. Earlier generations had of course done the same. In the late nineteenth and earlier twentieth centuries a great deal of indigenous poetry was written, especially in southern Africa, by writers like the Zulu B.W. Vilakazi and the Sotho B.M. Khaketla. Some of this southern African poetry had a religious flavour and some simply tried to echo Western topics; other examples were little more than efforts to use the newly-acquired skill for treating local subjects. But in many of these poems there was a conscious effort to stay close to the techniques of indigenous poetry, as in *The train* (no. 47), while others contained some protest against the racial situation (as in Vilakazi's work).

Writing in the local language has indeed become, since the colonial era, a way of reasserting African culture. Both Gladys Casely-Hayford in the 1940s and the Nigerian Frank Aig-Imoukhuede in the late 1950s used the West African pidgin dialects in writing poetry. In 1981 the Nigerian novelist, Chinua Achebe, put together a volume of poems that he and colleagues had written in Igbo under the title *Aka Weta*. Achebe's contribution to that volume is a dedicatory poem to the late poet Christopher Okigbo, written with phrases and a structure taken from a well-known Igbo folk song. Such an effort on the part of an established writer like Achebe illustrates the strength of the modern writer's attraction to the oral tradition.

One other way in which modern African poets have tried to return to their roots is by echoing the musical basis of the traditional poetry. As we observed above, many kinds of oral poetry use music in one form or another: whether in the actual singing of songs, or in the meaningful control of tonal accents (as in Yoruba), or else in the playing of musical instruments to provide background rhythm. Modern poets are aware how incapable writing is of achieving these ends, but some of them make an effort to come close to them nevertheless. In *Choice* (no. 13), the Malagasy poet Ranaivo uses the call-and-response structure of the *hain-teny* folk song of his people: here one character sings and another responds. Clark also uses that structure in the short *Streamside exchange* (no. 64), which clearly has a folk song quality. Clark, incidentally, grew up partly in the same Urhobo clan from which the call-and-response poem *The Woes of Independence* (no. 33) comes; his poem echoes the strains he heard in his early youth.

Another significant instance of the modern African poet's return to the musical basis of the traditional poetry is in his recourse to rhythm. Senghor pays tribute to African rhythmic music in *Relentlessly she drives me* (no. 15) and *Prayer to masks* (no. 76); although writing in a European language and in a modern European poetic style, he has shown his attachment to the rhythmic background of traditional African poetry by suggesting the local instruments to which many of his poems should be recited (as in no. 28, for example). Okigbo has followed him by composing some of his poems for 'flutes' and 'slit-drums.' Other poets have gone further to imitate the sounds of some of these instruments in their poems. Nnamdi Azikiwe does so in an early (1928) nationalist poem titled *Drum language*, which begins:

'Godogba, Godogba, Godogbam gba!'
The tomtom drums the secret news:
'The white devils are on the loose,
'Be careful of their crafty ruse,
'Godogba, Godogba, Godogbam gba!'

And the modern Ghanaian poet Atukwei Okai uses various drum echoes in his volume of poems titled *The oath of the Fonton-from* and elsewhere.

The significance of this rhythmic element in modern African poetry can be seen in the use of repetition. As stated earlier, although repetition is a valuable means of emphasising an important point or a pressing need, it is basically the product of the emotional excitement which music inspires. Modern African poets are as conscious as their European counterparts of the emphatic value of repetition, but when they use it they are frequently more anxious to lend to their poetry a certain musical quality which reflects the rhythmic basis of the traditional poetry. This is particularly true of poets from West Africa where a strong musical tradition has continued to survive. Anyone who is not familiar with the predominance of repetitive drum rhythms in Ghanaian culture will probably dismiss Okai's *Elavanyo concerto* (no. 27) as monotonous in its use of repeated sounds (alliteration, rhyme, assonance, etc.). But for one who understands that tradition, Okai is basically transferring to the printed page the kind of sounds that he grew up hearing.

The borrowing has, however, not been one-sided; it is inevitable that the oral tradition will be influenced to some extent by the literate culture with which it has lived side by side for some time. One such literate culture is Islam, which has existed in Africa since the middle ages and made deep inroads into the traditional life and thought of the people. Islamic literature came in the Arabic script, and many traditional African singers and poets, who have been converted to Islam, have imbibed some of the structures and idioms characteristic of Arabic poetry. Poetry from the Swahili and Somali, whose languages have had a long contact with Arabic, are good examples of the influence of literacy on traditional African culture (see nos. 59 and 93).

The Islamic influence has also been felt in the content of traditional African poetry, as may be seen in one of the versions of the Sunjata legend collected by Professor Gordon Innes from the Gambia. This version was narrated by the *griot* Banna Kanute, who obviously has some contact with Islam. To demonstrate what a special figure the hero Sunjata is, Banna portrays him in an interesting light. He tells us that Sunjata's father had lost all his previous sons in Prophet Mohammed's war against unbelievers at Khaibar; to compensate him for this loss, the Prophet prayed to Allah to send Sunjata's parents a special child; shortly after, Sunjata's mother was transformed from an aged woman to a fourteen-year old girl, and conceived Sunjata. In the oral heroic poetry the heroes are usually portrayed as special figures; here, ideas from the Islamic literature have helped the narrative poet create an even more unique personality — one blessed by divine will.

Furthermore, after Sunjata was born the tyrant Sumanguru, anxious to prevent him from becoming a threat to his rule, consulted various sorcerers to seek out how best to destroy the child. To undertake such a serious task, some of these sorcerers did what every devout Muslim would do under the circumstances: retire into the desert for forty days, offer forty *rak'a* (rounds) of prayers to Allah, and fast for the entire period. They even reported seeing a creature in their visions who spoke to them, in a form of Koranic Arabic, to the effect that Sumanguru was destined to be destroyed by the child. The idea of vision alone carries some mystery; the incomprehensible Arabic text recited by each sorcerer makes the whole business even more terrifying. Here, surely, is an oral poet who has used the available resources from the surrounding Arabic culture in the best interest of his art.

Despite these similarities and borrowings, however, there are a few notable differences between oral and written African poetry. Some of these differences are not really fundamental ones, but are due mainly to the fact that the writer exists in a different social and political climate from that in which the oral poetry has traditionally had its place. For instance, in traditional praise-singing the poet does everything possible to glorify his subject; he knows that for him to be well rewarded (with gifts) he has to make the subject happy, so the negative aspects of the subject's life are often twisted to appear positive. But the modern poet does not have to praise anyone to survive. As some of the poems under *Praise* will show, there is considerably less cheerfulness in modern praise poetry than in the traditional form. The modern writer is driven to celebrate a figure less for his own sake than as a reaction against the painful circumstances surrounding that figure. In other words, while traditional praise poetry celebrates a figure for his own sake and as an unchallenged master of his world (as shown in nos. 17, 20, 22, etc.), modern praise poetry admires him rather for showing much courage despite the problems surrounding him (as seen in, for example, nos. 27 and 28).

Indeed, most modern African poetry differs from the traditional one in tone largely because it concentrates more on the problems of present-day social and political life. This is not to say that the traditional poet has no worries or grudges with his society; in societies marked by widespread oppression, such as South Africa, a good deal of oral poetry is still directed against the general situation. On the whole, however, the writers, including the poets, have assumed the duty of drawing attention to social and political evil in nearly every kind of subject they deal with. The situation of affairs in Africa is generally painful, and this is reflected more by the writers, who have become the voice of conscience in a continent that is increasingly dominated by Western-educated people, than it is by the oral tradition. This touch of harshness can be found in various themes in this anthology: for example, in love (no. 7), praise (no. 26), the environment (no. 49), and appeal (no. 76).

Another important change that has occurred between oral and written poetry is in the area of coverage. The oral poet was traditionally very much limited to the small local or ethnic environment with which he was familiar, mainly because the means of communication by travel was generally severely limited. Thus the oral traditional poet seldom refers to communities beyond his immediate ethnic or geographical neighbours, commenting mainly on those with whom his people have been associated in trade, war or other experiences: for instance, in Yoruba poetry there are negative references to nearby Dahomey (now Benin Republic), and the Somali poet speaks admiringly of 'the gold of Nairobi.' But the world of the modern poet is far wider. Education has exposed him to very distant societies, giving him adequate knowledge of events in places he may never have been: the war in Vietnam was so well covered by the press that Kariara need not have visited the scene of the fighting to capture the horror that we feel in his *Vietnam* (no. 84). Besides, African poets have been giving us a picture of distant places ever since they have been journeying there to study: for instance, Lenrie Peters' *Autumn burns me* (no. 53) very likely refers to Britain where he studied and practised medicine for a long time. The significance of the poet's area of experience may be seen in the basic attitudes of the two kinds of poetry. Traditional African poetry is somewhat narrower in its outlook, viewing the world more from the angle of its own limited local interests. But the modern poet, even when he condemns other nations, does so mainly in the interest of justice in the larger human sense.

Perhaps the truly fundamental difference between the oral poetry and the written will be found in the circumstances of performance; if the text of an oral poem is properly recorded, it may reveal certain qualities which suggest the conditions under which it was performed. Poetry performed by a dance group may show a tendency toward a duplication of various lines, especially if the performance requires that the leader 'call' a line and the others 'respond' to it: such is the case, for instance, in *Attack traders* (no. 31).

On the whole, too, it could be said that poetry performed for public entertainment might reveal the effort that the performer makes to give the audience a satisfactory event — such as singing a song several times over (though collectors are frequently not patient enough to record all the repetitions), or, as in *Sunjata summons his generals* (no. 79), making digressions either to clarify certain details or to give members of the audience some pride in their history and culture. In other cases, the performer may wish to impress the audience as to how much skill and wisdom he possesses and how fast he can dispense them; he will thus end up, as in the *Salute to Fabunmi* (no. 21), repeating various phrases many times in different combinations. All this gives the oral poetry performed before a (sometimes quite critical) audience a certain quality of fullness and the sense of a communal event. And because the oral poet is not always sure what kind of audience or what kind of reaction he is going to meet, there is frequently an impromptu, unplanned character in the text of his poetry or the order in which the ideas are arranged. This may be seen in *The odo-masquerade* (no. 18).

But the modern poet works under considerably different conditions. To start with, he is much happier writing in an isolated room where there are no distractions. Whereas, for instance, the *odo* masquerade poet derives some inspiration from the scribe whose speed of copying he seeks to match with his own speed of chanting, the writer would be completely put off by a singer performing in the room where he writes. This absence of a live audience has two implications. First, because he does not have to cope with any distractions, the writer has time to arrange the argument of his poetry in an orderly way. Thus, where orally performed poetry often has a certain loose, impromptu quality in the order or movement of its ideas, written poetry progresses in a logical order carefully plotted for it by the poet.

Secondly, because there is no live audience to please or account to, there is frequently an abstract, impersonal element in written poetry. That spirit of sharing and participation for which traditional culture is well known is noticeably lacking in modern literate culture. When, for instance, the oral poet speaks about his own interests or experiences, he frequently involves other people besides himself: thus in *Katini's complaint* (no. 29) the poet invokes the name of the chief Wani as he complains about a messenger's victimisation of him; in *Kodzo the imbecile* (no. 30) the aggrieved poet similarly calls on his accompanists, the 'questioners'; and in *The Woes of Independence* (no. 33) the *udje* poet invites his 'comrades' to detail the problems that independence has brought to the society. This sense of fellowship is relatively rare in the written poetry. Although some modern poets try to reflect the traditional spirit in their poetry, the very circumstances in which they do their job (a private room instead of a public forum) and the medium which they employ (cold print instead of a warm interaction with an audience) make it clear that this kind of poetry is first and foremost a private enterprise. And because the poet is trying to appreciate the world around him through the inner paths of his private mind and conscience, much modern African poetry is rather difficult to understand: we have good examples in the poetry of Soyinka (no. 55) and Okigbo (no.74).

Another notable difference between oral and written poetry is in size of material. Many of the oral poems in this anthology seem short — such as *Coward, crawl back*! (no. 77). But they are frequently sung through many repetitions in which the singers (especially the leader) make variations to the occasional word, to the facial expression, to the tone of emphasis, etc. The performers want to please the audience, and it will not do to sing a short snatch and walk away! A faithful recording of the performance of a song will set down the full text of the song as it is sung through several variations; but many collectors simply give us the bare, short text, partly from impatience and partly on the feeling that the variations are insignificant. The modern poet, again because he has no one in front of him to please, does not need to go through repetitions or variations and so cuts his material rather economically to the essential statement. Whereas in oral poetry the fuller the text is, the more pleasing the performance, in written poetry tightness and economy are more often upheld as the proof of poetic skill. This is another reason why the modern poetry is so difficult.

One final difference between oral and written poetry that is worth mentioning has to do with technique. In oral poetry there are various ways of emphasising ideas or situations. If, for instance, a character in a song is supposed to shout, the performer will raise his voice to make the point; if a soft speech is required, the performer will lower his voice; if the performer wishes to indicate fright, he will either tighten his brows or lower them; and so on. Unfortunately, the alphabetic script used in writing is a set of symbols representing only sounds, and is not equipped to convey some of these dramatic moments that arrest the attention of the audience of an oral performance. But there are a few non-alphabetical symbols used in writing which are valuable for indicating certain situations. For instance, when in *Their behaviour* (no. 63) Dennis Brutus wishes to mention a fact about human nature of which we should all be ashamed, he 'hides' it in brackets. To indicate how the ugly sounds of propaganda went on and on during the Nigerian civil war, J.P. Clark in *The casualties* (no. 82) uses running dots. And so on. With the movement of poetry from the open square to the pages of a book, the poet has lost the capacity for arresting our attention physically and has therefore opted for tricks of print that will appeal to our imagination.

On the selection and arrangement of poems in this anthology

A few words need to be said about the thematic approach which has been adopted in compiling this anthology. Other anthologies of African poetry have previously been published, emphasising either the landmarks from generation to generation (the historical approach) or else the spread of authors from one region of the continent to another (the geographical approach). While these approaches are useful in their respective ways, the method used in this anthology should provide a clearer focus, by allowing us first to identify some of the major concerns of African poetry and secondly to appreciate the variety of approaches and attitudes – whatever the medium of expression, period or area of origin. This method also seems the most suited for highlighting some of the best pieces of oral poetry available in the continent – a tradition which has been poorly served in most earlier anthologies.

The thematic approach used here is an attempt to include some of the best elements of the historical and geographical approaches. As far as the historical growth of modern African poetry goes, every generation has been represented here – from the anglophone 'pioneer' poetry (Osadebay) and the negritude movement (Senghor, Diop), through the immediate post-independence generation (Soyinka, Awoonor), to the new radical voices of today (Cheyney-Coker, Ofeimun, Mtshali). I have also tried to cover as much of the geographical spread of sub-Saharan Africa as possible in both the oral and written poetry: from the horn of Africa (Ethiopia, Somalia) to the south (Zimbabwe, South Africa), and from the west (Senegal, Gambia) to the east (Kenya, Uganda). But the main strength of the anthology remains in its concentrating on principal themes and illustrating them with the best available pieces of poetry. Admittedly, in such an anthology it is extremely difficult to represent the work of any one poet in as much detail as if the book was entirely about him. But some of the most outstanding poets of today (such as Brutus, Clark, Senghor and Soyinka) have three to five poems assigned to each of them across several themes. In these ways we are able to appreciate not only a wide range of poetic skills from the continent but also the varied skills of a handful of geniuses.

A large proportion of poems in this anthology were originally in languages other than English – in indigenous African languages and in continental European languages (French, Portuguese). As far as the content or message of each of these poems is concerned, we simply have to trust the judgment of the translators and their knowledge of the languages concerned. Some of them, especially those dealing with European languages, have benefited from authoritative advice as well as careful study. The poems of Senghor are a good case. Although he writes in French he also uses English very competently, so that he has been able to give excellent supervision to the work of his principal translators (John Reed and Clive Wake) in handling the very delicate French in which the poems were originally written.

The oral poetry, however, presents a special problem. There are instances in which a translator is simply unable to handle the stylistic peculiarities of the indigenous language – even when the language is his own. Take the *Salute to Fabunmi* (no. 21), which Professor Adeboye Babalola collected in his native Yoruba and has turned into English. Lines 20–21 of the poem read thus:

> Ó pa fún Akintólá torítorí.
> Ó pa fún Oníròkò tolètolè
> He once killed a game animal and gave it, head and all, as a
>   gift to Akintola.
> He once killed a game animal and gave it, foetus and all,
>   as a gift to Oniroko.

Babalola has of course got the literal message of each line perfectly well. But no amount of toying with the English will produce an equivalent effect to that achieved by the tonal variation between the two lines in the Yoruba. In fact, the point of these lines is not simply that Fabunmi gave wild game to Akintola and Oniroko. The more important point is suggested by the tonal changes. The accents in the first line are high, while those in the second line are low. On the one hand, the tonal changes suggest the easy generosity of Fabunmi in giving gifts to a wide range of personalities. On the other hand, the kingship of Ibadan (here held by Balogun Akintola) is higher in the traditional hierarchy than the kingship of Iroko; the use of high and low tones here is one effective way of suggesting the relative powers of the two rulers. Finally, there is a certain musical effect intended not only in the tonal changes but also in the substitution of a *t-r* combination of sounds with a *t-l* combination. These are some of the unique qualities of oral poetry that are lost in most of the published translations.

One final problem with most translations of oral poetry published to date is that they do not give us an insight into the *performance* of the poems which, as I observed above, provides the best guide for understanding the oral quality of the poetry. Many a translation reads like bad English poetry mainly because the translator has eliminated those elements which reveal the original pieces as true products of an oral performance – elements such as repetition, humming sounds, exclamatory particles, names and titles addressed to patrons or members of the audience, evidence of participation by various people at the scene of performance, and so on. In this anthology I have simply had to use the best material I could find though some of the pieces are not as representative of the oral performance as one would have wished. But where I have found texts which read very much like the stuff of the oral performance, I have not hesitated to use them: nos. 4, 18, 21, 48, and 79 are some of the best examples here. This point has been raised mainly to remind students and scholars of oral poetry that a proper understanding of this kind of art depends fundamentally on proper methods of collecting and recording.

In each section, the modern poetry is arranged in the alphabetical order of the authors' names. For the oral poetry, where the performer's name is known, I have indicated it. However, since most of the oral poems have been recorded without their performers' names (which is wrong, in my view), I have had to arrange all the oral poems in each section in the alphabetical order of the ethnic groups from which they come.

How to use the anthology

In this anthology, I have tried to give as wide a variety of poems under each theme as possible. For instance, under *Love* I have included poems that deal with love between man and woman; love for mother or child; love of country or race; the joy and disappointment of love. Under *Criticism*, there are poems of personal abuse; of social criticism; of political criticism. And so on. Those who are reading the anthology mainly for pleasure and personal enlightenment can absorb as much of it as possible. But those studying this book for course or certificate examinations may prefer to concentrate on no more than eighty poems on the whole; possibly ten poems in each section, carefully picked.

I have moved the notes on the poems to the end of the anthology so that the reader can make an effort to understand the poem on his own before consulting the notes. Whether or not one is reading for an examination, it is always profitable to try to enjoy a poem and even to project one's imagination into the world of images utilised by the poet. It is only after the reader has made a sincere effort to penetrate the meaning of the poem that it becomes rewarding to consult the notes.

Some attempt has been made to provide a detailed commentary and notes to each poem, for the benefit not only of students but of the general reader. Students are particularly encouraged to give attention to *three* elements in each commentary that are necessary for an understanding of the poem:

(1) The *context* or background, not only in the sense of the culture or society from which the poem comes but also (as in the case of oral poetry) the situation within which such poetry is performed. This will go some way in explaining the message of the poem.

(2) The *message*. Usually it helps to read a poem aloud two or three times over; after a few such readings the meaning or message of the poem will hit the reader 'in the head', so to speak. But to appreciate that message fully, the reader will have to play close attention to the poet's technique.

(3) The *technique*. By this is meant a variety of means of achieving effectiveness: (a) the structure or order in which the poet organises his ideas, e.g., the successive build-up in *What a fool he is!* (no. 2), the repetitive structure in *Sunjata summons his generals* (no. 79), the parallel relationship between real rain and metaphorical rain in *I think it rains* (no. 55), the development of episodes in *Elavanyo concerto* (no. 27), or the use of rhymed endings in some modern poems; (b) the images

33

or mental pictures by which the poet tries to appeal to our imagination and so make his point effectively — such as *The odo-masquerade* (no. 18) calling himself a 'gong' or Okigbo referring to himself as a 'wagtail' (bird) in *Heavensgate* (no. 74), and the use of words in other ways that are suggestive; (c) the mood or attitude of the poet, such as joy and pride in *A mother to her first-born* (no. 5), sadness in *Katini's complaint* (no. 29), defiance in *I anoint my flesh* (no. 45), submission in *Heavensgate* (no. 74), and so on.

The context and message of each poem are discussed in the general commentary; matters of technique are treated partly in the commentary and partly in the line notes which also explain other kinds of references in the poem. The questions at the end of each set of notes are intended as aids to further understanding of the poem, while the general questions from page 266 are aimed to test the reader's grasp not only of the themes treated in the anthology but of various issues in African poetry raised in this introduction.

Once again, I regret that I do not have space enough to represent as many poets, communities or pieces as might satisfy all and sundry. But I believe that the hundred poems I have brought together here will give us a representative picture not only of the major concerns of African poetry but also of the varied achievement of that poetry across generations and communities. I do not by any means wish to leave the impression that the ways in which I have classified the poems are the only ones possible; but they are valid ones, and I am confident that they provide us with a useful means of coping with the ever-increasing volume of poetry being published today in books and journals. I hope that the various introductions and notes here will help to put the material of the poetry in the proper light. Most of all, I hope that this anthology will have helped to give the oral poetry of Africa the attention that it so richly deserves.

Isidore Okpewho
Ibadan University
September 1984

PART TWO
The anthology

Love

Because love is one of the most fundamental sentiments felt by man, it has remained a favourite subject in the poetry of any age or culture. There are many kinds of love, but here we have concentrated on three major ones. The first is sexual love or love between man and woman: here we examine it either as a joyful or satisfying relationship (nos. 3, 4, etc.), as the source of anxiety (nos. 1, 14) or of disappointment (nos. 2, 12). Then there is family love, as love of child (no. 5) or love of mother (no. 9). And finally there is nationalistic love: by this is meant either love of one's country or what we may call patriotic love (no. 6), or else love of one's race (no. 7). Some poets are able to achieve rather interesting combinations. For instance, Dennis Brutus expresses his patriotic love by conceiving an intense romance with the rural landscape (no. 6); and Senghor, as in his negritude poetry generally, embraces the landscape and culture of Africa through the image of a woman.

Love is such a basic human feeling that the modern African poets need not go to their oral traditions for ideas. But a few have been moved to borrow some elements of technique from these traditions. Thus Flavien Ranaivo follows the pattern of call-and-response in the *hain-teny* folk-song tradition of his native Madagascar, and Senghor sets his two poems here to traditional Senegalese musical instruments.

1 Where has my love blown his horn?

(ACHOLI, UGANDA)

Where has my love blown his horn?
The tune of his horn is well known.
Young men of my clan,
Have you heard the horn of my love?

5   The long distance has ruined me, oh!
The distance between me and my companion.
Youths of my clan,
Have you heard the horn of my love?

The shortage of cattle has ruined my man!
10   The poverty of my love.
Young men of my clan,
Listen to the horn of my love.

Where has my love blown his horn?
The tune of his horn is well known.
15   Young men of my clan,
Listen to the horn of my love.

2 What a fool he is!

(AMHARA, ETHIOPIA)

When I asked for him at Entoto, he was towards Akaki,
So they told me;
When I asked for him at Akaki, he was towards Jarer,
So they told me;
5   When I asked for him at Jarer, he was at Mendar,
So they told me;

39

When I asked for him at Mendar, he was towards Awash,
So they told me;
When I asked for him at Awash, he was towards Chercher,
So they told me;
When I asked for him at Chercher, he was towards Harar,
So they told me;
When I asked for him at Harar, he was towards Djibouti,
So they told me;
When I asked for him at Djibouti, he had crossed the sea,
Or so they said:
I sent to find him a hundred times,
But I never found him.
I sit by the fire and weep:
What a fool he is
To hope he will ever find anyone to equal me.

3 I will satisfy my desire

(BAGIRMI, NIGERIA)

I painted my eyes with black antimony
I girded myself with amulets.

I will satisfy my desire,
you my slender boy.
I walk behind the wall.
I have covered my bosom.
I shall knead coloured clay
I shall paint the house of my friend,
O my slender boy.
I shall take my piece of silver
I will buy silk.
I will gird myself with amulets
I will satisfy my desire
the horn of antimony in my hand,
Oh my slender boy!

40

4 Nyagumbe! Nyagumbe!

(CHOPI, MOZAMBIQUE)

	BRIDE:	Nyagumbe! Nyagumbe!
		Why do you refuse?
	BRIDEGROOM:	I am refusing.
		In my heart
5		is the love
		of refusing.
	BRIDE:	I will go
		to the band of men.
		Father! Father!
10		Nyagumbe refuses.
	FATHER:	Why does he refuse?
	BRIDE:	He is refusing.
		In his heart
		is the love
15		of refusing.
		I will go
		to the hearth.
		Mother! Mother!
		Nyagumbe refuses.
20	MOTHER:	Why does he refuse?
	BRIDE:	He is refusing.
		In his heart
		is the love
		of refusing.
25	MOTHER:	Go to the bin!
		Procure beans!
		Cook! Cook!
		Serve! Serve!
	BRIDE:	I will go
30		to the boys' hut.
		Nyagumbe! Nyagumbe!
		Here are beans.
		Why do you refuse?
		I will go
35		to the band of men.
		Father! Father!

		Nyagumbe refuses.
	FATHER:	Why does he refuse?
	BRIDE:	He is refusing
40		in his heart.
		I will go
		to the hearth.
		Mother! Mother!
		Nyagumbe is refusing.
45	MOTHER:	Why does he refuse?
	BRIDE:	He is refusing
		in his heart.
	MOTHER:	Go to the fowl-run!
		Catch a cock!
50		Kill! Kill!
		Cook! Cook!
	BRIDE:	I will go
		to the boys' hut.
		Nyagumbe! Nyagumbe!
55	BRIDEGROOM:	What is the meat?
	BRIDE:	The meat is a cock.
	BRIDEGROOM:	What is the cock?
	BRIDE:	The cock is a cockerel.
		Why do you refuse?
60	BRIDEGROOM:	I am refusing.
		In my heart
		is the love
		of refusing.
	BRIDE:	I will go
65		to the band of men.
		Father! Father!
		Nyagumbe refuses.
	FATHER:	Why does he refuse?
	BRIDE:	He is refusing.
70		I will go
		to the hearth.
		Mother! Mother!
		Nyagumbe refuses.
	MOTHER:	Why does he refuse?
75	BRIDE:	He is refusing
		in his heart.
	MOTHER:	My child! My child!
		Love him! Love him!

42

BRIDE: I will go
80   to the boys' hut.
        Nyagumbe! Nyagumbe!
        I did love you!
        He is laughing!
        Why are you laughing?
85 BRIDEGROOM: I am laughing
        In my heart
        is the love
        of laughing!

5 A mother to her first-born

(LANGO, UGANDA)

Speak to me, child of my heart.
Speak to me with your eyes, your round, laughing eyes,
Wet and shining as Lupeyo's bull-calf.

Speak to me, little one,
5   Clutching my breast with your hand,
So strong and firm for all its littleness.
It will be the hand of a warrior, my son,
A hand that will gladden your father.
See how eagerly it fastens on me:
10   It thinks already of a spear:
It quivers as at the throwing of a spear.
Oh son, you will have a warrior's name and be a leader of
     men.
And your sons, and your son's sons, will remember you
     long after you have slipped into the darkness.
But I, I shall always remember your hand clutching me so.
15   I shall recall how you lay in my arms,
And looked at me so, and so,
And how your tiny hands played with my bosom.
And when they name you great warrior, then will my eyes
     be wet with remembering.

And how shall we name you, little warrior?
20 See, let us play at naming.
It will not be a name of despisal, for you are my first-born.
Not as Nawal's son is named will you be named.
Our gods will be kinder to you than theirs.
Must we call you 'Insolence' or 'Worthless One'?
25 Shall you be named, like a child of ill fortune, after the
        dung of cattle?
Our gods need no cheating, my child:
They wish you no ill.
They have washed your body and clothed it with beauty.
They have set a fire in your eyes.
30 And the little, puckering ridges of your brow —
Are they not the seal of their finger-prints when they
        fashioned you?
They have given you beauty and strength, child of my
        heart,
And wisdom is already shining in your eyes,
And laughter.

35 So how shall we name you, little one?
Are you your father's father, or his brother, or yet another?
Whose spirit is it that is in you, little warrior?
Whose spear-hand tightens round my breast?
Who lives in you and quickens to life, like last year's melon
        seed?
40 Are you silent, then?
But your eyes are thinking, thinking, and glowing like the
        eyes of a leopard in a thicket.
Well, let be.
At the day of naming you will tell us.

O my child, now indeed I am happy.
45 Now indeed I am a wife —
No more a bride, but a Mother-of-one.
Be splendid and magnificent, child of desire.
Be proud, as I am proud.
Be happy, as I am happy.
50 Be loved, as now I am loved.
Child, child, child, love I have had from my man.
But now, only now, have I the fullness of love.

44

Now, only now, am I his wife and the mother of his first-
    born.
His soul is safe in your keeping, my child, and it was I, I, I,
    who have made you.
55 Therefore am I loved.
Therefore am I happy.
Therefore am I a wife.
Therefore have I great honour.

You will tend his shrine when he is gone.
60 With sacrifice and oblation you will recall his name year by
    year.
He will live in your prayers, my child,
And there will be no more death for him, but everlasting
    life springing from your loins.
You are his shield and spear, his hope and redemption from
    the dead.
Through you he will be reborn, as the saplings in the
    Spring.
65 And I, I am the mother of his first-born.
Sleep, child of beauty and courage and fulfilment, sleep.
I am content.

6 Nightsong: Country

DENNIS BRUTUS

All of this undulant earth
heaves up to me;
soft curves in the dark distend
voluptuous-submissively;
5   primal and rank
the pungent exudation
of fecund growth ascends
sibilant clamorously:
voice of the night-land
10   rising, shimmering,
mixing most intimately
with my own murmuring —
we merge, embrace and cling:
who now gives shelter, who begs sheltering?

7 Dry your tears, Africa!

BERNARD DADIÉ

Dry your tears, Africa!
Your children come back to you
Out of the storms and squalls of fruitless journeys.

Through the crest of the wave and the babbling of the
     breeze
5   Over the gold of the east
and the purple of the setting sun,
the peaks of the proud mountains
and the grasslands drenched with light
They return to you
10   out of the storms and squalls of fruitless journeys.

Dry your tears, Africa!
We have drunk
From all the springs
    of ill fortune
15   and of glory

And our senses are now opened
    to the splendour of your beauty
    to the smell of your forests
    to the charms of your waters
20   to the clearness of your skies
    to the caress of your sun
And to the charm of your foliage pearled by the dew.

Dry your tears, Africa!
Your children come back to you
25 their hands full of playthings
and their hearts full of love.
They return to clothe you
in their dreams and their hopes.

8 For Melba

KEORAPETSE KGOSITSILE

Morning smiles
In your eye
Like a coy moment
Captured by an eternal
5 Noon and from yesterdays
I emerge naked
Like a Kimberley diamond
Full like Limpopo after rain
Singing your unnumbered charms.

9 To the anxious mother

VALENTE MALANGATANA

Into your arms I came
when you bore me, very anxious
you, who were so alarmed
at that monstrous moment
5   fearing that God might take me.
Everyone watched in silence
to see if the birth was going well
everyone washed their hands
to be able to receive the one who came from Heaven
10 and all the women were still and afraid.
But when I emerged
from the place where you sheltered me so long
at once I drew my first breath
at once you cried out with joy
15 the first kiss was my grandmother's.
And she took me at once to the place
where they kept me, hidden away
everyone was forbidden to enter my room
because everyone smelt bad
20 and I all fresh, fresh
breathed gently, wrapped in my napkins.
But grandmother, who seemed like a madwoman,
always looking and looking again
because the flies came at me
25 and the mosquitoes harried me
God who also watched over me
was my old granny's friend.

10 I will cling to your garment

ERIC S. NG'MARYO

I will cling to your garment like a wild grass seed:
I will needle your flesh
And pray
That my insistent call for you
5   Be not met with
A jerky
Removal
From your garment;
And a throw into the fire,
10 But that
You will drop me on to the fertile ground of
Your favour.

11 Without you

ODIA OFEIMUN

In your absence
my life is all a stammer
hunted down
by a non-existent tomorrow

5   I feel guilty
of sins I have not committed
borne on the wings
of incessant fears

Without you,
10 my earth suffers a demise of colours
as when a ghost leaves a house
at night
the light goes out

12 Love apart

CHRISTOPHER OKIGBO

The moon has ascended between us
Between two pines
That bow to each other

Love with the moon has ascended
5 Has fed on our solitary pines

And we are now shadows
That cling to each other
But kiss the air only.

13 Choice

FLAVIEN RANAIVO

Who is that making her steps clatter on the firm earth?
— She is the daughter of the new chief-over-a-thousand
— If she is the daughter of the chief-over-a-thousand,
Tell her night will soon be falling
5 And I would trade all the coral-red loves
For a hint of her friendship.

— Who is she coming from the north?
— It is the sister of the widow scented with rose-apples.
— Tell her to come inside at once,
10 I will make her a fine dinner.
— She will not touch it I know:
She will take a little rice-water
Not because she is thirsty
But because it is her whim to please you.

14 I came with you

LÉOPOLD SÉDAR SENGHOR

[*For khalam*]

I came with you as far as the village of grain-huts, to the
gates of Night
I had no words before the golden riddle of your smile.
A brief twilight fell on your face, freak of the divine fancy.
From the top of the hill where the light takes refuge, I saw
the brightness of your cloth go out
5   And your crest like a sun dropped beneath the shadow of
the ricefields
When the anxieties came against me, ancestral fears more
treacherous than panthers
— The mind cannot push them back across the day's
horizons.
Is it then night for ever, parting never to meet again?
I shall weep in the darkness, in the motherly hollow of the
Earth
10   I will sleep in the silence of my tears
Until my forehead is touched by the milky dawning of your
mouth.

15 Relentlessly she drives me

LÉOPOLD SÉDAR SENGHOR

[*For two balafongs*]

Relentlessly she drives me through the thickets of Time.
My black blood hounds me through the crowd to the
    clearing where white night sleeps.

Sometimes I turn round in the street and see again the
    palm tree smiling under the breeze.
Her voice brushes me like the soft lisping sweep of a wing
    and I say
5 'Yes it is Signare!' I have seen the sun set in the blue eyes of
    a fair negress.
At Sevres-Babylone or Balangar, amber and *gongo*, her scent
    was near and spoke to me.
Yesterday in church at the Angelus, her eyes shone like
    candles burnishing
Her skin with bronze. My God, my God, why do you tear
    my pagan senses shrieking out of me?
I cannot sing your plain chant that has no swing to it, I
    cannot dance it.
10 Sometimes a cloud, a butterfly, raindrops on my boredom's
    window-pane.
Relentlessly she drives me across the great spaces of Time.
My black blood hounds me, to the solitary heart of the
    night.

Praise

Praise

In many ways the themes of love and praise are related to one another, especially because they are both rooted in the feeling of admiration. Here, however, we are concentrating on those praise poems that celebrate the role or achievement of the subject. Some of these are powerful or important leaders of people or ideas, such as Shaka the Zulu, the Emir Ali, the American civil rights leader Martin Luther King, or the Italian physicist Galileo. Others are small people who nevertheless show significant examples and inspire us with their deep commitment to whatever they do: such as the Shona blacksmith (no. 19), the dutiful Senegalese 'second-class private' (no. 28), or even the dancing girl (no. 23) who teaches the poet Clark the beauty of being closely united with one's traditional culture.

Some of the modern poets here echo the spirit of the traditional praise song: for instance, both Mtshali and Okai celebrate the achievements of bygone leaders as a rallying cry for present-day men of action, and again Senghor sets his praise song to a traditional musical instrument. But the traditional poetry differs from the modern one in a number of significant ways. In the first place, the practice of self-praise which is highly favoured in the traditional culture (see nos. 16 and 18) is extremely rare in modern poetry, perhaps because these days it is considered awkward for one to praise oneself openly. The second difference is in the critical element. Since his livelihood depends on his performance, the traditional praise poet prefers to please rather than offend: whatever criticism there is in the song is usually subdued, or else offered in the spirit of benevolent cautioning (see no. 20). On the contrary, African poetry since the colonial period is mostly critical or combative, and the modern poet, who does not have to praise anyone to survive, uses even the opportunity of praise to take up an argument: poems by Mtshali, Okai, and Kassam here are examples of this tendency.

One notable characteristic of traditional praise poetry is exaggeration: by making his subject larger than life, the poet is able to justify the special attention he is giving to it and to gain handsome rewards. Except for poems that consciously echo the oral tradition, the tendency toward exaggeration is weak in modern praise poetry which, at any rate, has little interest in the kind of material gains that motivate the oral poet.

16 A warrior sings his praises

ERINESTI RWANDEKYEZI (BAHIMA, UGANDA)

I Who Am Praised thus held out in battle among foreigners
 along with The Overthrower;
I Who Ravish Spear In Each Hand stood out resplendent in
 my cotton cloth;
I Who Am Quick was drawn from afar by lust for the fight
 and with me was The Repulser Of Warriors;
I Who Encircle The Foe, with Bitembe, brought back the
 beasts from Bihanga;
5 With Bwakwakwa, I fought at Kaanyabareega,
Where Bantura started a song that we might overcome
 them.

Thus with my spear, I and Rwamujonjo conquered
 Oruhinda;
The Banyoro were afraid on the battlefield of Kahenda;
The cocks of Karembe had already crowed;
10 I Who Am Nimble with The One Whom None Can
 Dislodge felled them at Nyamizi.

At Nkanga, I seized my spear by its shaft-end;
At Kanyegyero, I The Binder Of Enemies took them by
 surprise;
Thereafter was I never excluded from the counsels of
 princes, nor was Rwangomani;
I Who Rescue With The Spear had seized him so that we
 might fight together.

17 Ali, Lion of the World!

(HAUSA, NIGERIA)

Great Visitor, Son of Abdu,
Water it is that drowns whoever goes against it,
It overwhelms even the mighty ferryman;
Mighty conqueror, Sire of Danrimi, ruthless and cruel.

5   Who does not know Abdu's son?
Lord of the Battleline, when it's raining he is on the march
In search of a fight, is Ali!
     Ali Lion of the World, Grandson of Conqueror Dabo!
Even at night he is on the march
10 In search of a fight, is Ali!
     Ali Lion of the World, Grandson of Conqueror Dabo!
With soothsayers he goes on the march
In search of a fight, does Ali!
     Ali Lion of the World, Grandson of Conqueror Dabo!
15 With bowmen he goes on the march
In search of a fight, does Ali!
     Ali Lion of the World, Grandson of Conqueror Dabo!

Let us be up and going, Great Conqueror:
If they say, 'It is dark,'
     bring a lamp (says he), that is its remedy;
20 If they say, 'Rain,'
     put on a mat (says he), that is its remedy;
If they say, 'Thorns,'
     put on sandals, says the Great Conqueror.
     Lion of the World, Grandson of Conqueror Dabo!

In the war against Damagaram, Amadu son of Tanimu
Fled without looking back.
25 He was taking the bad news home with him.
The first wife said, 'Where is your horse, my Lord?'
So the wives asked!
The second asked, 'And where is your cloak?'
The third said, 'Where is your staff, my Lord?'
30 And the fourth said, 'Where is your lance, my Lord?'

Cease asking so many questions!
They are all with Ali, Lord of the World.
Said Amadu, 'There is a Tuareg in Kano:
If there had been seven like him,
35   I would not have come back to Damagaram.'
Well, it was not a Tuareg:
It was our leader, the Emir himself,
Refusing to flee, putting others to flight!

Captain of our spearhead, Giant among men,
40   Mighty Conqueror, leader of our horse and foot:
Who does not know Abdu's son,
The slippery slope, the downfall of the unwieldy?

18 The odo-masquerade

(IGBO, NIGERIA)

May the congregation here listen,
Listen
For it's the *Odo* that hears the market din
The *Odo* that lives near the *Nkwo*-market,
5   Speaking his mind — his eternal mind:
I say to you,
No other *Odo* gnaws into my trunk
And into my branches
Except the one of Ugwu-Odegbulu line,
     Okpoko
10 Who thundered and ate his visitor;
I am the *Odo* who feeds on the market din —
I *Ogene* the bell for calling conferences,
I, the beaked-singer that rips open the maize-cob,
I, the mysterious tripod used for cooking
15 So that the pot can stand erect,
Two of my three legs give way
And the pot falls off, rolling
Seeking the eternal cook.

I ask the creator-scatterer of locusts
20 To please retreat a pace
For Almight *Odo* son of Diuyoko is girded with cloth
And is going in peace —
If soldier ants advance, one advances,
If they retreat, one retreats;
25 He who has a basket should bring it to the wilderness
For the numberless locusts
Are hovering in a host in the wilderness.

I, the *Ozo* who killed an elephant
I, the *Ozo* who wore palm-leaves and rejected the hoe,
30 I, the *Ozo* who took his title on *Eke* day
And displayed at the village square on *Olie* day;
I, the beaked-singer
I, the thorny weed never used as a carrying pad;

I, the branch of the Inyi-tree that becomes a medicine —
35 The killer of other trees —
I am the wood-pecker
That destroys trees,
The tree we consecrated
Has ever been my walking-stick —
40   Ha — Ha — Ha — Ha —

I am the *Odo* that flew straight and touched the whole
     Igboland
The *Odo* living in the square of the King of Contentment
The *Odo*, whose gate is the *Ngwu* tree;
I am like the child who did a hard journey fast
45 And was said to have raced under supernatural influence
I am the craftsman of the spirit world.

I am a gong:
The gong is inspired
And it begins to talk:
50 I am the gong with a melodious voice,
The crowd is thick here,
The white ants are fluttering
They are in clusters;
My *uturu*-voice
55 Is singing in the *Odo*-fashion;
I've come, I've come, I've come,
Son of the Almighty *Odo*:
The copyist cannot pick up
All that flows from my voice, what I am singing,
60 I, the *Uturu*.

19 In praise of the blacksmith

(SHONA, ZIMBABWE)

Today this place is full of noise and jollity.
The guiding spirit that enables my husband to forge makes
    him do wonders.
All those who lack hoes for weeding, come and buy!
Hoes and choppers are here in plenty.
5 My husband is a craftsman in iron,
Truly a wizard at forging hoes.
Ah, here they are! They have come eager to find hoes.
Ah, the iron itself is aglow, it is molten red with heat,
And the ore is ruddy and incandescent.
10 My husband is an expert in working iron,
A craftsman who sticks like wax to his trade.
On the day when the urge to forge comes upon him,
The bellows do everything but speak.
The pile of slag rises higher and higher.
15 Just look at what has been forged,
At the choppers, at the hoes, at the battle axes,
And here at the pile of hatchets, large and small.
Then look at the double-bladed knives and the adzes.
Merely to list them all seems like boasting.
20 As for fowl and goats, they cover my yard.
They all come from the sale of tools and weapons.
Here is where you see me eating at ease with a spoon.

20 Moshoeshoe

(SOTHO, LESOTHO)

You've been saying there's no one at Kholu's:
The spear of someone from Kholu's is stabbing.
It stabbed a man's leg, he couldn't stand!
He supported himself by a tree, Binders.
5   Ram, butt, Kali of the Beoana,
Butt, the cowards are afraid,
They see when the darkness spreads.
It has no teeth, the Binders' lion,
As for the people, it only nibbles them!
10   Tyopho was devoured by the Binders' hyena,
When its three cubs kept it company,
The spotted hyena of the people from RaMatlole's.
He tried with a thorn tree to block the door,
He defended with a baby's cradle-skin!
15   The husband of Mokali, the aged leopard,
The husband of Mokali and RaNtheosi,
The flashing shield of RaNtheosi,
The flashing shield of RaMasopha,
Which is bright with fire.
20   The waistcoat of cloth,
The one who clings fast to the black and white cow!
The black white-spotted ox once flexed its muscles,
And Kobo's kaross was left on the branches,
Was left in the bushes, on the ridge,
25   Black white-spotted ox, though you've come with
         gladness,
Yet you have come with grief,
You have come with cries of lamentation,
You have come as the women hold their heads
And continually tear their cheeks.
30   Keep it from entering my herds:
Even in calving, let it calve in the veld,
Let it calve at Qoaling and Korokoro.
To these cattle of our village it brings distress,
It has come with a dirge, a cause of sadness.
35   Thesele, the other one, where have you left him?

61

21 Salute to Fabunmi

(YORUBA, NIGERIA)

FIRST HUNTER:
Oolo of Iware Forest, why is it that we no longer see
   Fabunmi, he who snatches a tree branch from a
   monkey's grip?
Husband of Layemi, a man who confidently aims and
   shoots at a black colobus monkey.
He who snatches a tree branch from a monkey's grip, father
   of Ajani.
He who breaks a tree branch against an old female monkey
   as he shoots her dead.
5   He who snatches a tree branch from a monkey's grip.
A relation of Elekede.
Owner of many guns, a man who stalks an animal in the
   forest, making a trail quickly like the rainbow in the sky.
Man who hangs ponderously from a tree like a swinging,
   broken branch.
Rainbow in the forest associated with a trail made for
   tracking an animal.
10 Fired bullets landing with a thud in an animal's abdomen.
He who kills a black colobus monkey and ceremoniously
   rubs its hand against the ground.
The enterprising hunter who kills a porcupine near a
   kolanut tree.
He is so good at shooting that he is vainglorious about his
   skill.
Citizen of Iware, he who snatches a tree branch from a
   monkey's grip, husband of Layemi.
15 We sadly miss Fabunmi, the man who fixes his gaze long
   and hard on one.
He who confidently aims and shoots at a black colobus
   monkey.

SECOND HUNTER:
Hey! Thank you very much! Ha!
Oolo of Iware Forest!
Why is it that we no longer see Fabunmi?

62

20 He once killed a game animal and gave it, head and all, as a
gift to Akintola.
He once killed a game animal and gave it, foetus and all, as
a gift to Oniroko.
He once killed a game animal and gave it to them at Oyo,
waving his right to the animal's skin.
The short cannon cracks repeatedly.
Father of Ajani.
25 Why is it that we no longer see Fabunmi, the man who
confidently shoots at a black colobus monkey?
Even if someone was the youngest of a set of triplets,
Or the youngest of a set of quadruplets,
Or a person on whose head was a cap concealing a pair of
twins,
When on a visit to Fabunmi at home,
30 Such a person would eat maize gruel in loaves with meat
from a monkey's head.
Oolo of Iware Forest!
Why is it that you no longer see Fabunmi, the man who
daily kills a chimpanzee?
The smart hunter, citizen of Alediji, a priest of the god
Ogun, a frequenter of the forest trails.

22 Shaka

(ZULU, SOUTH AFRICA)

Dlungwana, son of Ndaba!
    Ferocious one of the Mbelebele brigade,
Who raged among the large kraals,
So that until dawn the huts were being turned upside-
    down.
5   He who is famous as he sits, son of Menzi,
He who beats but is not beaten, unlike water,
Axe that surpasses other axes in sharpness;
Shaka, I fear to say he is Shaka,
Shaka, he is the chief of the Mashobas.
10 He of the shrill whistle, the lion;
He who armed in the forest, who is like a madman,
The madman who is in full view of the men.
He who trudged wearily the plain going to Mfene;
The voracious one of Senzangakhona,
15 Spear that is red even on the handle.
    The open-handed one, they have matched the
        regiments,
They were matched by Noju and Ngqengenye,
The one belonging to Ntombazi and the other to Nandi;
He brought out the one with the red brush,
20 Brought out by the white one of Nandi.
    They called him to Mthandeni despising him,
They said 'We cannot compete in dancing with this
    Ntungwa from up country,'
Whereas he was going to annihilate Phakathwayo in the
    return competition.
    The small beast of consent flying like a flag,
25 Why did the ferocious one consent?
Why has he accepted Godolozi,
Thinking that he was on this side at Nandi's place,
Whereas he was far away at little Ntombazi's place?
    The sun that eclipsed another with its rays,
30 For the present it eclipsed the one of Nthandeni.
    There are two words for which I am grateful,
I am grateful for that of Mphandaba and that of

Ndungenkomo,
Saying 'The string of beads does not fit the neck';
Please inquire from the people of Zinkondeni,
35　They said He who is frustrated they would stab at
　　　Hlokohloko,
The curdled milk got spilt and the dish got broken . . .

　　　　Young raging one of Ndaba!
He lives in a great rage,
And his shield he keeps on his knees;
40　He has not let them settle down, he keeps them in a state of
　　　excitement,
Those among the enemy and those at home.
　　　Mandla kaNgome!
He crossed over and founded the Ntontela regiment,
They said he would not found it and he founded it.
45　　　He who attempted the ocean without crossing it,
It was crossed by swallows and white people.
　　　He who sets out at midday, son of Ndaba, or even
　　　afternoon;
Pursuer of a person and he pursues him persistently,
For he pursued Mbemba born among the Gozas,
50　He pursued him until he put him at Silutshana,
He found the reed-bed of young boys,
But it was only the spirits of the place.
　　　Axe of Senzangakhona,
Which when it was chopping worked very energetically.
55　　　He who saw the cattle right on top of the hill,
and brought them down by means of long spears and they
　　　came down,
He washed his face in tears.
　　　Ngibi naNgwadi!
Little leopard that goes about preventing other little
　　　leopards at the fords.
60　Finisher off! Black Finisher off!

23 Agbor dancer

JOHN PEPPER CLARK

See her caught in the throb of a drum
Tippling from hide-brimmed stem
Down lineal veins to ancestral core
Opening out in her supple tan
5 Limbs like fresh foliage in the sun.

See how entangled in the magic
Maze of music
In trance she treads the intricate
Pattern rippling crest after crest
10 To meet the green clouds of the forest.

Tremulous beats wake trenchant
In her heart a descant
Tingling quick to her finger tips
And toes virginal habits long
15 Too atrophied for pen or tongue.

Could I, early sequester'd from my tribe,
Free a lead-tether'd scribe
I should answer her communal call
Lose myself in her warm caress
20 Intervolving earth, sky and flesh.

24 Martin Luther King

AMIN KASSAM

Under Abraham's vacant eyes
He proclaimed a dream
A dream
That blossomed a sun
5 Where darkness had reigned
A dream
That bestrode the eagle
With ringing heart
Wheeling high above
10 Flailing truncheons thudding
On bare flesh
From rocky desert
He carved a valley
Where soil and clouds
15 Embraced and fused
With the voice of man
Buried in his neck

25 The birth of Shaka

OSWALD MBUYISENI MTSHALI

His baby cry
was of a cub
tearing the neck
of the lioness
5   because he was fatherless.

The gods
boiled his blood
in a clay pot of passion
to course in his veins.

10   His heart was shaped into an ox shield
to foil every foe.

Ancestors forged
his muscles into
thongs as tough
15   as wattle bark
and nerves
as sharp as
syringa thorns

His eyes were lanterns
20   that shone from the dark valleys of Zululand
to see white swallows
coming across the sea.
His cry to two assassin brothers:

'Lo! you can kill me
25   but you'll never rule this land!'

26 Bamako

AGOSTINHO NETO

Bamako!
Where the truth dropping on the leaf's sheen
unites with the freshness of men
like strong roots under the warm surface of the soil
5   and where grow love and future
fertilised in the generosity of the Niger
shaded by the immensity of the Congo
to the whim of the African breeze of hearts

Bamako!
10   there life is born
and grows
and develops in us important fires of goodness

Bamako!
there are our arms
15   there sound our voices
there the shining hope in our eyes
transformed into an irreproachable force
of friendship
dry the tears shed over the centuries
20   in the slave Africa of other days
vivified the nourishing juice of fruit
the aroma of the earth
on which the sun discovers gigantic kilimanjaros
under the blue sky of peace.

25   Bamako!
living fruit of the Africa
of the future germinating in the living arteries of Africa
There hope has become tree
and river and beast and land
30   there hope wins friendship
in the elegance of the palm and the black skin of men

Bamako!
there we vanquish death
and the future grows — grows in us
35 in the irresistible force of nature and life
with us alive in Bamako.

[1954]

27 Elavanyo concerto

(to Angela Davis and Wole Soyinka)

ATUKWEI OKAI

Cross. Banner. Swastika. Sickle.
Dross. Hammer. Floodfire. Spittle.

The sun is the centre of our system.

The leaning tower. Two stones. Revolution.
5 Summons to Rome. Burning Stake. The Inquisition.

The sun's not the centre of our system.

El Cordobes! El Cordobes!
There are some things I have to confess:
(The bulls and bulls you kill in the ring.)
10 When to the winds you all caution fling.

You still have things unto which to cling.
The bulls and bulls you kill in the ring
Alone have no prospects of wearing a sling.
The bulls and bulls you kill in the ring.

15 But when Galileo Galilei
Was thrown into the rot-ring of scorn,
The charging bull they hurled against him
Was armed to the horn and to the hoof
With the cudgel of hate and the spear of fear

70

20 And with the red-hot crowbar of anger.
   Galileo Galilei in the ring
   Was alone: his only weapon and friend
   Was time: and time was a mere toddler then.
   (And for time to mature in the marrow,

25 You certainly have to come tomorrow;
   Centuries and centuries after the morrow)
   And they said: Galileo Galilei,
   We hear you are not at home in the mind,
   We fear you must be counted with the blind.

30 You may think all your thoughts; you may,
   But your ideas shan't see the light of day;
   Your midday coughing hurts our midnight prayers.
   And you said: two is a crowd; even the
   Elements bear witness; the heavens

35 Hear evidence; the universe gives judgment.
   Place no mouldy margin upon what I
   Should imagine; and no single censor
   In hell or heaven shall tell me censor
   My sigh or sin. You retail a sick tale

40 Tailored to your taste. But toppling trees tell
   Another story. When in the lap of
   A man-blinded God, truth lies, lying like
   The soon-to-be-unlaced lips of a hell-
   Robed Iscariot the Judas jettisoned

45 Into the joyless jungle of seekers
   After the truth that shall not tear apart
   When torn apart, caterpillar canoes
   All crawl into the highway threshold
   Of a contourless anger; but the seed,

50 O God, is already in the soil; the
   Rains have already gone down to it.
   Elavanyo! Elavanyo! better
   Times cannot be too far away. I
   Sit here watching the stars. Elavanyo.

55 Hei ... Galileo Galilei ... My eyes
    are watering, their teeth are tightening, your lips
    are quivering, and our solo-song slows
    down to a silent stop; Hallelujah Chorus
    cracks upon the shock-rock of an anti-
60 truth cataract.

    O ... Galileo ... Galilei ... you fold
    your face like a preying mantis pawned for
    a pound of maize; and we erase all
    trace, taking no chances with cheating
65 charcoal-sellers who hold the hand of hands
    over the hovering hawk hankering after
    human flesh.

    Hei ... Galileo ... Galilei ... Time marks
    time in our tears, and the rivers of truth
70 renew their roar; fire fights flesh in their
    fears, and suns that shone should no more soar.

    O ... Galileo ... Galilei ... truth's lip-
    stick on your mind, green anger in their heart,
    scorners' thick mud on your shirt, black dark-
75 ness in their hair, dry dagger in some
    hand; and they crouch and come: advancing
    towards you, advancing towards me,
    charging against the very liver of
    truth.

80 Hei ... Galileo ... Galilei ... water
    walking, rainbow running, and the sky in
    our song; I hear them laughing, I see you
    sneezing, murderous thunder under their
    tongue. Rays of knowledge pierce their eyes, smoke of
85 truth blocks their nose; and the fire in the
    flesh, and the rainfall on the rock, and the
    myre in the mesh, and man shall not talk? amen ...

    O ... Galileo Galilei ...
    O ... Galileo Galilei ...
90 Grave and grievous galley-groans all relay
    The grandeur grinding of the painful play

72

Of rude rods on souls that forlornly pray
But whom suffering shall soon surely slay
On a particular forthdawning day.
95 They love this earth, but their bursting breath gives way.
They love this life, but their spirits won't stay.
The candlelight of knowledge and truth holds sway . . .
Inquisition fires faint-die away . . .
O, Elavanyo . . . Galileo
100 O, Elavanyo . . . Galilei.

28 Taga for Mbaye Dyob

LÉOPOLD SÉDAR SENGHOR

[*For tama*]

Mbaye Dyob! I will speak your name and your honour.

Dyob! I will hoist your name to the high mast of the ship
    returning, ring your name like the bell that sounds
    victory
I will sing your name Dyobene! you who called me master
    and
Warmed me with your fervour in the winter evenings
    around the red stove that made us cold.
5 Dyob! You cannot trace back your ancestry and bring order
    into black history, your forefathers are not sung by the
    voice of the *tama*
You should have never killed a rabbit, who went to ground
    under the bombs of the great vultures
Dyob! you who are not captain or airman or trooper, not
    even in the baggage train
But a second-class private in the Fourth Regiment of the
    Senegal Rifles
Dyob! I will celebrate your white honour.

10 The girls of Gandyol will make you a triumphal arch with
    their curved arms, arms of silver and of red gold

73

Make you a path of glory with their precious cloths from
the Rivers of the South.
Then they will make you with their mouths a necklace of
ivory better to wear than a royal garment
Then they will cradle your steps, their voices will mingle
with the waves of the sea
Then they will sing 'You have faced more than death, more
than the tanks and the planes that defy all magic
15 'You have faced hunger, you have faced cold, and the
humiliation of captivity.
O bravely, you have been the footstool of *griots* and clowns
You have put new nails in your cross so as not to desert
your companions
Not to break the unspoken pact
Not to leave your load to your comrades, whose backs bend
at each new start
20 Whose arms grow weak each evening when there is one less
hand to shake
And the face grows darker lit by one less look, the eyes
sunken, reflecting one less smile.'
Dyob! from Ngabu to the Walo, from Ngalam to the Sea
will rise the songs of the amber virgins
Let them be accompanied by strings of the *kora*, let them be
accompanied by the waves and the winds
Dyob! I speak your name and your honour.

Criticism

Here we concentrate on poetry that attacks whatever causes offence – whether individuals, communities or institutions. The attack may be either private or public. Under private criticism we may consider *lampoons* or the poetry of personal abuse, whereby the poet ridicules those whom he simply dislikes or takes his revenge on those who have done him wrong (nos. 29, 30, 35). Lampoons were widespread in traditional culture, not only because they helped to discourage certain excesses in the society but also because they gave individuals one means of relieving their pent-up emotions. So widespread was this form of poetry that in some societies it was a recognised form of art, such as *halo* among the Ewe of Ghana and *udje* among the Urhobo of Nigeria. Nowadays, however, the law of libel discourages the practice of one individual recklessly offending another. But some modern African poets are tending towards reviving the tradition of abuse poetry: here Kofi Awoonor manages to capture the two most outstanding characteristics of this kind of poetry, its sauciness and sensationalism.

Although it is not always easy to draw a line between private and public criticism, the latter addresses itself to issues concerning an entire community or even human society at large. Some of the traditional pieces here reveal how sensitive the oral poet is to matters of social conduct (nos. 31, 32) and of political well-being (no. 33). The rest of this section is devoted to the modern poet's reactions to the social (nos. 34, 38, 44), political (nos. 37, 39, 42) and religious (nos. 36, 40) issues which – either singly or jointly – in his judgement create an unhealthy climate for existence.

29 Katini's complaint

KATINI (CHOPI, MOZAMBIQUE)

Kapitini, you make trouble.
You find me in my hut having taken cider.
Kapitini, you have only just been made a messenger, yet
    you send Malova to come and catch me.
What have I done?

5 Kapitini, you make trouble.
Wani, son of Chivune!
Bakubakwane said to me,
'Don't waste your time with *Timbila*,
Go and build your hut.'

10 You woke up early in the morning to look for your
    sjambok and watch, Dibuliani
Kapitini, you beat both of us, me and my wife.
What have I done?
So my Mashewani died.

I heard them trying to hush it up.
15 Chipaupau, son of Madandani, was there.
Dibuliani spoke about me in the presence of strangers and
    they told me.
Even Fainde was there.
Why don't you tell me to my face?

Kapitini, you make trouble.
20 You find me in my hut having taken cider.
Kapitini, you have only just been made a messenger, yet
    you send Malova to come and catch me.
What have I done?
Kapitini, you make trouble.

30 Kodzo the imbecile

KOMI EKPE (EWE, GHANA)

Hm hm hm. Beware.
I will place a load on Kodzo's head.
Nugbleza informed me that
It is the women of Tsiame
5   Who goaded Kodzo into my song.
Questioners, this became the evil firewood
he'd gathered; his hands decayed,
his feet decayed.
I am the poet; I am not afraid of you.
10   Kodzo, winding in the air, his anus agape
his face long and curved
like the lagoon egret's beak.
Call him here. I say call him
and let me see his face.
15   He is the man from whom the wind runs,
          the man who eats off the farm
          he hasn't planted;
his face bent like the evil hoe
on its handle. Behold, ei ei ei
Kodzo did something. I forgive him his debt.
I will insult him since he poked
20   a stick into the flying ant's grove.
Amegavi said he has some wealth
And he took Kodzo's part.
The back of his head tapers off
as if they'd built a fetish hut
          on his breathing spot.
25   His face wags, a fool with a white ass.
The monkey opened his anus
in display to the owner of the farm.
The lion caught a game, alas,
his children took it away from him.
30   Kodzo's homestead shall fall,
          shall surely fall.
Questioners, let evil men die
Let death knock down the evil doer.

78

If I were the fetish in the creator's house
That will be your redemption.
35 Kodzo, this imbecile, evil animal
who fucks others' wives fatteningly
his buttocks run off, his teeth yellow
his penis has wound a rope around his waist
pulling him around and away,
40 his backside runs into a slope
his eye twisted like the sun-inspector,
he has many supporters in Tsiame
his mouth as long as the pig
blowing the twin whistle.
45 Something indeed has happened.

31 Attack traders

(IGBO, NIGERIA)

'Attack' traders were not good wives,
I am speaking of married women;
'Attack' traders were not good wives:
They made Biafran money with a vengeance,
5 They made Biafran money with a vengeance,
Tied their bundles to their cloth end to walk about,
Tied their bundles to their cloth end to walk about:
Before their husbands could speak twice, they would
    explode,
'By what are you bigger than I am? That is enough for you!
10 How much do you say you paid my parents?
How much do you say you paid my parents?
I will untie my cloth end and pay you,
I will untie my cloth end and pay you!'
At the end of the war,
15 'Master, lend me a little money to buy some ingredients.'

32 Lamba courts

(KELELA, ZAMBIA)

Mothers, I have been to many courts
To listen to the cases they settle:
They settle divorce cases,
They talk about witchcraft cases,
5 They talk about thefts,
They talk about tax defaulting
And refusing to do tribute-labour,
But the things I saw at Mushili's court,
These things I wondered at!
10 From nine o'clock in the morning
To four o'clock in the afternoon,
The cases were only adultery!
Then I asked the court messenger,
'Do you have any different matters to settle?'
15 The court messenger said, 'No,
There are no other matters.'
It is just like this in Lambaland —
There are no assault cases,
There are no theft cases:
20 These are the cases in the courts of Lambaland.

33 The woes of independence

(URHOBO, NIGERIA)

LEADER:

Fortitude indeed we need
A mistaken step warns against carelessness in a repeat
    action
Oh, innocence has cost the pangolin its life!
Our songs are like sugar
5 A sewing needle pierces a point once only
Gongs are chiming once again
Djudju is a major divinity
Ogude, a powerful communal deity
Every year we worship him
10 Renew his charms and renovate the shrine
These are signs of his impending festival
Spectators hear a marvellous story!
The much-talked-about self-government is now our
    undoing
Colleagues hold well the song for me

GROUP:

15 News came from Benin blacks would govern themselves
That the white men had exploited us for too long; so the
    UAC folded up in anger
The first few years were very pleasant
No one ever thought regret would follow
'After independence price of palm produce would soar' said
    a slogan
20 'Rubber trade would boom' screamed another
Oh, with corn they have lured the fowl into a trap
When the referendum time drew near
Kinsmen in foreign lands were summoned home
'Demo, Power, Zik, *Okokoroko*!'
25 The more you drown a calabash the more it floats! the
    campaign fever gripped everyone
Barely two years after, tumult of tax raids brought sleepless
    nights to all
'The police are in town, let no one brave the streets'

And the naughty children would taunt defaulters:
'*Kikighwo*, run fast!'
30 And a stampede would begin
Those who ran into gullies were countless
And the injured were a multitude
The swift of foot escaped paying that year
But a debt does not grow mouldy with time
35 Soon angry murmur filled the air:
'Should one defecate in the home for fear of tax?
The so-called liberation is now a curse.
We move stealthily like a fox prowling after a stray fowl
Independence has brought us woes.'
40 Whilst we fumed over this letters came from Benin that the
government was broke
Tax receipts for four, six years were demanded, for the poor
living was a nightmare
Our race for progress is now at bay
Demo, *Okokoroko*, One Nigeria!

34 Armanda

JARED ANGIRA

Armanda was a well-meaning lass:
Read anthropology at college,
Danced the tango quite a lot
Drank the whisky on the rocks,
5 Smoked Dunhill to the hills,
And drove men off their heads
By her beauty, the beauty of the peahen.

Armanda was a well-meaning lass:
Hated the kitchen and its bureaucracy,
10 Abhorred the cards and the bridge,
Disliked the chess and the radio,
Screamed at the telly,
And frowned at the Scrabble.

Armanda was a well-meaning lass
15 Until she turned the apple-cart
Marrying the semi-paralytic Ray;
That was 'true love', so she said,
And insisted that the crutches
Were part of Ray that sent her on heat
20 And tickled her most!

Armanda was a well-meaning lass
Until they flew to distant lands
To sow the seeds of *happiness*;
In her well meaning, thank God,
25 There is hell expanding each day.
She led him to the bank
Laying all the millions
Into Armanda who missed nothing
And misses nobody.

30 In her well meaning, thank heavens,
There is hell, heating each day.
She led him to the orthopaedics

83

Recommending a plastic thigh.
Henceforth, Ray too could dance the tango
35   And converse at cocktail parties
All without the 'tickling' crutches.

There is no perfection in this world:
The surgery a disaster,
Ray regressed to the wheelchair
40   And Armanda confined to sympathy.
The well-meaning eyes went shy
And the sight of love
Became the sight of pity.
Safe with the account,
45   Safe with the pills,
Suddenly she qualified as judge
To judge the quick and the slow.

Life between two people
Is but plastic association
50   When one is resigned to pity
When one must always give
And another ever receive,
If I must dress you up
And push your wheelchair,
55   You too must dress me up
And drive me to the beach
A meaningful marriage.

One evening as the wind blew
A piece of paper came floating
60   In the wind and as it rested on Ray's lap
He read what he had always expected one day,
      'Goodbye love, goodbye Ray,
      I thought I could change it
      But I have failed
65   And I've flown home.'
And Ray never thought
Of his millions in her name.

35 Songs of abuse: (i) To Stanislaus the renegade

KOFI AWOONOR

This is addressed to you, Stanislaus, wherever you are.
Listen you punk, the last time we met you were selling
   faulty guns in Addis
I heard you panting afterwards in a Cairo whorehouse
Before I knew you had split with my spring overcoat
5 a cashmere job I danced for in a bar in Kabul.
I heard you were peddling fake jewelry to Pueblo Indians
and Washington hippies. The jail you occupied in
   Poonaville, Tennessee
was burnt down after you escaped; they could not eradicate
   the smell.
Verna wrote the other day, you remember Verna
10 the lean assed girl whose rent money you stole in Detroit,
she wrote to say you are still running around in her
   underpants.
What is this I hear about you preparing to settle in the
   Congo
to grow hashish in the valley of the Zaire?
I will be waiting for you; for every gun you buy
15 I shall command a thousand assegais, for every sword
a million Ashanti machetes and Masai spears
I am not afraid of you any more. Those days are past
when you stole my school fees and my catapult
and fled into the cove beyond bird island.
20 I too came of age.

36 I am ignorant of the Good Word in the Clean Book

OKOT P'BITEK

[*an extract*]

My husband
Looks down upon me;
He says
I am a mere pagan,
5 I do not know
The way of God.
He says
I am ignorant
Of the Good Word
10 In the Clean Book
And I do not have
A Christian name.
Ocol dislikes me
Because, he says,
15 *Jok* is in my head
And I like visiting
The diviner-priest
Like my mother!

He says
20 He is ashamed of me
Because when the *Jok*
In my head
Has been provoked
It throws me down
25 As if I have fits.

Ocol laughs at me
Because I cannot
Cross myself properly

          In the name of the Father
30   *And of the Son*
          And the Clean Ghost

     And I do not understand
     The confession,
     And I fear
35   The bushy-faced, fat-bellied padre
     Before whom people kneel
     When they pray.

          *

     I refused to join
     The Protestant catechist class,
40   Because I did not want
     To become a house-girl,
     I did not want
     To become a slave
     To a woman with whom
45   I may share a man.

     Oh how young girls
     Labour to buy a name!
     You break your back
     Drawing water
50   For the wives
     Of the teachers,
     The skin of your hand
     Hardens and peels off
     Grinding millet and simsim.
55   You hoe their fields,
     Split firewood,
     You cut grass for thatching
     And for starting fires,
     You smear their floors
60   With cow dung and black soil
     And harvest their crops.

     And when they are eating
     They send you to play games
     To play the board game

65   Under the mango tree!
     And girls gather
     Wild sweet potatoes
     And eat them raw
     As if there is a famine,
70   And they are so thin
     They look like
     Cattle that have dysentery!

     You work as if
     You are a newly-eloped girl!
75   The wives of Protestant
     Church teachers and priests
     Are a happy lot.
     They sit with their legs stretched out
     And bask in the morning sun,
80   All they know
     Is hatching a lot of children.

37 Abolish laughter first, I say

DENNIS BRUTUS

Abolish laughter first, I say:
Or find its gusts reverberate
with shattering force through halls of glass
that artifice and lies have made.

5   O, it is mute now – not by choice
and drowned by multi-choired thunder –
train wails, babies' sirens' wails:
jackboots battering the sagging gate
the wolfwind barks where the tinplate gapes,
10   earth snarls apocalyptic anger.

Yet where they laugh thus, hoarse and deep
dulled by the wad of bronchial phlegm
and ragged pleuras hiss and rasp
the breath incites a smouldering flame;
15   here where they laugh (for once) erect –
no jim-crowing cackle for a watching lord,
no sycophant smile while heart contracts –
here laugh moulds heart as flame builds sword.

Put out this flame, this heart, this laugh?
20   Never! The self at its secret hearth
nurses its smoulder, saves its heat
while oppression's power is charred to dust.

38 Peasants

SYL CHEYNEY-COKER

The agony: I say their agony!

the agony of imagining their squalor but never knowing it
the agony of cramping them in roach infected shacks
the agony of treating them like chattel slaves
5   the agony of feeding them abstract theories they do not
      understand
the agony of their lugubrious eyes and battered souls
the agony of giving them party cards but never party
      support
the agony of marshalling them on election day but never
      on banquet nights
the agony of giving them melliferous words but mildewed
      bread
10   the agony of their cooking hearths dampened with unuse
the agony of their naked feet on the hot burning tarmac
the agony of their children with projectile bellies
the agony of long miserable nights
the agony of their thatched houses with too many holes
15   the agony of erecting hotels but being barred from them
the agony of watching the cavalcade of limousines
the agony of grand state balls for God knows who
the agony of those who study meaningless 'isms in
      incomprehensible languages
the agony of intolerable fees for schools with no jobs in
      sight
20   the agony of it all I say the agony of it all
but above all the damn agony of appealing to their patience
Africa beware.! their patience is running out!

39 Loser of everything

DAVID DIOP

The sun used to laugh in my hut
And my women were lovely and lissom
Like palms in the evening breeze.
My children would glide over the mighty river
5   Of deadly depths
And my canoes would battle with crocodiles.
The motherly moon accompanied our dances
The heavy frantic rhythm of the tomtom,
Tomtom of joy, tomtom of carefree life
10   Amid the fires of liberty.

Then one day, Silence ...
It seemed the rays of the sun went out
In my hut empty of meaning.
My women crushed their painted mouths
15   On the thin hard lips of steel-eyed conquerors
And my children left their peaceful nakedness
For the uniform of iron and blood.
Your voice went out too
The irons of slavery tore my heart to pieces
20   Tomtoms of my nights, tomtoms of my fathers.

40 Easter penitence

MICHAEL J. C. ECHERUO

O crucible,
O furnace.
  from the darkness and delirium
  the emptiness of another ecstasy.

5 O crucifix,
O chalice.
  from the remnants and fragrance
  the heartburn of Eastern sacrifice.

O sunrise!
10 Bird of glory at dawn
  Bird of wonder at dawn
  Reigning for ever in glory!

Pilgrim of Emmaus
speaking to him in their tongue
15 arguing.
And he answered only in a word.
  Raca!
O thou God!

Speak again.
20 *Raca!*
  left thy child in the fog
  left thy bug in the sun
O thou God!

  miserere.
25 oil water and light
crucible O, and the crucifix.
  O God.

41 Yes, Mandela, we shall be moved

KEORAPETSE KGOSITSILE

Yes, Mandela, we shall be moved
We are Men enough to have a conscience
We are Men enough to immortalise your song
We are Men enough to look Truth straight in the face

5 To defy the devils who traded in the human Spirit

For Black cargoes and material superprofits
We emerge to sing a Song of Fire with Roland

We emerge to prove Truth cannot be enslaved
In chains or imprisoned in an island inferno
10 We emerge to stand Truth on her two feet We emerge

To carry the banner of humanism across the face of the
Earth

Our voice in unison with our poet's proudly says
'Change is gonna come!'

42 When this carnival finally closes

JACK MAPANJE

When this frothful carnival finally closes, brother
When your drumming veins dry, these very officers
Will burn the scripts of the praises we sang to you
And shatter the calabashes you drank from. Your
5 Charms, these drums, and the effigies blazing will
Become the accomplices to your lie-achieved world!
Your bamboo hut on the beach they'll make a bonfire
Under the cover of giving their hero a true traditional
Burial, though in truth to rid themselves of another
10 Deadly spirit that might otherwise have haunted them,
And at the wake new mask dancers will quickly leap
Into the arena dancing to tighter skins, boasting
Other clans of calabashes as the undertakers jest:
What did he think he would become, a God? The devil!

43 How can I sing?

ODIA OFEIMUN

I cannot blind myself
to putrefying carcasses in the market place
pulling giant vultures
from the sky

5 Nor to these flywhisks:
how can I escape these mind-ripping scorpion-tails
deployed in the dark
with ignominious licence
by those who should buttress faith
10 in living, faith in lamplights?

94

And how can I sing
when they stuff cobwebs in my mouth
spit the rheum of their blank sense
of direction in my eyes
15 — who will open the portals of
my hope in this desultory walk?

Yet I cannot blunt my feelers
to cheapen my ingrained sorrow
I cannot refuse to drink from
20 the gourd you hold to my lips

A garland of subversive litanies
should answer these morbid landscapes
my land, my woman

44 Pedestrian, to passing Benz-man

ALBERT OJUKA

You man, lifted gently
out of the poverty and suffering
we so recently shared; I say —
why splash the muddy puddle on to
5 my bare legs, as if, still unsatisfied
with your seated opulence
you must sully the unwashed
with your diesel-smoke and mud-water
and force him buy, beyond his means
10 a bar of soap from your shop?
a few years back we shared a master
today you have none, while I have
exchanged a parasite for something worse.
But maybe a few years is too long a time.

45 I anoint my flesh (Tenth day of fast)

WOLE SOYINKA

I anoint my flesh
Thought is hallowed in the lean
Oil of solitude
I call you forth, all, upon
5 Terraces of light. Let the dark
Withdraw

I anoint my voice
And let it sound hereafter
Or dissolve upon its lonely passage
10 In your void. Voices new
Shall rouse the echoes when
Evil shall again arise

I anoint my heart
Within its flame I lay
15 Spent ashes of your hate —
Let evil die.

The Environment

The Environment

All poetry is, in a sense, an observation. The very surroundings and conditions in which the poet lives provide his most immediate material.

Many poems in the oral tradition are devoted to observing those aspects of nature that relate to man's sources of livelihood: an example here is the Yoruba poem *The baboon* (no. 48), obviously connected to the hunting life. Such evidence has led some scholars, especially anthropologists, to conclude that African oral literature has fundamentally a *functional* value, in the sense that it reflects practical concerns. But it is clear from the brilliant description of the baboon that the poet is guided more by a sense of physical appeal than by practical interests.

Modern African environmental poetry owes very little to the oral tradition. The modern African poet seems more inclined to follow the example of the European poets in their positive (romantic) or negative portraits of the environment. It is possible to discover some common concerns in the traditional and modern poetry — such as a reflection of the poet's personal feelings in his description of the environment (less so in no. 47 than in no. 53) and a condemnation of the urban environment (nos. 46, 47); but such similarities can only be explained on the basis of the poets' human feelings, they do not reflect an imitation of the oral tradition.

46 The sky

(EWE, GHANA)

The sky at night is like a big city
where beasts and men abound,
but never once has anyone
killed a fowl or a goat,
5 and no bear has ever killed a prey.
There are no accidents; there are no losses.
Everything knows its way.

47 The train

B. M. KHAKETLA (SOTHO, LESOTHO)

Tjhutjhumakgala, beautiful thing of the White man,
There's a steel rope tethering this black bovine,
As for a woven rope, he would break it!

It is, indeed, the Mother-of-smoke-that-trails-behind,
5 A Madman, Weaver-of-a-*towane*-grass-hat,
Creator-of-fog even while the skies are clear,
Churner-of-clouds even while the winds are still,
Leaving us covered with blackness;
Smoke billows up, and sparks fly,
10 As when a bonfire is fed with dry weeds.

Its speed, this Bringer-of-sorrow,
Creates a wind-storm, shaker-of-things-that-are-still,
And the grasses and the trees sway madly back and forth,
Moving fast and being in simulated flight;

15 And the frog croaks in wonder from the stream,
And the antbear refuses to leave his hole,
Strange too is the swirling dust of the whirlwind,

And it seems that wind-storms are coming,
Powerful winds raised with magic power;
20 And many doubt not it's the Day of Judgement,
And forsakers of the faith think once more of prayer!

The train is spiteful, Little-Black-One,
It took away my brother and he was lost forever,
My heart was sore, tears welled in my eyes,
25 And flowed like rivers down my cheeks,
And there I stood crying aloud with grief!

Millipede of the fields, Dark-brown-coloured-one,
Your feet are a thousand, puny ones are they.
Draw yourself in haste and keep abreast of time,
30 Draw yourself in haste that they may come into view
The mountains of my homeland – Souru, Letlwepe,
    Ntshupe,
And also such as Mmaseepho and Sekitshing.

48 The baboon

ODENIYI APOLEBIEJI (YORUBA, NIGERIA)

Laare.
Opomu who teaches a dog how to hunt successfully.
Having mastered the technique of hunting, the dog eats up
    Opomu.
O baboon.
5 I greet you, possessor of hard-skinned swollen buttocks,
Having a whip in each hand.
Whom the hunter pursues and in the process besmears his
    smock with earth.
Animal speckled all over his body like a patient cured of
    severe smallpox. Wearer of a cap enhancing the face,
    drummer in the forest.
He who covers his mouth with slab-like jaws.
10 Animal from whose hands the hunter has not received a
    wife, yet who receives self-prostration homage from the
    hunter.

100

Immediately I see him on the ground, I carefully hide
	myself.
While he was away from home, an extra share of occiput
	was reserved for him.
On his arrival, he started crying for an extra share for his
	mouth.
He who, after raiding a farm, returns to his perch, his
	mouth hanging down like a Dahomean's pocket.
15	Possessor of eyes shy like a bride's, seeing the farmers' wives
	on their husbands' farms.
Bulky fellow on the *igba* tree, uncle to the Red Patas
	Monkey.
Gentleman on the tree-top, whose fine figure intoxicates
	him like liquor.
Ladoogi whose mouth is protuberant and longish like a
	ginning rod.
Whose jaws are like wooden spoons and whose chest looks
	as if it has a wooden bar in it.
20	Whose eyes are deep-set as it goes a-raiding farms, even the
	farms of his relatives-in-law.
Four hundred while going through the farm.
Twelve hundred when returning to the bush.
He said it was a pity
It was the farm of his relatives-in-law,
25	Otherwise he would have eaten two hundred more.
He whom his mother gazed and gazed upon and burst out
	weeping,
Saying her child's handsomeness would be the ruin of him.
Possessor of a hair-denuded posterior.
He whose claws are mischievously sharp, he who defiantly
	stares at human beings.
30	Whose female's udders are never left in peace, nursing
	mother who continually clings to the branches of trees.

[*Song*]
Stout and noisy,
A baboon I saw on my forest farm, as it was munching
	away.

[*Refrain*]
Stout it was, munching away.

49 Ibadan

JOHN PEPPER CLARK

Ibadan,
     running splash of rust
and gold — flung and scattered
among seven hills like broken
china in the sun.

50 Daybreak

SUSAN LWANGA

O dawn
Where do you hide your paints at night
That cool breath, that scent
With which you sweeten the early air?

5   O dawn
What language do you use
To instruct the birds to sing
Their early songs
And insects to sound
10   The rhythm of an African heartbeat?

O dawn
Where do you find the good will
To speed the early traffic on its way,
Rouse the cold drunkard
15   And send your askaris and barking dogs
To chase thieves to their dens?

O dawn
Whose cold breath makes young boys and girls
Glad of a warm sheet,
20 Enflames the dreams of unmarried ones,
And brings familiar noises
To gladden the hearts of the married.

51 The sweet brew at Chitakale

JACK MAPANJE

The old woman squats before a clay jar of *thobwa*
She uncovers the basket lid from the jar and
Stirs attention with a gourdful of the brew.

The customers have all been here: cyclists
5   In dripping sweat have deposited their coins
In the basket gulping down their share,

Pedestrians on various chores have talked
Before the exchange and then cooled their
Parched throats to their money's worth,

10 But this bus passenger bellows for a gourdful
From the window, drinks deliberately slowly until
The conductor presses the go-button –

The woman picks up the pieces of her broken
Gourd, and dusting her bottom, again squats
15 Confronting her brew with a borrowed cup.

52 Sunset

OSWALD MBUYISENI MTSHALI

The sun spun like
a tossed coin.
It whirled on the azure sky,
it clattered into the horizon,
5   it clicked in the slot,
and neon-lights popped
and blinked 'Time expired', as on a parking meter.

53 Autumn burns me

LENRIE PETERS

Autumn burns me with
primaeval fire. Makes my skin
taut with expectation,
hurls me out of summer fatigue
5   on to a new Bridge of Sighs.

Somewhere I feel the heart
of the earth pumping, and down below
it bleeds in a million ripples.
I drop a sweet memory into
10 the flow and the cascading grips me with fascination

Great trees in transit fall
are made naked in langour of shame
solitary like actors on a stage
like stars, orphans, celebrities,
15 politicians, uncomfortably mysteriously like you and me.

But I will not mourn the sadness.
I will go dead-leaf gathering

for the fire in a slice of sunlight
to fill my lungs with odours of decay
20 and my eyes with mellowed rainbow colours

I will go creeping down tasselled
latticed tree-avenues of light
and listen to squirrel tantrums
punctuate the orchestration of autumn silence
25 and hold in my hand the coiling stuff of nature

Then I will love
Yes love; extravagantly under
the flutter of dying leaves
and in a shadow of mist
30 in wonder; for autumn is wonder and wonder is hope.

54 An African thunderstorm

DAVID RUBADIRI

From the west
Clouds come hurrying with the wind
Turning
Sharply
5 Here and there
Like a plague of locusts
Whirling
Tossing up things on its tail
Like a madman chasing nothing.

10 Pregnant clouds
Ride stately on its back
Gathering to perch on hills
Like dark sinister wings;
The wind whistles by
15 And trees bend to let it pass.

In the village
Screams of delighted children
Toss and turn
In the din of whirling wind,
20 Women —
Babies clinging on their backs —
Dart about
In and out
Madly
25 The wind whistles by
Whilst trees bend to let it pass.

Clothes wave like tattered flags
Flying off
To expose dangling breasts
30 As jaggered blinding flashes
Rumble, tremble, and crack
Amidst the smell of fired smoke
And the pelting march of the storm.

55 I think it rains

WOLE SOYINKA

I think it rains
That tongues may loosen from the parch
Uncleave roof-tops of the mouth, hang
Heavy with knowledge

5 I saw it raise
The sudden cloud, from ashes. Settling
They joined in a ring of grey; within,
the circling spirit

Oh it must rain
10 These closures on the mind, binding us
In strange despairs, teaching
Purity of sadness

And how it beats
Skeined transparencies on wings
15 Of our desires, searing dark longings
In cruel baptisms

Rain-reeds, practised in
The grace of yielding, yet unbending
From afar, this your conjugation with my earth
20 Bares crouching rocks.

56 The stone speaks

M. B. ZIMUNYA

I am old and age-less
young and youth-less
living and life-less
dead without death.

5   I'm Silence.

Old.
Older than Moses and Jesus;
older than Greece and Rome;
than the river and the ruins;
10 than Mwenemutapa and Rhodes;
than Chaminuka,
older than all.

Moment.

Reflection

Reflection

The poems in this section are dominated by a certain philosophical or else moralistic tone. Many of the reflective poems of the oral tradition are of the moralistic kind, largely because these poems were traditionally used for educating the younger citizens on the values of the society. This was done either through direct teaching, as in the Kanuri poem (no. 57), which shows an Islamic influence; or through riddles and proverbs (as in no. 58); or else through folktales which use animal and other symbols for illustrating elements of conduct, as in no. 61 which comes from *ifa* tradition, the storehouse of Yoruba traditional wisdom and morality. This does not mean, however, that abstract reflection is unknown in traditional African poetry: *On variety* (no. 60) is an example of poetry which uses biological elements to drive home a psychological point.

Some modern African poets endeavour to echo the reflective quality of their oral traditions. Space does not allow us here to consider, for instance, the use of proverbial form in both traditional and modern reflective poetry from Ghana. But Dadié's poem here has something of that mystical flavour which is contained in *The well* (no. 58), and in *Streamside exchange* (no. 64) Clark explores the uncertainty of man's future in an arrangement which definitely has a folk-song element to it. Otherwise, modern African reflective poetry owes very little to the oral tradition. It can hardly perform the function of educating the youth in the way that the traditional poetry did: a large proportion of the readers are not even Africans. The tendency towards abstract reflection – as we can see in the poems by Angira and Zimunya here – is therefore much stronger in the modern poetry.

57 On truth

(KANURI, NIGERIA)

One thread of truth in a shuttle
Will weave a hundred threads of lies.
Vomiting one's liver cures the most severe biliousness;
The hatching of an egg is unpleasant for the shell:
5 Do not match yourself against Providence.
God is all-powerful:
He prevents the eye from seeing the eyelashes.
Eggs become lice:
The small man becomes the great man.
10 Stick to the truth:
Truth is like the light of dawn,
Untruthfulness is like darkness at sunset.

58 The well

(SUSU, GUINEA)

There is a well
that has five kinds of water.
There is sugared water
and salty water.
5 There is tasteless water
and bitter water.
The fifth water is red
red like blood.
This well is the head.

59 On companionship

(SWAHILI, KENYA)

Give me the minstrel's seat that I may sit and ask you a
    word, my friends.
Let me ask for what reason or rhyme women refuse to
    marry?
Woman cannot exist except by man, what is there in that
    to vex some of them so?
A woman is she who has a husband and she cannot but
    prosper.
5 Cleave unto your man and his kinsmen will become jealous
His kinsmen have planted cocoyams but the fruit they reap
    is dum-palm nuts!
We think you plant the borassus palm, the teak, the mnga
    and the solanum tree.
When man goes on the road he goes with a friend, for he
    who walks alone has no good fortune.
As man goes through life soon he is pierced by the thorn,
10 Or the sand-mote enters his eye and he needs a friend to
    remove it.
Likewise I give you advice, the rich man and the poor man
    join hands across the shroud.
Better a loin-cloth without disgrace than the fine-flowered
    shawl of shame.

60 Life's variety

(YORUBA, NIGERIA)

Why do we grumble because a tree is bent,
When, in our streets, there are even men who are bent?
Why must we complain that the new moon is slanting?
Can anyone reach the skies to straighten it?

5 Can't we see that some cocks have combs on their heads,
      but no plumes in their tails?
   And some have plumes in their tails, but no claws on their
      toes?
   And others have claws on their toes, but no power to crow?
   He who has a head has no cap to wear, and he who has a
      cap has no head to wear it on.
   The Owa has everything but a horse's stable.
10 Some great scholars of Ifa cannot tell the way to Ofa.
   Others know the way to Ofa, but not one line of Ifa.
   Great eaters have no food to eat, and great drinkers no
      wine to drink:
   Wealth has a coat of many colours.

61 The lion refused to perform sacrifice

(YORUBA, NIGERIA)

The twisted wooden stump which crosses the road in a
   crooked way.
Ifa divination was performed for the Lion,
On the day he was going into the forest to hunt for
   animals.
He asked whether the hunting expedition to which he was
   going
5 Would give him abundant rewards.
He performed divination because of that.
He was asked to perform sacrifice so that he might triumph
   over his enemies.
But the Lion boasted that nobody was bold enough to work
   against his interest.
He said that he would not perform sacrifice.
10 Before long, the Lion went into the forest to hunt.
Esu turned himself into wind,
And followed him.
When the Lion got into the forest,

He saw one *ira*,
15 And he killed it.
But as he was trying to open up its internal organs,
Esu plucked a fruit of the *afon* tree,
And threw it against the Lion's hips.
As soon as it landed on his hips,
20 The Lion ran away.
Before he returned,
Esu carried away the animal.
When the Lion returned,
And searched for a long time without seeing the animal,
25 He looked for another animal.
But the same thing happened.
When the Lion became very hungry,
He hastened to go and perform sacrifice.
After he had performed sacrifice,
30 He went back into the forest to hunt for animals,
And Esu did not frighten him again.
He started to dance,
He started to rejoice.
He said, The twisted wooden stump which crosses the road
   in a crooked way.
35 Ifa divination was performed for the Lion
On the day he was going into the forest to hunt for
   animals.
He was told to take care of the divinities.
He was told that it would be a good thing,
If he performed sacrifice.
40 It is not a long time,
It is not a distant date,
Come and meet us in conquest.

62 An evening libretto

JARED ANGIRA

Sometimes I feel
The presence of space
A large hall
In my heart
5 And I invite all
And they trudge along
Responding to the call.

And alas, alas,
What a disappointment
10 Not even one of them
Finds a standing space
A heart full of every vice
Full of escape into the mystic.

And I watch them go
15 With guilt on my conscience,
Each one of them
Wishing to try elsewhere.

What tragedy
That the outsiders
20 Must come
To confirm the full
Occupancy of the heart.

The irony of life
That at times you believe
25 That you know yourself best
Only to discover
The great self-deception.

63 Their behaviour

DENNIS BRUTUS

Their guilt
is not so very different from ours:
— who has not joyed in the arbitrary exercise of power
or grasped for himself what might have been another's
5   and who has not used superior force in the moment when
       he could,
(and who of us has not been tempted to these things?) —
so, in their guilt,
the bared ferocity of teeth,
chest-thumping challenge and defiance,
10   the deafening clamour of their prayers
to a deity made in the image of their prejudice
which drowns the voice of conscience,
is mirrored our predicament
but on a social, massive, organised scale
15   which magnifies enormously
as the private deshabille of love
becomes obscene in orgies.

64 · Streamside exchange

JOHN PEPPER CLARK

CHILD:
River bird, river bird,
Sitting all day long
On hook over grass,
River bird, river bird,
5 Sing to me a song
Of all that pass
And say,
Will mother come back today?

BIRD:
You cannot know
10 And should not bother;
Tide and market come and go
And so has your mother.

65 With purity hath nothing been won

TABAN LO LIYONG

with purity hath nothing been won
greece came not thru purity
christ died through the impure
only with impurity hath japan moved ahead
5   the american beast came about through things impure
purity kills creativity in the womb
impurity spreads with health
eve ate the apple for impuritys sake
my heart bless thyself
10   thou truckest not with things that are pure
impurity fills you up like angels of god
thou art greater than earth and hell
for impurity limiteth the child in the cradle
impurity is boundless like my soul

66 Look at this globe

M. B. ZIMUNYA

Look at this globe
Enclosing the heart of light
Whose translucence
Allows light to pierce it
5   With needlets of rays
Whose glory traps the human eye.
I should rejoice
If my flesh
Weren't a light-proof bulb
10   Enclosing an ebony heart,
Whose rays of darkness
Beat those of light.

118

Appeal

Human beings are moved to make an appeal or a plea when they are faced with situations beyond their power. In traditional African culture such appeals are frequently addressed to spiritual forces like the supreme deity, subordinate gods, ancestors and protective spirits. With the infiltration of the traditional religion by foreign ones like Christianity and Islam, appeals are also often made to the supreme deities of these religions by the traditional folk.

In many cases the appeal is made, either individually (no. 70) or as a group (no. 68), to these divinities for a favour. In other cases the appeal takes the form of a consultation made through an intermediary, such as a diviner or ritual priest (no. 69). The client who makes the appeal has a problem, or desires to know from the gods the prospects of something he wishes to undertake; the intermediary carries out the consultation with the spiritual forces through a difficult medium of symbols that contain the clue to a solution or an answer to the client's request. In either case, the language of the traditional African poetry of appeal reveals a certain intensity of feeling.

The appeal is also deeply felt in the written poetry, although some of the personal warmth is lost in the movement from the oral performance to cold print. The divinity frequently addressed in modern African poetry is the Christian God. But religion is one of those acts that reflect the basic character and world-view of a people; and some African writers, anxious to reconcile themselves with their native traditions, have taken to addressing their traditional divinities in their poetry. The poems in this section by Ndu, Okigbo and Senghor are striking examples of this tendency.

Appeals may, of course, be addressed to individuals or authorities also. Osadebay's poem here is one such appeal.

67 Drum appeal

(AKAN, GHANA)

The path has crossed the river.
The river has crossed the path.
Which is the elder?
We made the path and found the river.
5 The river is from long ago,
The river is from the Creator of the universe,
Kokon Tano,
Birefia Tano.
River-god of the King of Ashanti,
10 Noble river, noble and gracious one,
When we are about to go to war,
We break the news to you.
Slowly and patiently I get on my feet.
Slowly and patiently I get on my feet.
15 Ta Kofi, noble one,
Firampon condolences!
        condolences!
        condolences!
Ta Kofi, noble one,
20 The drummer of the Talking Drum says
He is kneeling before you.
He prays you, he is about to drum on the Talking Drum.
When he drums, let his drumming be smooth and steady.
Do not let him falter.
25 I am learning, let me succeed.

68 Rain-making litany

(LANGO, UGANDA)

[*Recitative*]
We overcome this wind.   [*Response*]
                                                We overcome.
We desire the rain to fall, that it be poured
    in showers quickly.   Be poured.
Ah! thou rain, I adjure thee fall. If thou
    rainest, it is well.   It is well.
A drizzling confusion.   Confusion.
5   If it rains and our food ripens, it is well. It is well.
If the children rejoice, it is well.   It is well.
If it rains, it is well. If our women rejoice,
    it is well.   It is well.
If the young men sing, it is well.   It is well.
A drizzling confusion.   Confusion.
10 If our grain ripens, it is well.   It is well.
If our women rejoice.   It is well.
If the children rejoice.   It is well.
If the young men sing.   It is well.
If the aged rejoice.   It is well.
15 An overflowing in the granary.   Overflowing.
May our grain fill the granaries.   May it fill.
A torrent in flow.   A torrent.
If the wind veers to the south, it is well.   It is well.
If the rain veers to the south, it is well.   It is well.

69 The White Bagre

(LoDAGAA, GHANA)

[*opening lines*]

Gods,
ancestors,
guardians,
beings of the wild,
5 the leather bottles
say we should perform,
because of the scorpion's sting,
because of suicide,
aches in the belly,
10 pains in the head.
The elder brother
slept badly.
He took out some guinea corn
and hurried along
15 to the diviner
who poured out his bag
and then said,
let's grasp the stick.
They did so
20 and he picked up 'deity'
and he picked up 'the wild'
and he picked up 'sacrifice'.
He picked up 'deity',
that was what
25 he picked up first.
He picked out 'deity'
and began to ask,
What 'deity'?
Deity of childbirth?
30 Deity of farming?
Deity of daughters?
Deity of grandfathers?
Deity of grandmothers?

Deity of the bowstring?
35 Deity of chicken breeding?
You reject them all.
Deity of meetings?
The cowries fell favourably:
it was so.
40 The elder
began to think,
got up quietly
and hurried off
to his father's house.
45 He called his children
to come,
and they came there
thinking to themselves
it was a call to eat.
50 They ran there,
met together
and the elder
got up and went out
to stand on a pile of earth.
55 Taking some ashes
and cold water,
he began to spurt it out
spurted it over the children
saying,
60 'I spurt it over you.
If you see
shea fruit,
don't eat them.
If you see
65 new crops,
don't eat them.'
He told the children
they could go down.
When they got home
70 the elder
lay down to sleep
but tried in vain.
So he got up
and went again
75 to the diviner's house

124

to pour out the bag
and he asked him
about his fear.
'What sort of fear is it?'
80 'It is not fear.
Last night
when I lay down,
I didn't sleep.
That is why
85 I got up and came here,
came to ask
if you know
whether you can help me
in this matter.'
90 So he spoke
and went home.
He went back
and reached his house,
and as he got there,
95 see the children
who have gathered around.
In the evening
they came together
and he told them
100 he had been
to enquire
at the diviner's
and was told
it was the deity
105 that has come
from the front,
that is pointing
with the right hand,
that has come
110 to stay here,
that has come
bringing childbirth,
that has come
bringing good hunting.
115 He has not come to return.
So he spoke
and paused.

'And yet
you children
120   don't want to farm,
don't want to raise chickens.
You don't want
to possess
the truth.
125   And yet
the problems
are beyond us,
we, the initiates.
The first men
130   searched in vain
and they went
and deceived us,
we, the living ones.
They went away
135   and they should have
taken it along
to the land of the dead.
But they left it
for us
140   and we search in vain.'
And so it was
that he took cold water
and took ashes
and said,
145   'It is good health
that I want.'
He spat out the water
so it spurted over them.

70 To Ogun

(YORUBA, NIGERIA)

Now I will chant a salute to my Ogun.
O belligerent One, you are not cruel.
The Ejemu, foremost chief of Iwonran Town,
He who smartly accoutres himself and goes to the fight.
5 A butterfly chances upon a civet-cat's excrement and flies
    high up into the air.
Ogun don't fight against me.
Don't play with me.
Just be to me a giver of good luck.
You said you were playing with a child.
10 I saw much blood flowing from the girl's private parts.
Ogun don't fight against me.
Don't play with me.
You said you were playing with a boy.
I saw much blood flowing from the boy's private parts.
15 Ogun, don't fight against me.
Don't play with me.
You were playing with a pigeon.
The pigeon's head was torn from its neck.
Ogun, don't fight against me.
20 Don't play with me.
You were playing with a sheep.
The sheep was slaughtered with a knife.
Ogun, don't fight against me.
Don't play with me.
25 You were playing with a male dog.
The male dog was beheaded.
Ogun, don't fight against me.
Don't play with me.
O Belligerent One, you are not cruel.
30 The Ejemu, foremost chief of Iwonran Town,
He who smartly accoutres himself and goes to the fight.
A butterfly chances upon a civet-cat's excrement and flies
    high up into the air.

There were initially sixteen chiefs
In the town called Ilagbede, of these the paramount chief
    was Ejitola,
35   Ejitola Ireni, son of Ogun, the blacksmith who, as he speaks,
    lightly strikes his hammer upon his anvil repeatedly.
Son of he who smashes up an iron implement and forges it
    afresh into new form.
Son of he who dances, as if to the *emele* drum music, while
    holding the hollow bamboo poles used for blowing air
    upon the coal embers fire in his smithy. He who swells
    out like a toad as he operates the smithy's bellows.
I will chant a salute to my Ogun.
O Belligerent One, you are gentle, the Ejemu, foremost
    chief of Iwonran, He who smartly accoutres himself and
    goes to the fight.
40   Some people said Ogun was a failure as a hunter.
Ogun therefore killed a man and packed the corpse into a
    domestic fire.
Then he killed the man's wife and packed her corpse
    behind the fireplace.
When some people still said that Ogun was a failure as a
    hunter,
The sword which Ogun was holding in his hand,
45   He stuck into the ground on a river bank.
The sword became a plant, the plant now called *labelabe*.
Hence the saying 'No ceremony in honour of Ogun can be
    performed at the river-side,
Without *labelabe's* getting to know of it.'
It is I, a son of Akinwamde, who am performing.
50   I do good turns for people of good appearance.

71 A plea for mercy

KWESI BREW

We have come to your shrine to worship –
We the sons of the land.
The naked cowherd has brought
The cows safely home,
5   And stands silent with the bamboo flute
Wiping the rain from his brow;
As the birds brood in their nests
Awaiting the dawn with unsung melodies;
The shadows crowd on the shores
10   Pressing their lips against the bosom of the sea
The peasants home from their labours
Sit by their log-fires
Telling tales of long ago.
Why should we the sons of the land
15   Plead unheeded before your shrine,
When our hearts are full of song
And our lips tremble with sadness
The little firefly vies with the star,
The log-fire with the sun
20   The water in the calabash
With the mighty Volta;
But we have come in tattered penury
Begging at the door of a Master.

72 Dear God

DENNIS BRUTUS

Dear God
get me out of here:
let me go somewhere else
where I can fight the evil
5 which surrounds me here
and which I am forbidden to fight
— but do not take from me my anger
my indignation at injustice
so that I may continue to burn
10 to right it or destroy.

Oh I know
I have asked for this before
in other predicaments
and found myself most wildly involved

15 But if it be possible
and conformable to your will
dear God,
get me out of here.

73 Afa (before Chukwu at dusk)

POL NDU

[an extract]

Here again, Igwekala
I bend low and whisper:

when the rains went
and the sun over-spent
5   hours in violet eves
old hoes hung low on eaves;

now pilgrim birds troop across the dimmed horizon,
and bereaved kites abandon smoky fields
for tunes of frustrated loneliness

10   tell me, my true-god,
what holds back your hand?

Four rays meet:
in a circle;
and the circle, a spark
15   that breaks,
fluid-crawling furrows of the four lines,
into extra ripples
and extra cycles

Your silence speaks infinite light,
20   fathomless love and flowing pity,
invincible quantum of unhatched glory
to leap suddenly into strange mutilation,
smearing sweet myrrh on fragmented shells and limbs,
dipped in grease and oil

25   The stainless brand
hall-marking eternity,
here.

74

Heavensgate: (i) the passage

CHRISTOPHER OKIGBO

Before you, mother Idoto,
    naked I stand;
before your watery presence,
    a prodigal

5   leaning on an oilbean,
lost in your legend.

Under your power wait I
    on barefoot,
watchman for the watchword

10   at *Heavensgate*;
out of the depths my cry:
give ear and hearken ...

Dark waters of the beginning.

Rays, violet and short, piercing the gloom,
15   foreshadow the fire that is dreamed of.

Rainbow on far side, arched like boa bent to kill,
foreshadows the rain that is dreamed of.

Me to the orangery
    solitude invites,
20   a wagtail, to tell
the tangled-wood-tale;
a sunbird, to mourn
a mother on a spray.

Rain and sun in single combat;
25   on one leg standing,
in silence at the passage,
the young bird at the passage.

Silent faces at crossroads;
    festivity in black ...
30   Faces of black like long black
        column of ants,

behind the bell tower,
into the hot garden

where all roads meet:
35 festivity in black . . .

O Anna at the knobs of the panel oblong,
hear us at crossroads at the great hinges

where the players of loft pipe organs
rehearse old lovely fragments alone —

40 strains of pressed orange leaves on pages,
bleach of the light of years held in leather:

For we are listening in cornfields
among the windplayers,
listening to the wind leaning over
45 its loveliest fragment . . .

75 Young Africa's plea

DENNIS CHUKWUDE OSADEBAY

Don't preserve my customs
As some fine curios
To suit some white historian's tastes.
There's nothing artificial
5 That beats the natural way
In culture and ideals of life.
Let me play with the whiteman's ways
Let me work with the blackman's brains
Let my affairs themselves sort out.
10 Then in sweet rebirth
I'll rise a better man
Not ashamed to face the world.
Those who doubt my talents
In secret fear my strength
15 They know I am no less a man.
Let them bury their prejudice,
Let them show their noble sides,
Let me have untrammelled growth,
My friends will never know regret
20 And I, I never once forget.

76 Prayer to masks

LÉOPOLD SÉDAR SENGHOR

Masks! Masks!
Black mask red mask, you white-and-black masks
Masks of the four points from which the Spirit blows
In silence I salute you!
5   Nor you the least, the Lion-headed Ancestor
You guard this place forbidden to all laughter of women, to
    all smiles that fade
You distil this air of eternity in which I breathe the air of
    my Fathers.
Masks of unmasked faces, stripped of the marks of illness
    and the lines of age
You who have fashioned this portrait, this my face bent
    over the altar of white paper
10 In your own image, hear me!
The Africa of the empires is dying, see, the agony of a pitiful
    princess
And Europe too where we are joined by the navel.
Fix your unchanging eyes upon your children, who are
    given orders
Who give away their lives like the poor their last clothes.
15 Let us report present at the rebirth of the World
Like the yeast which white flour needs.
For who would teach rhythm to a dead world of machines
    and guns?
Who would give the cry of joy to wake the dead and the
    bereaved at dawn?
Say, who would give back the memory of life to the man
    whose hopes are smashed?
20 They call us men of coffee cotton oil
They call us men of death.
We are the men of the dance, whose feet draw new strength
    pounding the hardened earth.

War

War

The experience of war has always been a fierce one in any age or community. In many traditional African poems this fierceness takes an interesting turn. In the traditional culture, war was regarded as one solid way for a man to prove his manhood and earn respect among his people: poetry composed in this spirit would naturally reflect a certain eagerness for war, and we can see that in the examples here from the Acholi, the Kipsigis, and even from the Mandinka legend of Sunjata. Occasionally, however, we may detect some mellowness of tone in the traditional war poetry; this is particularly so when the poem has been composed by the losing side for whom the experience of war was not a very pleasant one (see no. 80).

Some of that fierceness of tone which we find in the traditional poetry is also present in the modern poetry. If we look at the poems here relating to the guerrilla struggle against the Portuguese in Angola and Mozambique (nos. 83, 86) and to the Zimbabwean experience (no. 81) we will find some manly tone of anger from people who believe that their land or their manhood has been violated. Nevertheless, the modern African poetry of war shows greater humane consideration than the traditional one. This may be partly because, as communities have learnt over time to understand each other and accommodate each other's characters, there is a greater interest in peaceful coexistence today than in the days of our ancestors. The sense of accommodation may also be due to the scale of damage that is done in modern warfare. The scene of a war fought with guns and bombs is far bloodier, the toll of destruction more frightening, than in a war fought with spears and arrows. The haunting quality of Kariara's poem (no. 84) justly reflects the lasting horror of modern warfare.

77 Coward, crawl back!

(ACHOLI, UGANDA)

Coward, crawl back into your mother's womb
We are sons of the brave,
Sons of stubborn people.
The coward has blocked my path completely.
5 Who is that calling my name
And arguing stupidly?
We are sons of the brave, sons of stubborn people,
The coward has blocked my path completely;
Coward, crawl back into your mother's womb.

78 The army is going to war

(KIPSIGIS, KENYA)

Child's mother *oo wo ho*
Child's mother *oo wo ho*
Put the pot on the fire *oo wo ho*
Put the pot on the fire *oo wo ho*
5 The one which can hold a head *oo wo ho*
The army is going to war *oo wo ho*
The army is going to war *oo wo ho*
You don't know where *oo wo ho*
The army is going to war *oo wo ho*
10 The army is going to war *oo wo ho*
To Mangorori *oo wo ho*
Oye leiyo oo wo ho
Oye leiyo oo wo ho
Arap Tombo *oo wo ho*
15 Arap Tombo *oo wo ho*
Repair the bridge *oo wo ho*
So the army may pass *oo wo ho*
Oye leiyo oo wo ho

137

Arap Mama *oo wo ho*
20 The army is going to war *oo wo ho*
The army is awake *oo wo ho*
The army is going to war *oo wo ho*
To capture the Kipsiyabe *oo wo ho*
Arap Tombo *oo wo ho*
25 Repair the bridge *oo wo ho*
So the cattle may pass *oo wo ho*
I praise those warriors *oo wo ho*
When there is a scare they kneel *oo wo ho*
Then leap up and bellow *oo wo ho*
30 Then leap up and bellow *oo wo ho*
Like the elephant *oo wo ho*
My brother's wife *oo wo ho*
Pack the food in the war bag *oo wo ho*
The army is awake *oo wo ho*
35 The army is going to war *oo wo ho*
To kill the Masai *oo wo ho*
To kill the Masai *oo wo ho*
To drive the cattle *oo wo ho*
Which is dark brown *oo wo ho*
40 Which is brown *oo wo ho*
With a white tip of the tail *oo wo ho*
My brother's wife *oo wo ho*
Sharpen the spear for me *oo wo ho*
Then rub it with fat *oo wo ho*
45 The army is going to war *oo wo ho*
You don't know where *oo wo ho*
To Mangorori *oo wo ho*
To kill Jaluo *oo wo ho*
To capture cattle *oo wo ho*
50 Which are passing by *oo wo ho*
They ford *oo wo ho*
The widè Kipranye *oo wo ho*
The army has gone *oo wo ho*
To Mangorori *oo wo ho*
55 Through the rocky gorge *oo wo ho*
To kill Mayo *oo wo ho*
Oye leiyo oo wɔ ho
Oye leiyo oo wo ho
Oye leiyo oo wo ho

138

79 Sunjata summons his generals

BAMBA SUSO (MANDINKA, GAMBIA)

[*an extract*]

Sunjata told his griot, 'You must summon my leading men,'
Those who were known as leading men
Are what we Westerners call army commanders,
And what the Easterners call men of death.
5   When he had summoned the leading men,
Kurang Karang Kama Fofana came —
A far-seeing man and a man who speaks with authority,
Kama crossed to the other side of the river with iron shoes,
Kama crossed the river with iron shoes.
10   He and one thousand,
Four hundred
And forty-four bowmen.
Sunjata declared, 'The time for battle has not yet arrived,
    Tira Makhang has not come.'
He told his griot, 'Call my leading men.'
15   Suru Bande Makhang Kamara came —
Foobali Dumbe Kamara,
Makhang Koto Kamara, Manding Saara Jong,
Jukuna Makhang Kamara, Baliya Kamara,
Makhang Nyaame Kamara, Nyaani Saara Jong.
20   He too came with one thousand,
Four hundred and forty-four bowmen.
Sunjata told him, 'The time for battle has not yet arrived,
    Tira Makhang has not come.'
Sunjata said to his griot, 'Call the important men.'
He called them.
25   Sankarang Madiba Konte came —
Sankarang Madiba Konte, Wuruwarang Kaaba and
    Dongeera,
Ganda who instils courage,
Ganda who deprives of courage,

Ganda, master of many arts.

30 Faa Ganda killed his in-law on Monday,
Next Monday Faa Ganda became provincial governor;
They say that you should not give your daughter to Faa
    Ganda,
Killer of his in-law.
He and one thousand,
35 Four hundred,
And forty-
Four bowmen
Answered the call of Naareng Daniyang Konnate at
    Dakhajala.
Sunjata said to him, 'The time for fighting has not yet
    come, Tira Makhang has not come.'
40 Sankarang Madiba Konte demanded, 'Is Tira Makhang
    better than all the rest of us?'
Sunjata replied, 'He is not better than all the rest of you,
But he fights a morning battle,
He fights an evening battle,
And we join with him in the big battle.'
45 Sankarang Madiba Konte was Sunjata's grandfather;
He was angry, and he took out an arrow and fired it.
The arrow hit Muru,
It hit Murumuru,
It hit Gembe,
50 It hit Gembe's bold son,
It hit Seega, the Fula, in his navel.
That is why the griots say to members of the Konte family,
'Arrow on the navel Faa Ganda.'
They say that if you see an arrow on a forehead,
55 It is Faa Ganda's arrow,
Because anyone who is shot in the forehead –
If anything has cut his head open –
Will not live.
Any serious illness which attacks you in the abdomen also
    never leaves you alive.
60 That is why they say, 'Arrow in the navel Faa Ganda,
Arrow in the forehead Faa Ganda'.
They call him 'Firer of the red arrow'.
He it was who shot the arrow
And slew Susu Sumanguru's father upon the hill.
65 All seven heads,

140

It was his arrow which smashed them all.

> Sukulung Kutuma's child Sukulung Yammaru,
> You are right, many great matters have passed,
> Let us enjoy our time upon the earth.
70 A time for action, a time for speaking, a time for
>   dying; knowing the world is not easy.
> If you call a great man, no great man answers your
>   call;
> You must lay your hand upon the earth;
> Many a great man is under the ground, a youthful
>   king.
> Had the ground a mouth, it would say, 'Many great
>   men are under me.'
75 Maabirama Konnate, cats on the shoulder, Simbong
>   and Jaata are at Naarena,
> Your griots suffered when you were not there.
> Ah, you have an army,
> You seize and you slay,
> Sheikh 'Umar, man of war, war goes well for you.
80 (AMADU *asks*: At that time was he preparing to wage war
>   against Susu Sumanguru?
> BAMBA: He declared that he would not become king of
>   Manding
> Until he and Susu Sumanguru had first joined battle.)
> They were at that point
> When Sora Musa came —
85 Kiliya Musa,
> Nooya Musa,
> Wanjagha Musa,
> Bera Senuma,
> Sangang Senuma,
90 Maadikani Senuma,
> Konsikaya Koli Kumba, eye red as Bureng gold.
> He too with one thousand, four hundred
> And forty-four bowmen
> Answered the call of Sunjata Konnate at Dakhajala.
95 Sunjata declared, 'The time for fighting has not yet come,
>   Tira Makhang has not arrived.'
> Sora Musa asked him, 'Naareng, is Tira Makhang better
>   than all the rest of us?'
> Sunjata answered him, 'He is not better than all you others.
> He fights a morning battle, he fights an evening battle,

Then we join with him in the big battle.'

100 (AMADU: Make clear to us which families, with which
    surnames,
Trace their descent from Tira Makhang.
BAMBA: When you hear the name Sora Musa,
If someone is called by the surname Dumbuya, that is
    Suuso.
If someone is called by the surname Kuruma, that is Suuso.
105 If someone is called by the surname Danjo, that is Suuso.
If someone is called by the surname Geyi, that is Suuso.
All of these are descended from Sora Musa.
If someone is called by the surname Njai, that is Konte.
If someone is called by the surname Jara, that is Konte.)
110 When Tira Makhang rose up —
That Tira Makhang is the great Taraware.
(AMADU *asks inaudible questions.*
BAMBA: The Tarawares' surname is Tira Makhang.
The surname Dambele is Tira Makhang.
The surname Jebate is Tira Makhang.
115 The surname Job is Tira Makhang.
The surname Juf is Tira Makhang.
The surname Saane is Tira Makhang.
The surname Maane is Tira Makhang.
The descendants of Tira Makhang are all scattered,
120 Their surnames are all changed in this way,
But the original surname of all of them was Taraware.)
Tira Makhang was descended from Siisi,
Siisi fathered Taamana,
Taamana fathered Kembu,
125 Kembu fathered Kembu and Teneng,
And the latter fathered Tarakoto Bullai Taraware.
From that the griots say,
'Kirikisa the man who accompanies the king,
The man who rides horses to death and kills anyone who
    gainsays him.'
130 (AMADU: Then the warriors arrived.)
When Tira Makhang was coming,
He said, 'Wrap me in a shroud,
Because when I see Susu Sumanguru, either I put him in a
    shroud or he puts me in a shroud.
That is my declaration.'
135 He called his wives,

142

And he put them in mourning,
And he declared, 'When I see Susu Sumanguru,
If he does not do this to my wives, then this is what I will do
    to his wives.'
He then lay down upon a bier,
140 And they carried it on their heads and came and laid it at
    Sunjata's feet,
And Tira Makhang said to him, 'There is no need to make a
    speech;
As you see me,
When I see Susu Sumanguru,
Either he will kill me and they will wrap me in a shroud
    and lay me upon a bier
145 Or else I will kill him and they will wrap him in a shroud
    and lay him upon a bier.'
(AMADU: At that time they were preparing for battle, but
    they had not yet set out.
BAMBA: War had not yet broken out.
At that time they were preparing for battle.)

When the leading men had responded,
150 The army rose up
And battle was joined at Taumbaara.

80 The fall of Kaabu

AMADU JEBATE (MANDINKA, GAMBIA)

[*an extract*]

At that time, of the Fulas who had come with the Almani
    of Timbo,
Those who remained outside did not exceed three hundred
    men.
All the rest were within the walls of the town.
You would plunge into human blood up to your knees;
5 Blood was soaking the walls and they were collapsing.
They fought on;
The swords stuck to their hands;
Human blood was gushing forth like a spring.

They fought with each other and fought with each other
    till finally they drew their knives.
10 Knives were ineffective;
Finally even hand to hand fighting became impossible; they
    all just stood still and looked at each other.
They had fought themselves to a standstill.

Janke Waali looked at his senior griot and said to him,
'You must get out.
15 I am going to bring about a terrible disaster.'
The griot said, 'Who am I going to tell this to?'
He said, 'Let us remove to safety some of our younger
    members who can carry on our lines.'
The other replied, 'Yes, I think we should do that,
Because our muscles are old.
20 You and I have enjoyed good times;
Hard times are now here, and we shall all suffer them.'
Then one princess,
One female griot,
One prince,
25 One male griot –
These he handed over to his *jinn*,
And he moved off with them.

It passed the Futa men.

The Almani of Timbo looked behind him like this and saw them going;

30 He said, 'There goes that mute *jinn* of his taking his griots away and some members of his family.'

The *jinn* knew everyone, but they did not see it.

Whenever fighting was hard, the *jinn* used to help Janke Waali.

It was in control of their oracle, Tamba Dibi.

Janke Waali had loaded a pistol and it lay on the ground; he had spread a big lion-skin in one of the powder magazines.

35 He gave orders, 'Open the powder magazines and pour their contents on top of each other.'

The griot was saying, with added embellishments,

'On a day for living a man will not die; likewise on a day for dying no head will escape.'

He added, 'There is an expression "A *kooring's* white bones", but not "A *kooring's* white hair".

Today's death and a fresh grave.'

40 They evacuated all the strongholds,

Till nothing remained except king Janke Waali's stronghold.

A little Futa man suddenly appeared

And shouted, 'Elephant! Elephant!'

He said, 'Princess, today you will go and huck millet for my mother in Futa.'

45 She said, 'The millet which I huck for your mother, You won't be able to keep in your stomach.'

She took a pestle and hit him over the head.

She dragged him some distance, then laid him on the ground and sat on him; she said to him, 'Someone else will go to Futa and report what has happened, but it won't be you.'

Janke Waali said to a slave, 'Now, how are they?' He said, 'Now, no-one can touch his opponent.'

50 Janke Waali said, 'Now has the time of our annihilation come.'

Oh! Oh!

The white man's crazy merchandise!
Janke Waali fired the pistol.
The seventy powder magazines
55 All exploded simultaneously.
The stronghold spun round and round seven times.
Janke Waali himself did not die inside the fortifications,
Nor did Kumancho Saane,
The woman on whose account the war was fought.
60 The Futa men were wicked; they drew her with a *kaatimo*.
She went and hid under the leaves of a young palm tree to
    the west of the fort.

As to Janke Waali,
The gunpowder hurled him outside,
For he had said to her, 'What shall we do?', and she had said
    to him,
65 'Sir, the tree which produced you as a flower produced me
    as a fruit.
If that were not so, we would have turned our backs on the
    gunpowder, but now let us face it.'
He said to her, 'Come, let me tie a strip of cloth over your
    eyes', but she refused.

The whole of Kaabu went mad.
A tiny remnant of the Futa army remained.
70 The Almani of Timbo came and stood,
And said, 'Great heavens,
A prince of Kaabu never gives up.
I am thinking about God's attitude towards me, for I have
    taken many a life here.'
The Almani wept.
75 The Futa man was distressed; he became a rubber tree.
Even tomorrow, if you go there and scratch it, blood will
    come out.
He could no longer move;
He lost his power to perform wonders.
However much he tried, he was to the west of the
    fortification.
80 If anyone disbelieves me, he should go there and have a
    look.

81 Take up arms and liberate yourselves

(SHONA, ZIMBABWE)

[*an extract*]

Our ancestor Nehanda died with these words on her lips,
'I'm dying for this country.'
She left us one word of advice
'Take up arms and liberate yourselves.'

5   Aren't you coming with us to fight?
Aren't you really?
We are running about carrying sub-machine guns
We carry anti-air missiles
'Take up arms and liberate yourselves.'

10 Chitepo died with these words on his lips
'I'm dying for the fatherland.'
He left us one word of advice,
'Take up arms and liberate yourselves.'

Father Chitepo died in the thick of the struggle,
15 Saying, 'Now I'm dying for the fatherland.'
His last words for us were,
'Take up arms and liberate Zimbabwe.'

Hence we are going to the war front,
We hit the enemy and run carrying sub-machine guns,
20 We brandish anti-air missiles.
'Take up arms and liberate yourselves.'

Now we are in the thick of it,
Running up and down with our guns,
Our anti-airs too.
25 'Take up arms and liberate your fatherland.'

82 The casualties

JOHN PEPPER CLARK

The casualties are not only those who are dead;
They are well out of it.
The casualties are not only those who are wounded,
Though they await burial by instalment.
5   The casualties are not only those who have lost
Persons or property, hard as it is
To grope for a touch that some
May not know is not there.
The casualties are not only those led away by night;
10 The cell is a cruel place, sometimes a haven,
Nowhere as absolute as the grave.
The casualties are not only those who started
A fire and now cannot put it out. Thousands
Are burning that had no say in the matter.
15 The casualties are not only those who escaping
The shattered shell become prisoners in
A fortress of falling walls.

The casualties are many, and a good number well
Outside the scenes of ravage and wreck;
20 They are the emissaries of rift,
So smug in smoke-rooms they haunt abroad,
They do not see the funeral piles
At home eating up the forests.
They are the wandering minstrels who, beating on
25 The drums of the human heart, draw the world
Into a dance with rites it does not know

The drums overwhelm the guns . . .
Caught in the clash of counter claims and charges
When not in the niche others have left,
30 We fall,
All casualties of the war,
Because we cannot hear each other speak,

Because eyes have ceased to see the face from the crowd,
Because whether we know or
35 Do not know the extent of wrong on all sides,
We are characters now other than before
The war began, the stay-at-home unsettled
By taxes and rumours, the looters for office
And wares, fearful every day the owners may return,
40 We are all casualties,
All sagging as are
The cases celebrated for kwashiorkor,
The unforeseen camp-follower of not just our war.

83 The people went to war

ANTONIO JACINTO

On the matting
bathed in the blackness
with which smoke cuts off the sun
Mother Lemba,
5   lost in present memories of her absent husband,
puts ointment on her son.

Kaianga's wife is weeping

Kaianga has gone to war, Kaianga has gone to war

In the solitary township
10   lights and shadows play silently between the huts
children sleep
old people dream
dogs sit panting
flies buzz round the dunghill
15   and from the roofs, threads of water drip
— life affected by the absence of men —

The sun burns an open question

The people have gone to war, the people have gone to war
when will they come back?
20   and no wing cuts the empty sky
Kaianga has gone to war, Kaianga has gone to war
I don't know if he'll come back

The people have gone to war, the people have gone to war
I do know: the people will come back.

84 Vietnam

JONATHAN KARIARA

The field was full of bruised babies
Blood, hardening
Slowly stealing on ashen faces
Painted open lips.
5 Women sat reclining
Monuments of peace
Sculptured by death.
The river heaved, eased
Flowed on
10 The river was gay
Flowing on
For this field was frozen in blood
And the river was leaving.
Boots had trodden this field
15 Booby traps (set by those
Who had left with the river)
Had gripped babies
In silence.

In the field the dead women
20 Sighed
Remembering the dull thud
Of the metal fist
Of the interrogator
(These were not the sons of rice)
25 Remembered
The steely cold of a gun
Placed against the temple
Seeking entrance
No more, no more
30 Betrayal

The useless pain of snatching
Life from the fertile flood.
In that moment
The women were winnowed

35 (The dross drifted with the river)
The seed was sown
In blood
Other sons of rice would sprout
Sheathed
40 For those women
Were sowing
In blood.

The field was rich for
This was not despair
45 This was fate, pestilence
This silence was not acquiescence
This was patience
This death was eloquent
This was not new
50 This was the plague of the year before
This would be wiped out.
This was never to be forgotten
For this was not war
As other wars are wars
55 For chroniclers
These other sons
Had been sent to stir the spirit
(Their blood mingled with the sons of rice)
They would smell this
60 In the field which
The women
Had sown
In blood.

This seed would spread
65 Sealed in the marrow
Would spread
In the insane twitch of the mouth
Of those who sailed with the river
Would spread
70 To the House of Bone
For the river had flowed.

85 Evacuation

POL NDU

Distance
explodes
with cannon

Fire flakes
5   rain with
fire balls

the shrieking
the sleeping
the naked
10 the ragged
the clothed

melting
in the frenzy

weird things
15 herding nowhere

reset
the tents
in sulphur
or in sun

86 A militant's poem

JORGE REBELO

Mother
I have a gun of iron
your own son
he whom one day you saw
5   chained
(and wept
as though the chains had bound
and cut
your own hands, your own feet)
10   your son is free now, Mother,
your son has a gun of iron
My gun
I will scatter all the chains
I will open all the prisons
15   I will destroy all the tyrants
I will give the land back to our people.
Mother, it is beautiful to fight for freedom
in every bullet I shoot, there is a message of justice
and old dreams wake like birds.
20   In the hour of combat, in the battle front
your image comes close to me.
It is for you too I am fighting, Mother,
that you should not have tears in your eyes.

87 Camp 1940

LÉOPOLD SÉDAR SENGHOR

Suddenly a stormy evening has laid waste the garden of lovers

The white lilac is beaten down, the scent of the lilies has faded

The lovers have left for the breeze-swept Islands and the Rivers of the South.

A cry of disaster has gone from end to end of the cool fresh country of wines and songs

5 Like a sword of lightning piercing its heart, from the East to the West.

A huge village of huts made of mud and branches, a village crucified on two pestilent ditches.

Hatred and hunger ferment together there in the torpor of a deadly summer.

A great village circled by the frozen spitefulness of barbed wire

A great village under the tyranny of four machine guns, always ready to take offence.

10 And the noble warriors beg for cigarette butts

Fight dogs over bones, dispute the dividing of cats and dogs in dreams.

But only They have kept the innocency of their laughter, only They the freedom of their fiery soul.

Evening falls, a sob of blood that sets free the night.

They watch over the great pink children, their great blond children their great white children

15 Who toss and turn in their sleep, haunted by the fleas of care and the lice of captivity.

The stories told through the African evening lull them, and the low voices that espouse the paths of silence

And lullabies gently, lullabies drumless, without the beat of black hands clapping

— That will be for tomorrow, siesta time, the epic dream

Cavalcade of sunlight on the white savannahs and
   unending sands.
20 The wind is a guitar in the trees and the barbed wire is more
   melodious than harpstrings
   The roofs bend down to listen, stars smile with their
   sleepless eyes;
   Up high above, their face is dark, dark blue.
   The air grows gentle in the village of mud and branches
   And the earth grows human as the sentries, the roads
   beckon them to freedom.
25 They will not go. They will not leave their fatigues nor
   their duty of joy.
   Who will do the lowliest jobs if not those who were born
   noble?
   Who will dance on Sundays to the drumming of mess-tins?
   And are they not free in the freedom of their destiny?

   Suddenly a stormy evening has laid waste the garden of
   lovers
30 The white lilac is beaten down, the scent of the lilies has
   faded
   The lovers have left for the breeze-swept Islands and the
   Rivers of the South.

Death

Death

There are on the whole two main attitudes to death. One is to see it as a depressing end to human life and to feel a great sense of loss at the departure of someone very close or fear at the prospect of death. The other is the more positive attitude of exploring the benefits that may be derived from death or of accepting death philosophically as an unavoidable experience.

In many traditional African societies, *dirges* (i.e. songs of death) are sung by women around a body lying in state; such songs often reveal a sense of helplessness and loss, invariably accompanied by weeping and wailing, as in our Akan example or the one from the Igbo. Men do, of course, feel overcome by the death of someone very close. But dirges sung by men are more likely to concentrate on recalling the glorious history of the deceased or to take a rather manly stand: here the Acholi poem is remarkable for its dry-eyed light-heartedness; the Ewe poet 'says not nay; he agrees' to whatever death may bring; and the Yoruba chant paints a boisterous picture of death as taming the limitless ambitions of men.

Because it is composed mostly outside the immediate circumstances of loss – and mostly by men – the modern African poetry of death reveals little of the sense of helplessness we see in (for example) the Akan dirge (no. 89). Some are marked by a certain dignified sense of loss, as Echeruo's *Distanced*. Others reveal a startling irreverence that may be found in a large proportion of the poetry written today: in *Post Mortem*, for example, Soyinka starts by announcing a comparison between a corpse and beer as objects kept in cold storage. While the traditional poetry treats death (regarded in some communities as a god) with considerable respect, the modern poet has frequently handled it with some of the piercing criticism that he brings to other subjects. However, as the poems by Awoonor and Mustapha here reveal, some African poets are demonstrating increasing attachment to traditional views and attitudes to the subject.

88 If death were not there

(ACHOLI, UGANDA)

If death were not there,
Where would the inheritor get things?
The cattle have been left for the inheritor;
Ee, how would the inheritor get things?
5 The iron-roofed house has been left for the inheritor;
Ee, if death were not there,
How would the inheritor get rich?
The bicycle has been left for the inheritor;
This inheritor is most lucky;
10 Ee, brother, tell me,
If death were not there,
Ugly one, whose daughter would have married you?
A wife has been left for the inheritor;
Ee, inheritor, how would you have lived?
15 The house has been left for the inheritor;
If death were not there,
How would the inheritor get things?

89 Mother! Mother!

(AKAN, GHANA)

Mother! Mother!
Aba Yaa!
You know our plight!

Mother! you know our plight.
5 You know that no one has your wisdom.
Mother, you have been away too long.
What of the little ones left behind?

Alas!
Who would come and restore our breath,
10 Unless my father Adom himself comes?
Alas! Alas! Alas!
Quite often it is a struggle for us!

It is a long time since our people left.
Amba, descendant of the Parrot that eats palm nuts, hails
      from the Ancestral Chamber.

15 I cannot find refuge anywhere.
I, Amba Adoma,
It was my grandfather that weighed gold
And the scales broke under his weight.

I am a member of Grandsire Kese's household:
20 We are at a loss where to go:
Let our people come, for we are in deep distress.
When someone is coming, let them send us something.
Yes, I am the grandchild of the Parrot that eats palm nuts.

90 Zanu's death

AMEGA DUNYO (EWE, GHANA)

Our Adzima drums have stepped out;
who will listen to the songs of sorrow?
who put death's rope on the ram's neck
and yet the ram refused to move?
5 Call the poet's supporters, call his chorus.
I do not know what I've done.
We went afar looking for wealth.
Ekuadzi went to the land of spirits
leaving his kinsmen behind.
10 Mothers of children cried into sobs.
The winds of the grave blow here.
My mother's child died;
Death is adamant, death is very adamant.
Shall I sing the Christian's song
15 about angels circling a throne
and the heavens opened
so my mother's child shall see the promised kingdom?
The boat has arrived on the other shore.
Who heard the songs of sorrow?
20 Dunyo says not nay; he agrees.
Go and tell the elders;
when they go to death's homeland
and see how affairs are,
let them come and inform their offsprings.
25 I will stay till Zanu returns;
if it were so, I will await his return.
And so Death locked the door waiting for me
waiting to come and uproot
what lies in life's field.
30 I leave the rest to the chorus
I leave the rest to my songsters.

91 Widow's lament

(IGBO, NIGERIA)

Six times the widow recalls the death of her husband:
When early yam-planting season sets in
She cries in memory of her husband and retires dejected;
The second, during the cutting of yam props,
5 Who will supply her in time with bamboo?
She cries, stopping after she has cried a lot;
The third, when helplessly she sees her palm nuts ripe,
Would she defy custom and climb a palm tree?
Widowhood has led to labour hiring for the cutting of the
      palm bunch
10 Which service was rendered free in our early days;
The fourth, her husband's absence in the meeting of the
      kindred,
Who will inform the widow of the deliberations?
The fifth, when a festival is in progress,
Who will send the widow to Eke-Ututu market for festival
      fowl?
15 The last she cries uncontrollably for the deceased husband
Is the day she is drenched in her unrepaired thatched
      house,
That day she knows nothing is as painful as losing a
      husband.

92 The earth does not get fat

(NGONI, MALAWI)

The earth does not get fat. It makes an end of those who
      wear the head plumes.
We shall die on the earth.
The earth does not get fat. It makes an end of those who act
      swiftly as heroes.
Shall we die on the earth?

162

Listen O earth. We shall mourn because of you.
Listen O earth. Shall we all die on the earth?

The earth does not get fat. It makes an end of the chiefs.
Shall we all die on the earth?
The earth does not get fat. It makes an end of the women
chiefs.
Shall we die on the earth?

Listen O earth. We shall mourn because of you.
Listen O earth. Shall we all die on the earth?

The earth does not get fat. It makes an end of the nobles.
Shall we die on the earth?
The earth does not get fat. It makes an end of the royal
women.
Shall we die on the earth?

Listen O earth. We shall mourn because of you.
Listen O earth. Shall we all die on the earth?

The earth does not get fat. It makes an end of the common
people.
Shall we die on the earth?
The earth does not get fat. It makes an end of all the beasts.
Shall we die on the earth?

Listen you who are asleep, who are left tightly closed
in the land.
Shall we all sink into the earth?
Listen O earth the sun is setting tightly.
We shall all enter into the earth.

93 Poet's lament on the death of his wife

RAAGE UGAAS (SOMALI, SOMALIA)

Like the *yu'ub* wood bell tied to gelded camels that are
    running away,
Or like camels which are being separated from their young,
Or like people journeying while moving camp,
Or like a well which has broken its sides or a river which
    has overflowed its banks,
5   Or like an old woman whose only son was killed,
Or like the poor, dividing the scraps for their frugal meal,
Or like the bees entering their hive, or food crackling in the
    frying,
Yesterday my lamentations drove sleep from all the camps.
Have I been left bereft in my house and shelter?
10   Has the envy of others been miraculously fulfilled?
Have I been deprived of the fried meat and reserves for lean
    times which were so plentiful for me?
Have I today been taken from the chessboard (of life)?
Have I been borne on a saddle to a distant and desolate
    place?
Have I broken my shin, a bone which cannot be mended?

94 But for death

(YORUBA, NIGERIA)

[an extract]

SECOND OJE:
Offspring of Abilodesu, listen to my words.
One with disordered head pad.
Offspring of one whom the drums hail with rebellious
    strains.
But for death,
5 Adisa, listen to my sermon,
Three persons would have designated themselves God the
    King.
Now ask me, say, who are they?

FIRST OJE:
Who are they?
However it may be, explain it
10 Because a woman will always open wide the door of the
    feared one.

SECOND OJE:
A rich man would have designated himself, God the King
What of the medicine man?
He would have designated himself, God the King.
On the day death would kill the rich man
15 Money would be of no avail
On the day death would kill the medicine man
The charm that locks up man's intentions,
The one that stupefies one
The one that makes one look like a fool
20 The one that arrests one's movements:
Indeed, everything will perish.
On the day death will kill the great priest
Gentle winds will carry off all his papers.

FIRST OJE:
It is true, it is perfectly so.
25 Death kills a herbalist
As if he learns no Ifa.

Death kills the medicine man
As if he possesses no charms.
Death kills a great priest
30 As if he does not cry unto God the King.
I look up
I look down below
I see no two kings known as God the King.
No king like Balaratu who is called the doer of great deeds.

SECOND OJE:
35 It is true, it is perfectly so.
Don't let it exceed two at a time.
It is now the turn of Raaji Ajani . . .

95 Stop the death-cry

KOFI AWOONOR

Let all of you stop the death-cry
and let me hear.
It is home; I stood at death's door
and knocked throughout the night.
5 Have patience and I shall pay the debt.
Suppose I had someone
Someone who will call me the dove
and it will run and come to me.
I have something to say I want to say
10 But it surpasses saying.
The dove says it is the soft voice
Which takes gifts from elders.
The prepared-for war is never surprised
So have patience
15 and I will pay the debt.
I knocked at death's door all night.
It was only the sleeping crow who came.
'Go back and prepare your gods
and then come back.'
20 So I left; I am seeking to prepare my gods.
I am seeking; I am seeking.

96 Distanced

MICHAEL J. C. ECHERUO

Tolling.

Were it the hangman's only
Of doom,

Yet would it tell
5   A hundred miles from here
(Good friend!)
What only the losers know

That death kills
And the spirit lives
10 And memories haunt
Both living and dead.

97 Gbassay — blades in regiment

MUKHTARR MUSTAPHA

Push a porcupine quill into
My quaint eyes
Then plunge an assagai into
My fibroid face
5   Then slash my neck and stain
The tortoise back rich with my blood

Force a rug needle into my narrow
nose: force it right into my
Indigo marrow.

10 List my tongue and tie it
With a rope from a tethered goat

Lacerate my ribs with deep sanguine
gutters splattering blood like a
Bellow in full blaze – blazing yellow

15 Disembowel my belly and feed the
Hawks that hover there hourless-
timeless black blue sky
And inside a crater bury
My ears.
20   'Is it death?'

98 What is death like?

ERIC S. NG'MARYO

What is death like?
Is it like a flash of lightning
Or a clap of thunder
In a night of storm
5 Then eternal stillness
And dark?

Is it like a sudden opening
Of a secret door
Like the vaginal opening
10 To a newly born,
Then colour, variety and –
Life?

What is death like?

99 Isatou died

LENRIE PETERS

Isatou died
When she was only five
And full of pride
Just before she knew
5   How small a loss
It brought to such a few.
Her mother wept
Half grateful
To be so early bereft.
10 And did not see the smile
As tender as the root
Of the emerging plant
Which sealed her eyes.
The neighbours wailed
15 As they were paid to do
And thought how big a spread
Might be her wedding too.
The father looked at her
Through marble eyes and said:
20 'Who spilt the perfume
Mixed with the morning dew?'

100 Post mortem

WOLE SOYINKA

there are more functions to a freezing plant
than stocking beer; cold biers of mortuaries
submit their dues, harnessed — glory be! —

in the cold hand of death ...
5   his mouth was cotton filled, his man-pike
shrunk to sub-soil grub

his head was hollowed and his brain
on scales — was this a trick to prove
fore-knowledge after death?

10   his flesh confesses what has stilled
his tongue; masked fingers think from him
to learn, how not to die.

let us love all things of grey; grey slabs
grey scalpel, one grey sleep and form,
15   grey images.

PART THREE
Notes and questions

1 Where has my love blown his horn?

This is a brilliant example of a love song from a rural community. In it a young woman anxiously searches for her shepherd lover who wanders away, blowing his horn, in search of cattle (apparently as bride-price for the woman). The poem strikingly repeats some of its lines; this element of repetition is a mark both of the musical quality of the oral poetry and of the anxiety with which the woman looks for her man. Notice also the way in which the poet balances and rounds out the poem: stanza one introduces the search; stanzas two and three lament the plights first of the woman then of the man; and stanza four re-echoes the whole of stanza one as a closing refrain.

line 1 *horn* Shepherd boys usually play musical instruments to relieve the boredom of long hours of watching over their cattle. They also sometimes use the tunes either to recall their cattle or to attract others.

lines 9–10 In cattle-raising societies, a man's wealth is frequently measured in terms of the size of his herd; payments for services and other forms of social exchange (e.g. marriage) are also frequently made in cattle.

Questions

What effect does the repetition of the questions have in this poem?

Explain the phrase 'long distance' (line 5) in the context of the landscape in which the poem is set.

2 What a fool he is!

This song records the frustration and disappointment that accompanies the decline of love between husband and wife (or between two lovers). The feeling builds up as the woman wanders from one town to the next, coming to a climax when the man is reported to have crossed the sea (Indian Ocean). At that point the woman no longer cares for the validity or otherwise of the information she is given – notice the difference in tone between 'So they told me' and 'Or so they said' – and proceeds to dismiss the man. Many African oral poems are built on this pattern of accumulation of details (see *Nyagumbe! Nyagumbe!* (no. 4) for a similar example): the effect is to postpone the climax and so make the message or point of the song all the more striking when it comes.

Question

Discuss the difference in structure and effect between the last five lines of the poem and the preceding sixteen.

3 I will satisfy my desire

This song well captures the excitement with which a young woman prepares to have a romance with her lover. The Bagirmi are today largely Islamised; and though the religion has tended to discourage the singing of such songs as indecent and profane, many of them have survived. In structure this poem has some of that roundedness and balance which we saw in *Where has my love blown his horn?* Here the lady starts off her song with details about 'antimony' and 'amulets', and returns to them towards the close of the poem, perhaps to emphasise that her bodily charm is the most significant element in her preparations. By closing the poem with details with which it began, the poet reveals not only a sense of music (the repetition is a kind of refrain) but also a sense of poetic discipline.

line 1 *antimony* a dark, powdery substance often used as cosmetic.
line 10 *piece of silver* money.

Question

By what phrases does the poet convey the mounting effect of the lady's excitement?

4 Nyagumbe! Nyagumbe!

Dora Earthy, who collected this song, says: 'A young man named Nyagumbe starts off to seek a bride. He finds the girl he wants; but while he is staying at her parents' home, she shows no signs of returning his love. He therefore refuses to take the food she prepares for him. The girl's mother advises her to love the young man, and then all will be well. Nyagumbe is secretly amused at his own plans for winning the girl . . . After each line there is a humming refrain.'

By this sequence of dramatic exchanges the poet makes the point that, in the union between woman and man, the sentiment of love is more important than material benefits. One rather interesting aspect of this poem is the picture it paints of the traditional family. The father does not want to be bothered by all this frivolous encounter between boy and girl, and so maintains a dignified lack of favour; it is the mother that shares her daughter's anxieties and joins in the efforts to ensure her happiness. There is an underlying humour in the girl's frantically running about while the young man watches his plans working!

The fast-moving pace of the song emphasises the girl's anxiety. The frequent repetition of phrases also reveals the musical excitement with which the message of love is being conveyed.

line 8 This is an open space (*banza*) where the mature men gather together and chat near a fire or under a tree.
line 17 This is a fireplace in the women's hut where women sit in the evening and tell stories.
line 30 This is a hut where only young men and boys congregate.
line 58 A cock not old enough to crow. This is obviously considered a delicacy.

Questions

What do you feel the humming at the end of every line contributes to the song?

Try to reconstruct the whole poem as a play. You need not give the characters any more words than they already have in the poem, but try to put in as many stage directions as would bring out fully the various moods (e.g. anxiety) and actions (e.g. smiling) suggested by the statements of the characters.

5 A mother to her first-born

This beautiful poem will be properly understood if it is seen in the light of the traditional African household as well as views about children. To start with, there was a general tendency towards polygamy in the traditional African family. Of the several children born to the man of such a household, it was generally understood that the first-born – especially if he was a male – would inherit most if not all of the father's property when the latter died. We can therefore understand the special joy of the singer of this poem in being the mother of her husband's 'first-born'.

She has further reason to be happy she bore a male child. Female children were of course highly valued for the bride-wealth they brought at marriage. But the greatness of a household was measured more in terms of the male children in it: sons who would help their father on his farm, or who would swell the reputation of their family name by their various deeds of valour. So, although a man would smile on his wife if she bore him a daughter, he would look on her with special favour if she bore him a son.

Proof of the mother's joy and excitement can be seen in the frequent repetition of words and phrases as well as her childlike toying with ideas, as she celebrates a child who has done her proud.

line 3   *bull-calf* The Lango, like their neighbouring Acholi (see no. 1), are a cattle-raising community.
line 30   To *pucker* is to draw up into little folds.
line 59   A *shrine* was often set up in a traditional African household in honour of its ancestors. Sacrifices of food would occasionally be made to it and appeals and prayers (for the welfare of living members of the family) addressed to it.

Questions

What quality of the male child does this woman celebrate most in her son?

What picture do we get – especially from sections three, four and six of this poem – of the spiritual or religious life of the Lango?

6 Nightsong: Country

This is a unique kind of love poem. By identifying himself with the vitality of the rural landscape, the poet shows how very intensely he loves his country. We may best refer to this kind of sentiment as patriotic love.

There is a strong sensuous feeling in this poem. This may be explained by the circumstances (of imprisonment) under which the poet was living at the time of writing. The repressive politics of the apartheid government are aimed essentially at denying the Africans a right to their land and, in the end, at destroying their feeling of attachment to it. One logical reaction of a sensitive African is to intensify his hold and attachment to the land, and one way of doing this is by celebrating it in language of the deepest sensitivity. So strong is the attachment which Brutus demonstrates here, so closely does he embrace his land, that the situation described in the poem is very similar to that of a love romance between the poet and a sexually attractive woman. There is no obscene intention here – simply an expression of a sentimental and indestructible commitment to one's country through an acknowledgement of its beauty.

Brutus uses here a variation of the SONNET structure as a way of imposing some form or order on the chaos in which he lives. Several words are also either long or deliberately designed to be pronounced slowly and lazily so as to emphasise the easy, comfortable feeling of a romance: 'heaves', 'voluptuously-submissively', 'sibilant clamorously', 'shimmering', 'intimately', 'murmuring', 'sheltering', etc. Even the frequent use of *m* sounds somehow suggests a sigh and enhances the atmosphere of romance.

> *Country* (part of the title) Brutus plays here upon the dual meaning of 'countryside' and 'fatherland.'
>
> lines 2–3 *heave* and *distend* indicate sighing and stretching of the body.
> line 5 *primal* ancient; *rank* strong-smelling.
> line 6 *pungent exudation* sharp odour.
> line 8 *sibilant clamorously* hissing loudly.
> line 14 Because the poet and the land are now one and inseparable, it is difficult to tell which of the two of them gives or receives protection.

Questions

Why do you think the poet uses high-sounding words in expressing his feeling here?

In describing his sensuous attachment to his land, Brutus uses images reflecting most of the five human senses. Can you identify and discuss these?

7 Dry your tears, Africa!

Many African poets of the colonial period, especially negritude poets (of whom Dadié would be considered one), portrayed Africa in the image of a woman, whether a beautiful lady or a mother. The purpose of this was to represent the African race or culture as something to be admired, loved or respected and not despised or abandoned in favour of white culture. In this exceptionally tender poem, Dadié presents the image of Mother Africa being consoled by her sons who had abandoned her and gone on a journey. It is a poem of filial love conveying the sentiments of racial loyalty.

The journey referred to is both a literal and a metaphorical one. Dadié returned to live and work in his country Ivory Coast in 1947 after a long period away from it, studying and working in Senegal and visiting France. But implied also is a journey away from African culture. Many Africans during the colonial era were seen to be embracing the white man's culture and abandoning theirs; after a while, however, they came to realise the uniqueness and beauty of their own culture and its advantages over the foreign one. In these various respects, therefore, Dadié's poem is an act of rededication by 'prodigal sons' returning to their abandoned parent and re-declaring their love and loyalty.

The poem is dressed throughout with metaphors: 'tears', 'storm and squalls', 'springs', 'playthings', etc.; these reflect the spiritual depth of the feeling of love and loyalty. But the PERSONIFICATION of Africa adds a great deal of human warmth and tenderness to the sentiments of the poet. The statement 'Dry your tears, Africa', repeated in alternate stanzas, lends some rhythmic or musical movement – like alternate drum beats – to the poem as a way of lifting up the spirits of the sorrowing Mother.

line 3 The *storm and squalls* may refer to the black man's involvement in the Second World War which ended in 1945 (two years before Dadié's return to the Ivory Coast). The experience with the white man would then be seen as a *fruitless journey* in the sense that it has done the black man more harm than good.

lines 4–8 Over the seas and across all parts of the continent – east, west, and everywhere. The *proud mountains* are a reference to such heights as Kilimanjaro in east Africa and Futa Jalon in the west; the *grasslands* are for the savannah regions of western and southern Africa.

line 22 *foliage pearled by the dew* leaves adorned by pearls of dew-drops resting on them in the early morning.

Questions

What aspects of the African's contact with Europe would be seen as constituting 'ill-fortune' on the one hand and 'glory' on the other?

Discuss the images in this poem that convey a feeling of tenderness.

8 For Melba

From the United States where he has lived in exile since 1962, Kgositsile has emerged as one of South Africa's most outstanding poets. Much of his poetry is understandably angry, but a good number are also quite tender, as this title poem to one of his collections.

The poem is effective in a number of ways. First, the idea of morning smiling is a sensitive use of PERSONIFICATION; on the whole, in this poem, Kgositsile shows a strong feeling for the closeness between the beauty of nature and that of the human body. Secondly, the use of contrasts – one of the most effective techniques in poetry writing – may be seen here between 'moment' and 'eternal', and between 'captured' and 'emerge'. Thirdly, the repeated use of SIMILES ('like ... like ... like') reveals the musical excitement with which the young poet tries to express the joy of his loving admiration. Finally, the poet is so breathless in his excitement that he has omitted to use any punctuation until the very end of the poem.

line 3   *coy* shy.

line 5   *from yesterdays* Melba is a girl the poet met in America. To be able to portray his deepest feelings for her, he tries to cast his mind back to scenes from the South African homeland which he left years ago.

line 7   *Kimberley* an area in South Africa where precious stones are mined.

line 8   *Limpopo* a river in South Africa.

Questions

Do the words 'captured' and 'emerge' have any particular significance for a poet from South Africa?

The relationship between 'rain' and 'unnumbered charms' is called ASSOCIATION. In what way are the two images associated with one another?

9 To the anxious mother

In this tender poem the poet recalls, with love and appreciation to his mother, the first anxious moments of his birth. We may notice that, although the poem is addressed to the poet's mother, the poet tells us less about her than about the general scene surrounding his delivery (there is more interest shown, in fact, in the efforts of his grandmother than in the anxiety of his mother). The emphasis may be explained by the fact that, as a visual artist (a painter), Malangatana is more easily inclined to present a vivid scene than to engage in an abstract expression of gratitude. The poem remains, nevertheless, a fine expression of filial love, all the more striking for its simplicity.

Questions

What ideas or phrases in this poem would be most likely to reassure or gladden a mother?

From what point of view has the poet composed this piece: from the point of view of a grown man, or of a newborn baby? Examine the ideas in the poem for your answer.

10 I will cling to your garment

Ng'maryo's poetry is frequently marked by a certain agility and vitality. This is a good example of one such poem, in which a young man passionately professes his love to a girl who apparently has not yet given any encouragement to him.

Questions

What is the value of the many short lines used in this poem?

Identify three images (METAPHOR, SIMILE) used in the poem and show how effectively they have been used.

11 Without you

Odia Ofeimun is known mostly for poems which condemn the injustices in the social and political life of his country, Nigeria. This is one of the few poems – an early one at that – in which he has chosen a non-radical subject, although it may be argued that in 'non-existent tomorrow' the poet suggests that atmosphere of insecurity which constantly surrounds a nation marked by social and political inequalities. In any case, in this poem Ofeimun pays a simple tribute to a lady whose love has brought to his life a certain amount of stability, peace, and brilliance.

line 7   *wings* The endless fears within him are seen as putting him constantly in flight and so denying him peace of mind.

line 10   *my earth suffers a demise of colours* i.e. the world around me loses all brilliance and beauty. The brightness of the sun illuminates the world, revealing a variety of objects whose different colours make the world so lively and lovely. The lady is here likened to the sun, and in the next line to a ghost especially because ghosts are said to appear sometimes in shining white forms.

Questions

Explain the use of 'stammer' (line 2).

How successful is the poet's comparison of his lady to a ghost?

12 Love apart

Like Ofeimun, Okigbo is not known to have written many love poems. His published collection of poems, *Labryinths* (from which this early poem has been excluded) deals essentially with the poet's difficult search for an individual voice that will be put to the service of his community.

This poem contains one of the most powerful portraits of a dying love affair ever to be captured in African poetry. The poet has significantly chosen a moonlit night, which provides the right setting for expressing the sentiment of love; but the moonlight here only highlights the sharp separation between the lovers. It is also interesting that the lovers are compared to pines, which in the tropical landscape of Nigeria may be no other than whistling pines (*casuarina*). These trees are known for the very silent sounds they make even in the strongest wind. And now the life has gone completely out of them, for the love that sustained them has quite dried out; as they lean towards each other in their final gesture of affection, they are as empty of any feeling for each other as two intertwined shadows that make no actual physical contact.

The poem is successful in using very few words to describe a very powerful moment. There is also some mystery in the idea of love ascending with the moon; in folklore the moon is sometimes credited with some magical powers, and Okigbo seems to suggest here that the moon has drawn up with it the love between these two people. Whatever the case may be, this association of the images of the moon and silence lends a haunting effect.

Questions

What does 'bow' (line 3) tell us of the state of the relationship between the lovers?

What words in this poem convey the feelings of (a) emptiness, and (b) separation?

13 Choice

Ranaivo is well-known for translating many of the traditional love poems of his native Madagascar into French, and for modelling some of his own original poetry after these traditional forms. In this delightful little piece, the poet tries to uphold the virtues of honesty and simplicity in love over frivolous and materialistic concerns. The young man in the poem is interested in winning his women, both rich (chief's daughter) and poor (sister of poor widow) with material attractions. In the second stanza, however, the point is made that a lady may not be so much interested in material benefits as in the simple personal warmth of friendship.

In form as in message this poem somewhat resembles the Chopi poem *Nyagumbe! Nyagumbe!*, which also upholds love above material attractions. Ranaivo's poem is cast in the form of a dialogue between the amorous young man and a friend. This call-and-response sequence is no doubt indebted to the oral tradition; note also the repetition of phrases in this sequence ('Who is . . .', 'Go tell her . . .') which adds some musical charm to it. The poem is also arranged in SONNET form; not only with regard to its overall length of fourteen lines, but also in its internal shape – there is a slight contrast between the picture in the first stanza and that in the second (in the images or statuses of the ladies), and a twist in the last few lines (an urge for simplicity which contradicts the frivolity of the young man).

line 5   *coral-red loves*   Corals are the skeletons of little sea creatures which have formed, over a long period of time, into bright-coloured rocks and are often smoothed out into quite expensive jewellery. The phrase is a reference either to white women or to mulatto girls with rosy-red cheeks. As an island in the Indian Ocean, Madagascar came into frequent contact with European merchants on their way to the Far East. Whatever the case may be, the phrase suggests something that enjoys high social standing or at least a high estimation in the eyes of the man.

line 8   *rose-apples*   is obviously a reference to very cheap cosmetics. The widow cannot afford the sophisticated scents sold in the shops, and so takes her adornment from ordinary nature. The poverty of the girl is also suggested by the young man's offer to cook her a dinner, which implies that she may be hungry (or *thirsty*, line 13).

Questions

Why does the poet make the first lady walk with steps that 'clatter on the firm earth'?

Discuss the use of the phrase 'a little rice-water'. How is it effective?

180

14 I came with you

One of the most striking features of Senghor's poetry is the way in which he portrays the beauty of black womanhood with the most affecting imagery. This imagery frequently comes from his sensitive observation of the tropical environment of his native land. In his poetry – far more intimately than in that of other negritude poets – the beauty of the African world or culture is reflected in the beauty of the African woman, and vice versa.

This poem is marked by a tone of anxiety. The departure of the lady fills the lover with the fear that she may never return; a landscape of setting sun and growing darkness has been chosen as an appropriate background for the lover's uncertain feelings. However, this picture of anxiety is in many ways balanced by Senghor's moving portrait of the African landscape in the dusk: despite the setting which they provide for fears about a relationship, the images of grain-huts, of the sun dropping 'beneath the shadow of the ricefields', and of panthers and the Mother Earth reveal the poet's sentimental attachment to his native environment and its culture. The setting of the poem to a traditional musical instrument – a favourite technique of Senghor's – gives further proof of this attachment.

khalam a small three-stringed guitar.

line 1 *grain-huts* cylindrical mud huts in which grain like millet or rice is stored; *gates of Night* is a metaphor for twilight, the entrance from the final moments of daylight to the early period of darkness.

line 2 *golden riddle* the faint light of the sun played on her smile, so that it was not clear whether she was smiling out of friendliness or not. When a description (*golden*) is transferred from a familiar object (*sun*) to an unfamiliar one (*riddle*) in the same context, it is called a TRANSFERRED EPITHET.

line 3 *freak of the divine fancy* a wonder created (or conceived) by the mind of God.

line 5 *crest* her head or headwear.

line 6 *ancestral fears more treacherous than panthers* The fears – as to what the future holds – are called ancestral (i.e. ancient) because fears about the unknown have always afflicted man since time immemorial. They are compared here to panthers which lurk secretly for some time before striking their victims.

line 9 *motherly hollow of the Earth* Because it is the natural source of food or nourishment, the Earth is often pictured in traditionally agricultural societies as a mother nourishing her children (mankind). *Hollow* suggests a mother's womb, deep and inexhaustible (like the earth) in its sympathy and tenderness.

line 11 *the milky dawning of your mouth* Your mouth, tender as milk, as it kisses me awake in the morning.

Questions

The style of this poem is slightly complex. In what way is it related to the feelings of the lover?

Explain the phrase 'the silence of my tears' (line 10).

15 Relentlessly she drives me

Negritude poetry, written mostly in the days when many African countries were under French colonial rule, showed an obligation to reassert the lost pride of the African race. It frequently contained comparisons between African and European culture, so as to demonstrate the superiority of the former over the latter. One way in which Senghor and other negritude poets set up a suitable framework for such comparison was to address a poem to a loved one (real or imagined), and to glorify her with images and references which made her (and their) African background so much more attractive than the European culture with which they were surrounded.

This and the last poem are contained in a collection of mostly love poems by Senghor originally titled *Chants pour Signare*, written and published in France in 1949. The picture of the African environment which we see in these poems is therefore mainly a nostalgic one. It is particularly strong in this poem. It appears that the poet encountered a woman, here in France and far away from his native land, who continually ('relentlessly') forced him to think of African women back home. The woman is quite obviously fair-skinned ('fair negress'), and so prompts memories in the poet of such women back home (see below) and the African environment from which he has been away so long. She reminds him of moonlit nights (line 2), of other tropical scenes and scents (lines 3–6), and of the rhythmic African music which is so different from that of the European Roman Catholic Church (lines 7–9).

This embrace of African culture is again emphasised by the setting of the poem to a traditional musical instrument. The echoing of the first two lines of the poem in the last two also lends the poem a certain musical quality (compare a similar device in (no. 1) *Where has my love blown his horn?*).

> *balafong* a traditional xylophone.

line 1 *thickets of Time* crowded images of past experience. Senghor had been away from his native land since 1928 (when he left to study in France). The experiences which he had been through since then would, in retrospect, seem as crowded and confused as a thick bush, or thicket. By capitalising the word *time* Senghor may also be thinking of the larger African cultural history.

line 2 *the clearing where white night sleeps* the moonlit village in the midst of the tropical forest. The image of the sleeping night is an example of PERSONIFICATION.

line 4 *lisping sweep of a wing* gentle brush of the wing of a butterfly or a bird. This rather thin and tender touch is compared to a similar effect of the tongue on the teeth (lisping) of somone who cannot pronounce 's' and 'z' properly.

line 5 *Signare* (a word borrowed from the Portuguese) means a high-class lady. Such ladies were previously kept as mistresses by Portuguese settlers in Senegal. There are today many fair-skinned women in Senegal who are products and descendants of that association, and they enjoy a high social standing there. In the second sentence of this line, Senghor seems to be striving to reassert the African element (the tropical sun) against the European (blue eyes) in the woman.

182

line 6
Sevres-Babylone and *Balangar* are Senegalese towns. *Gongo* is a perfume which emits rather strong scent.

line 7
Angelus At certain hours of the day, especially at noon, every Roman Catholic church rings its bell, inviting the faithful to offer a prayer in memory of the act of the Angel Gabriel in announcing to the Virgin Mary that she would be the mother of Jesus. *Angelus* (meaning Angel) is the first word of this commemorative prayer.

line 10
Sometimes, in my boredom, I imagine a cloud or a butterfly falling on my window-pane like a drop of rain.

line 12
solitary heart of the night unperturbed village in the heart of the continent. *Night* here recalls the moonlit night of line 2; but in some of his other writing Senghor has been known to use the word (in terms of the darkness) as a colour symbol for Africa.

Questions

How much use does Senghor make in this poem of references to colour as a way of comparing African and European cultures?

In this poem, Senghor combines the tender sentiments of love with the strong feelings of nationalist politics. Can you identify the words and phrases which bring out these two elements of tenderness and strength?

16 A warrior sings his praises

The Bahima (singular: Muhima) are a cattle-raising people originally concentrated in the kingdom of Ankole in south-western Uganda, but found today in scattered settlements in the east as well. There are two basic forms of traditional poetry practised by the Bahima. One is the *ekirahiro* by which a man describes his cattle in glowing, exaggerated terms. This kind of poetry is usually performed when the cowherds are sitting together resting, usually in the evening after work. The second and more distinguished form is the *ekyevugo* or heroic chant, by which a man praises himself for his accomplishments in war or in cattle-raiding. 'In the past,' says H. F. Morris who collected a number of such chants, 'every well-brought-up Muhima was expected to be able to compose and recite these poems, for not only was their recitation a pastime for the evening, but there were also certain occasions on which it was necessary for a Muhima to recite a praise poem which he had composed. Among these were such occasions as when a man was given a chieftainship by the Omugabe [the paramount ruler of the Bahima]; when he dedicated himself to the Omugabe for service in battle; and when he visited his future father-in-law the night before his marriage. Furthermore, it was usual for a Muhima in the midst of battle to recite [his *ekyevugo*] in order to keep up his own and his companions' courage.'

This selection is an example of the *ekyevugo*. Such a composition is marked by hyperbolic language: the *omyevugi* (reciter) is anxious to portray himself in the most exaggerated terms. He may never have participated in battle, and the closest he may have come to an act of valour could be a scuffle with another cowherd at a cattle watering place. But he uses the traditional form and idiom of the *ekyevugo* as a metaphorical way of announcing his merits.

This particular poem relates to an actual battle (in 1865) between two clans of the larger Bahima group. It was composed by a certain Rwanyindo who took part in the fight, but was recorded several generations later (1955) from an informant Erinesti Rwandekyezi. Various names in the poem – Bihanga, Kaanyabareega, Oruhinda, Kahenda, Karembe, Nyamizi, Nkanga and Kanyegyero – are places where the fighting took place. The other names – Bitembe, Bwakwakwa, Bantura and Rwamujonjo – are of the composer's comrades in the fight.

Perhaps the most notable effect of this kind of poetry is that it leaves in us a certain sense of urgency, no doubt because the reciter is expected to praise himself with as many attributes as possible and with just as much speed. Although some of the vocal effects which make the *ekyevugo* attractive in the oral tradition are lost in translation, we can still feel the intensity of the performance as well as the lofty aims of the composition.

line 1 *foreigners* the invaded enemy. *The Overthrower* is a comrade. Other such praise names are in lines 3 and 10.
line 2 This is the cotton cloth worn by traditional Bahima over the shoulders.
line 6 The song is an *ekyevugo*, so as to incite the warriors to deeds of courage.
line 8 *Banyoro* is the general name for the invaded enemy.
line 9 'The idea conveyed here is that the hero fought on into the night and was still fighting when the cocks crowed' (Morris).
line 13 *Rwangomari* was the composer's master.

Questions

What is the effect of the preponderant use of the personal pronoun *I*?

Discuss those lines of this poem that best advertise the heroism of the reciter.

17 Ali, Lion of the World

There is an old protocol, going back a long way in African traditions, which is observed in the royal courts of the Western Sudan – especially in the palaces of the emirs of northern Nigeria. Whenever an important personality or ruler visits the emir, the presence of the visitor is announced with considerable fanfare by the attendant praise-singer or musician. The singer takes care to mention the various merits and achievements of the visitor – his ancestry, his deeds of valour, his wealth, and so on. This praise poem was obviously sung for Ali, an emir of Kano, as he paid one such visit.

One of the most striking things about this poem is the way the poet shifts from one tone of address to another in his dramatic recitation of the qualities of Ali. In stanza one the poet addresses Ali directly, with a proverb thrown in as a title; in stanza two the poet begins a long list of details illustrating Ali's stubborn thirst for battle with an indirect question; stanza three also illustrates Ali's doggedness, but it starts off dramatically with the tone of one of the general's colleagues during a military campaign and prepares us for the next stanza; in stanza four the poet assumes the plight of one of Ali's victims in a notable campaign; the last stanza brings us back once again to the dominant tones that we saw in the first two stanzas (direct, and indirect).

The repetition of various lines is also noteworthy for its role in emphasising the principal qualities of Ali: his hunger for war and his untiring energy. The narrative in stanzas four and five is equally significant; in the traditional African praise poetry a narrative episode or scene is frequently thrown into a series of independent details or lines of praise as a way of spicing up the recitation. Such an episode is usually short, and is usually no more than a vivid extension or illustration of one of the qualities mentioned. When, however, the story element dominates a poem glorifying a heroic figure, the poem is no longer a praise poem (PANEGYRIC) but an EPIC song in which the achievement of the hero in one major event is celebrated in exaggerated language and with full dramatic scope.

> *line 4* *cruel* This is not necessarily a negative EPITHET. In traditional culture, a man wins a great deal of admiration as a hero if he inspires fear in friends and foes alike.
>
> *line 8* *Lion of the World* In the traditional literature of the Islamic Western Sudan (of which the emirates of northern Nigeria were a part), the image of the rulers was frequently exaggerated. Some of this literature has been influenced by ideas from Oriental books which found their way to West Africa in the course of the centuries-old trans-continental trade. In these books the figures of notable warriors and rulers like Alexander the Great loom large; naturally, the poets of the oral tradition who have had access to these ideas and images frequently see their own rulers (however limited their areas of control) in the light of figures like Alexander the Great.
>
> *line 33* The Tuareg are a nomadic people who have spread from North Africa to the Sahelian regions of West Africa.
>
> *line 39* *spearhead* the section of an army that fights with spears.
>
> *line 41* *horse and foot* soldiers who fight on horseback and on foot.

Questions

Discuss the use of accumulation of details in this poem.

Comment on the use of exaggerated imagery in the portrait of Ali.

18 The odo-masquerade

Among the Igbo of Nigeria, masquerades perform to crowds of mostly adult citizens on important occasions, for example, when an important man dies or is taking a chieftaincy title. On such occasions, the masquerade poet sings praises of the important man, glorifying his family and achievements. But quite often the masquerader takes the opportunity to shower praises on himself. There may be other performers like him and he is aware of this; fired by this spirit of competition, he makes all kinds of exaggerated claims for everything from his dress to his achievements (none of which may ever have been attempted). This particular masquerade poet appears to have dressed himself with the mask of a bird: many of the metaphors used in the poem clearly put him in the light of a bird. But occasionally he abandons the bird-references to claim a variety of social achievements and attributes of power. We find in such self-praise the same spirit that underlies all praise poetry: the effort to be seen as a superman in a world of fierce physical competition.

Perhaps the most significant stylistic feature of this oral poem is the evidence of its context as a public performance. The very first line shows clearly that the poem was performed before a group of people; in the second line the command to 'listen' is repeated, perhaps emphatically, so as to ensure maximum attention from the noisy crowd. In line 6 the performer continues to impress himself upon his audience; in lines 50–55 he tells us what an effort he is making with his voice to please his crowd, and we also get an idea how large the crowd is. Even more interesting is the information about the man trying to record the performance with pen and paper: the masquerade poet brags that the copyist cannot keep pace with his performance! Here we have one of the distinct qualities of oral poetry: it gives us an idea of the context of its composition or performance more readily than written poetry cares to do.

lines 1–10   The bird metaphors come from the fact that the performer is wearing a bird mask. No performer has dared to stand up to him, other than the one wearing a mask of the *okpoko*-bird and he was driven to an act of madness for that.

line 5   *eternal* This indicates that the masquerade poet is discussing issues of large significance, and his statements should not be taken at surface level. It is quite clear that he is speaking in METAPHORS throughout.

lines 19–27   This is apparently a threat to another masquerader (here titled *creator-scatterer of locusts*) performing on the occasion. The *odo* masquerade poet is moving in peace with his group, but like soldier-ants they have a great capacity for acting together in the face of challenge. The *odo* is warning that the bothersome locusts (signifying his rival's powers) should be cleared out of the way to make room for his own performance.

line 28   *Ozo* a title taken in Igboland by those who have achieved some form of success – e.g. in military or economic life.

line 29   *palm-leaves* are worn by celebrants in ritual performances, sometimes by masquerades.

lines 30–31   Four market days make up the traditional Igbo week: Nkwo (see line 4 above), Eke, Olie and Afo.

line 42   *King of Contentment* He lives in the company of one who has everything he needs (either the king of his community or even God Himself). Either way, the masquerade poet is bragging about his social status.

Questions

Discuss some of the references here in which the masquerade poet brags about his supernatural powers.

Does this poem gain or lose any speed or intensity by not having any narrative episodes?

19 In praise of the blacksmith

Some of the more notable praise poetry to be found in traditional African societies is devoted to a glorification of labour – not, as we have seen so far, to an exaggerated portraiture of ruling figures by praise-singers looking for material rewards or of individuals projecting themselves. In this kind of poetry the sense of competition for supremacy (often with unfair advantages) is strikingly subdued and we get instead a sense of honest work. This poem has none of that imagery that raises the subject above the level of ordinary mankind; indeed, line 19 shows a touch of modesty on the part of the woman. This is praise poetry sung by simple folk doing honest work, not a glorification of privileged members of the society or of those who aspire to their company.

line 9 *ruddy* red (with fire).
line 14 *slag* particles of crude iron beaten out from the metal as it is being knocked into shape.

Questions

Discuss whether this poem can be considered a glorification of the occupation of blacksmith generally as well as of one particular blacksmith?

One basic problem in the thematic classification of poetry is that a poem may have certain elements which qualify it to be classified as much under one theme as another. What other theme might this poem come under?

20 Moshoeshoe

Moshoeshoe, son of Mokhachane and Kholu, was to all intents and purposes the founder of the Sotho kingdom, which developed largely with the progressive collapse of the Zulu kingdom after Shaka (see no. 22). By conducting frequent cattle raids into neighbouring territories he was able to increase the extent not only of his herd of cattle (a symbol both of wealth and of power in that part of Africa) but also of his area of control since the plundered people frequently came to recognise his power and his authority. He was particularly hostile to the Thembu, whom he raided on at least three different occasions. Unfortunately, on the third occasion (in 1835), although he came home with a lot of cattle, his brother Makhabane was killed during the fighting. While on the whole praising the fighting courage of Moshoeshoe, this poem nevertheless contains (as some praise poetry around such notable figures in traditional African society does) some mild criticism.

As in most oral praise poems, the emphasis here is on accumulation of praise EPITHETS. There are references to Moshoeshoe's exploits, especially against the Thembu, as a way of giving vivid illustration to the greatness of the hero. These are, however, told not in a clear coherent sequence but in brief references. This brevity adds to the 'charged' quality of the poetry. One notable stylistic feature of southern African praise poetry is also present in this poem: warriors like Moshoeshoe are frequently addressed by means of images of fierceness like weapons and wild animals. Here Moshoeshoe is variously referred to as ram (line

187

5), lion (line 8), hyena (line 10), leopard (line 15), ox (line 22), and flashing shield (line 17).

line 1 Addressed to the Thembu, who have been denying the presence of warriors among the Sotho.

line 4 *Binders* In many traditional African societies, there are ceremonies and rites initiating young boys to adulthood. During this period, each youth is expected to choose a (praise) name for himself. Moshoeshoe chose 'the Binder', and his army was later known under the name 'Binders'. The name probably refers to the way a warrior encircles the opponent and thus brings him under his control. Compare line 12 in *A warrior sings his praises* (no. 15).

line 5 As explained by M. Damane and D.B. Sanders who collected this poem: 'Moshoeshoe is here referred to as his ancestor, Kali. The Beoana were Kali's regiment' (see: *Luithoko: Sotho Praise Poems*, Oxford University Press, 1974).

line 7 *darkness* i.e. of war.

line 8 When this poem was composed, Moshoeshoe was an old man (see also line 15). But it is a credit to his ferocity that he still inspired fear in the enemy. The reference to toothlessness also brings a touch of humour to the poem.

lines 10—14 *Tyopho* was a chief living among the Thembu when Moshoeshoe raided them in 1835. These lines reflect Tyopho's desperate efforts — using the most ridiculous materials — to save himself from Moshoeshoe's force. *Mathlole* was Moshoeshoe's great-grandfather.

lines 15—19 *Mokali* and *RaNtheosi* are names for two of Moshoeshoe's wives. *Masopha* was a son of Moshoeshoe's.

lines 20—24 Further references to the 1835 raid against the Thembu (also called Kobo-e-Ngoka). *Waistcoat* apparently refers to the way Moshoeshoe clung steadily to an opponent in a fight. *Kaross* is a square garment made of sheets of leather sewn together.

lines 25—34 Moshoeshoe's victory over the Thembu was marred by the death of his brother Makhabane. The people mourn Makhabane, and the poet would not want his own herds of cattle contaminated by those won by Moshoeshoe in that ill-fated encounter. *Qoaling* is a mountain and *Korokoro* a stream several miles away from the Sotho capital, Thaba Bosiu.

line 35 *Thesele* is another name for Moshoeshoe, and *the other one* is Makhabane. Partly because the ruler was the absolute authority in the land, and partly because the poet's livelihood as a praise-singer depended on maintaining favourable relations with the ruler, the traditional praise-poet could not be too bold in his criticisms.

Questions

Discuss the shifts of mood in this poem.

Does Moshoeshoe emerge here as a positive or a negative figure? Support your view with references to the poem.

21 Salute to Fabunmi

This is an example of *ijala* or hunters poetry from the Yoruba of Nigeria. Among the Yoruba, the occupation of hunting is consecrated to the god Ogun, who is the god of iron and so patron of all crafts conducted with metal (e.g. gun for hunting). All hunters in any community are thus constituted into a guild or cult under the protection of Ogun; when one of them dies, elaborate rites are held, including the chanting of songs celebrating his greatness as a hunter. The salute to Fabunmi is one such chant, glorifying not only Fabunmi's hunting skills but his generosity and concern for others.

This poem makes very striking use of images and picturesque details in describing Fabunmi as a 'crack shot.' His act in shooting down a swinging monkey is seen as snatching the branch from the monkey's grip; the long speedy trail he leaves as he tracks an animal is likened to a rainbow in the sky; he is so accurate in his aim he can get an animal as small as a porcupine at the foot of a kolanut tree, apparently from a considerable distance; and we are even made to hear the sound of the bullet as it lands in an animal's abdomen.

But the more striking qualities of this poem derive from its background as an oral performance. *Ijala* poetry is normally chanted with a high, vibrato voice and with considerable speed. The element of speed accounts for some of the peculiar features of the poem. The challenge is for the performer to remember as many attributes of his subject as possible; but since his mind cannot always keep pace with the speed of his lips, he is forced to repeat many lines several times over so as not to halt the chanting. And yet there is a very musical effect to these repetitions which adds to the pressure and excitement under which the performer is working. Besides, the repetitions are saved from being monotonous by the fact that they come in various combinations and modifications. Notice, for instance, the changes to the text accompanying the phrase 'he who snatches a tree branch from a monkey's grip' in lines 1, 3, and 14; the varying environment of the phrase 'husband of Layemi' in lines 2 and 14; and of the phrase 'why is it that we no longer see Fabunmi?' in lines 1, 25, and 32.

Even more interesting is the exchange of performances between two hunters. In such exchanges – which are common in *ijala* performances – there is usually an atmosphere of competition between the two performers which adds to the excitement of the whole scene. Notice that the second performer uses a SIGNATURE at the start of his recitation ('Hey! . . . Ha!') – a lyrical device which helps him not only to prepare himself for the task but also to ensure the attention of the audience.

line 1 *Oolo* The protective divinity of Iware town.

line 11 'the traditional practice was that the hunter rubbed the palm of the left hand of the killed monkey against the ground' (see: S. A. Babalola; *The Content and Form of Yoruba Ijala*, Oxford University Press, 1966).

line 23 A very forceful metaphor. The sound of Fabunmi's rifle (which fires many times) is compared to the boom of a cannon (though this fires only once every charge).

lines 26–30 The persons referred to in lines 26–28 are evidently forbidden by custom to eat monkey meat. But so warm was Fabunmi towards his guests that, were these people to visit him, they would go so far as to eat the choicest part of the monkey (its head).

Questions

From the idioms used in this praise poem, would you consider it a realistic or an exaggerated portrait of the hunter Fabunmi?

Although this poem could be considered a dirge — i.e. a song performed at a time of death — what are the qualities of it that rescue it from the sadness which generally attends such occasions?

22 Shaka

Shaka was the legendary Zulu warrior and ruler of the nineteenth century. Son of a chief Senzangokhona and a powerful mother Nandi, he served his apprenticeship as a warrior under Dingiswayo (chief of the Mthethwa tribe), assuming the rulership of the Zulu at the death of his father (1816). Thereafter he evolved a formidable army and strategy which helped him to conquer and appropriate various ethnic groups around the Zulu. He died in 1828, stabbed to death by his brothers and colleagues.

Shaka was also noted for his skill as ruler and empire builder but in the oral tradition it is his military skill and fierce energy that get the greater share of glorification. This accounts for the emphasis placed in this poem on rage and martial energy; as in the praise of Moshoeshoe, there is a predominance of ferocious animals (lion, leopard) and fierce weapons (axe, spear) as metaphors for Shaka's destructive vigour. In a praise poem to such a figure as Shaka we can see the greatest premium placed by the oral tradition on sheer physical valour: many of the feats achieved by Shaka would be considered cruel and heartless by modern standards, but seen in the context of his times his ferocity would seem quite appropriate in an age when might was right. The images used throughout this poem confirm a preference for ferocity.

The poem also reveals the usual stress found in praise poetry of such notable figures, between independent phrases or lines of praise, and narrative episodes. It is hardly possible to sing the praise of one who led such an active life without feeling tempted now and then to narrate specific instances. However, the duty to heap praise upon praise is greater here than the urge to tell a story. The narrative episodes are therefore severely abbreviated, so much so that in many instances significant events (e.g., major battles) are alluded to very concisely (sometimes with proverbs). The result is poetry that is filled with complex allusions and highly suggestive metaphors.

This selection is made up of two segments (lines 1–36, 37–60) from a very long *izibongo* (praise poem). The numerous names refer mostly to Shaka's connections and conquests. Mbelebele, Mashoba, Mfene, Mthandeni, Zinkondeni, Hlokohloko and Silutshana are names of communities or ethnic groups among which Shaka conducted his military campaigns. Other important names are explained below.

line 1 *Dlungwana* is a 'praise-name meaning the rager or ferocious one'. *Ndaba* was Shaka's grandfather.
line 5 *Menzi* ('creator') was a praise-name of Senzangakhona, Shaka's father.
line 8 Frequently in praise poetry, the poet brings his own sentiments into play,

as a way of bringing the subject of his performance closer to him. See also lines 31–32.

line 15   The result of so much stabbing. This is a good instance of the ALLUSIONS (indirect or passing references) often found in praise poetry.

lines 16–36   These are allusions to two separate episodes in Shaka's military career. Shaka, the 'white' son of Nandi, lured Zwide, the 'red' son of Ntombazi into a war and defeated him: Noju and Ngqengenye were advisers of Shaka and Zwide respectively. Lines 21–36 refer to Shaka's victory over Phakathwayo. The latter had insulted Shaka in a dance competition in the Mthandein area, and Shaka retaliated with war in which he finally destroyed his rival. After Phakathwayo's death, there was rivalry for his chieftaincy among his brothers; Shaka consented to favour one of them, Godolozi, unaware that the latter was on the side of Zwide (Ntombazi's son) in his war with Shaka.

lines 32–33   These two prominent men in Phakathwayo's council had apparently encouraged their chief to make this insolent remark about Shaka's style of dancing.

lines 34–36   Phakathwayo's people had hoped to surprise and stab him to death but (as the Zulu proverb implies) their plans were destroyed.

line 42   According to Trevor Cope, who collected this poem, this is 'A praise name which may mean "Mighty Power"' (see Izibongo: *Zulu Praise Poems*, Oxford University Press, 1968).

lines 45–46   Shaka had sent a mission to the English King George, but the expedition did not get very far from Natal.

lines 49–52   This episode is unknown.

line 58   A praise-name of uncertain meaning.

Questions

Why is this praise-singer of Shaka grateful for the names of Phakathwayo's counsellors (lines 31–32)?

Comment on the usefulness of ALLUSIONS in this poem.

23 Agbor dancer

This portrait of a dancing girl was apparently suggested by a performance at a cultural festival. In it Clark celebrates the youthfulness and energy with which the girl dances; the ease and smoothness with which her movements blend with the background music; and the way in which the entire performance is rooted in the culture from which the girl comes.

The effectiveness of this poem lies, to a large extent, in the way that Clark manipulates the sounds within words, producing such musical effects as alliteration, assonance, and rhyme. Although these are devices that Clark has used frequently in his poetry, their musical benefits are particularly relevant to this poem in which he is celebrating someone connected with music (a dancer). Of the many examples of alliteration in this poem, we may recognise the *l* and *f* sounds in 'Limbs like fresh foliage' (stanza one); and the *m* and *tr* sounds in 'magic/Maze of music/In trance she treads the intricate' (stanza 2); and so on. One of the striking pictures that Clark wishes to expose in this poem is the way in which the body movements of the girl follow closely the beat of the music, very much as the surface of water trembles and forms ripples under the driving force of the wind. In a sense the *tr* (as well as *br*, *cr*, etc.) sounds help Clark at least to suggest these trembling and rippling effects. Notice also the rhyme scheme of the poem: Clark no doubt uses the harmony of sounds in the rhyming device to suggest the harmonious relationship between the girl, the music, and the culture.

The last stanza of the poem is significant. Having spent the three earlier stanzas admiring the ease with which the dancer fuses with her culture and its music, the poet is inevitably moved to comment sadly on how education has made him a prisoner to another culture and estranged him from his own. The celebration of traditional culture gives the poet an opportunity to condemn the effects of foreign culture on him.

lines 1–5 In this stanza the dancer is symbolically portrayed as a tree swaying (*tippling*) excitedly to the rhythm of drum music – all the way from its skin-covered trunk (*hide-brimmed stem*), through its veins that run in long lines, to its very aged centre. The flexible (*supple*) and dark-brown (*tan*) arms of the swaying dancer are pictured as the fresh leaves of the tree. *Ancestral core* may also be taken as a metaphor for the earth (to which the tree is rooted) as the ancient base of traditional culture.

lines 8–10 The delicate rhythms of the music are seen as ripples on the surface of a river flowing to the thick vegetation of a forest; in her wild swaying movements the dancer copes skilfully with those delicate patterns of the music as one riding on ripples.

lines 11–12 In many of his early poems, Clark follows the practice of some notable British poets (e.g. G. M. Hopkins) in transposing words and phrases from their usual order for poetic effect. These two lines would normally read 'Tremulous beats wake in her heart a trenchant descant' (i.e. high note); however, not only would *trenchant descant* sound rather ugly, but Clark is anxious to maintain his rhyme scheme and so finds it convenient to separate the two words for that purpose.

lines 14–15 Because they are uncovered by shoes, the girl's long toes are physical features uncorrupted or unspoilt (like virgins) by modern fashion. But they are, unfortunately, so twisted (either from too frequent dancing or from walking too long on the hard soil) that they cannot easily be described in writing or by word of mouth.

lines 16–17 The ELISION of the final *e* in *sequester'd* (separated, removed) and *lead-tether'd* (chained, imprisoned – here, to a foreign culture) is an old-fashioned technique in English poetry. *Scribe* is an old-fashioned word (meaning writer) which has been deliberately chosen to rhyme with *tribe*.

Questions

How does the message of this poem justify Clark's use of old-fashioned words and forms?

Identify and discuss the words in this poem that represent the contrast between union with traditional culture and separation from it.

24 Martin Luther King

This poem is a celebration of the great American Negro civil rights leader, Rev. Martin Luther King. For a long time in the history of the United States, the blacks had suffered severe discrimination and the brutality of policemen who attacked them with truncheons and trained dogs at the least provocation. Before he was assassinated in 1968 by a bigot, King led a number of protests against the injustice suffered by blacks. One of the most outstanding of these was the march on Washington, D.C., the seat of the United States government, in 1963 in which both influential whites and downtrodden blacks participated. Before the enormous crowd gathered to hear him speak on the grounds of the Lincoln Memorial monument, he delivered a moving speech which began with the words 'I have a dream . . .' In that speech Rev. King, a Baptist minister, frequently used Biblical language to declare his hope that one day peace and love would reign in the hearts of men not only in his country but across the earth. This poem glorifies the courage of Martin Luther King on the occasion of the speech.

line 1 The speech was made under the statue of Abraham Lincoln, the sixteenth president of the United States who signed the Emancipation Proclamation (1863) that proclaimed all American slaves free. The reference to 'Abraham' also evokes the image of the Biblical patriarch Abraham; in this way the poet tries to reflect the religious status of the subject of the poem (Rev. King) and to suggest the religious quality of his message of hope.

lines 6–11 The dream of peace and love overshadowed (*bestrode*) the authority of the American government, whose emblem shows the figure of an eagle. Here the poet reveals the vindictiveness (*ringing heart*) of the authorities (i.e. the police) as an eagle circling (*wheeling*) in flight and beating people with truncheons.

lines 12–17 There are essentially two images suggested here. On the one hand, there is the picture of Martin Luther King leading a large crowd who trampled the hard streets with so much pressure that they were reduced to dust which rose to the sky. On the other hand, building a fertile valley out of a desert suggests that King succeeded in converting hard-hearted Americans to his mission and in uniting all segments of the American society, both high (*clouds*) and low (*soil*), in his agitation. Whatever the case may be, the unification of separate entities – of earth and sky, or of the lowly and the mighty in American society – constituted the human message (*voice of man*) that King delivered with such deep commitment. Although King was not killed on this particular occasion, the phrase *buried in his neck* indicates that he was assassinated (1968) while spreading his message across the land.

Questions

Discuss the full meaning of the phrase *vacant eyes* (line 1).

The phrase *a dream* is used three times in this poem. What is the significance of the repetition?

25 The birth of Shaka

Oswald Mtshali is easily one of the most talented of those poets in South Africa today who have devoted their energies to portraying the ugly social and political situation in that country. This poem is a tribute to the most notable ancestor of the Zulu, the legendary warrior and nation-builder, Shaka. Mtshali has undertaken to celebrate Shaka in his poetry as a rallying cry for the black people of South Africa in their troubles today. In doing this he is performing a role very much like that of the praise-singers in traditional African society. Some of these praise-singers were attached to kings and warlords, and before his master went into battle it was the duty of the praise-singer to sing the glories of his master's ancestors so that he could fight nobly and bravely and so uphold the glory of his line. Mtshali must have felt a similar obligation to encourage the black people in their bloody struggles against the apartheid regime of South Africa.

It will be useful to compare this poem with the *izibongo* treated earlier in this section (no. 22), for Mtshali (himself a Zulu from Natal) has obviously borrowed some ideas from the oral tradition as he composed his poem. As in the earlier poem, the ferocity and fighting energy of Shaka are portrayed with the metaphors of the lion (stanza one) and war weapons like the shield (stanza three); the raging temper of Shaka is powerfully portrayed in stanza two; and in stanza five Mtshali even echoes the image of the swallows which the *izibongo* equally links with white seafarers.

There are, however, two striking differences between Mtshali's poem and the *izibongo*. The latter has confined itself to using images which relate specifically to Shaka as a Zulu leader. Although the traditional poets of South Africa are by no means unaware that the present political situation has its roots in the confrontation between their ancestors and white people, the racial element is much weaker in their praises of Shaka than the details of his victories. Mtshali's poetry, however, is deeply influenced by the bitterness of the present situation, and in it we feel the confrontation between the races more sharply. In stanza two the Africanness of Shaka's rage is emphasised by the fact that his blood was boiled in *clay* pots — utensils formed with material straight from the African soil. *Gods* in stanza two and *ancestors* in stanza four are the major figures in traditional African religion, and in them Mtshali seems to suggest that Shaka has been shaped in accordance with traditional African metaphysics. And in stanza five the colour differences between the races are highlighted by references to *dark* valleys and *white* swallows. While, therefore, we would call the *izibongo* a praise poem to a Zulu leader, we would more properly see Mtshali's as a praise poem to an African or black leader.

Another difference between the *izibongo* and Mtshali's poem is in the time periods which their portraits of Shaka cover. In the *izibongo* we are shown some of the military victories of Shaka; since the poet's interest is in the greatness of Shaka, he puts his emphasis on the heyday of his achievements. But Mtshali has at the back of his mind the history of black African struggle. His subject is seemingly the birth of Shaka, and indeed most of the poem deals with how Shaka's greatness was formed from the beginning. But at the end the poet introduces an incident which comes at the very end of Shaka's life, and the significance of that final threat lies in the fact that it is addressed as much by the poet to the present-day usurpers of the African land as by Shaka to his treacherous brothers.

lines 1–5 Shaka's father and mother were separated early in Shaka's life; Mtshali here suggests that Shaka's fierce temper had its roots in this early sense of loss he felt as a child. It is possible to read this image as a metaphor for the present-day situation in South Africa. Many children there lose their fathers as a result of the socio-political situation – the men are frequently taken away by the apartheid authorities on one pretext or another – and this may contribute to the impatience and frustration with which many children grow up (notably in Soweto, where Mtshali lives).

lines 14–18 *Thongs* are pieces of metal; *wattle* and *syringa* are types of trees.

lines 23–25 Shaka was stabbed to death by his brothers Dingaan and Mhlangana, who contested his kingship after his death. Dingaan had Mhlangana assassinated and became king of the Zulu. But the nation established by Shaka grew steadily weaker until it was annexed by the British settlers.

Questions

What effect is Mtshali trying to achieve with the alliterations in stanza two?

This poem begins and ends with the symbol of a cry. What do you suppose the poet is using this symbol for?

26 Bamako

Before African countries began winning independence from colonial rule in large numbers – starting with Ghana in 1957 – conferences were frequently held by groups of African intellectuals and freedom fighters, both inside and outside the continent. These conferences were intended mostly to draw attention to the greatness of African culture and the sense of unity among all African peoples (which was usually advertised by the term *pan-Africanism*), so as to strengthen the case for the liberation of Africa from colonial rule. One such conference was held in Bamako, capital of Mali, in 1954, when this poem was written.

As in the other poems discussed in this section, this praise poem sets out to celebrate achievement: in this case, the achievement of Bamako in giving Africans the opportunity and environment to sow the seeds of hope and build strong foundations for the future. In this poem, there is a very striking picture of a people determined to free themselves from centuries of subjugation and hopelessness; to 'dry the tears shed over the centuries' of slavery and to overcome the spiritual death which this subjugation has brought. The success of this struggle for liberation will depend on the determination and sense of purpose of the freedom fighters; but greater credit goes to the city of Bamako for inspiring new life in them, for sowing the seeds of hope in them, and for giving them a feeling of friendship and identity as Africans struggling under a unified cause. This prominent place given by the poet to Bamako is shown in the repeated exclamation of the name of the city at the beginning of each stanza.

There is also a generous use of abstract nouns: freshness, generosity, goodness, force of friendship, hope, etc. This is partly because the poet is spreading his vision over the entire expanse of the continent, and partly because at this point freedom is still an abstract idea which has not been realised in concrete terms by a vast majority of the peoples of Africa. However, the poet balances this element of abstractness by references to concrete objects like rivers, trees, soil and sky which portray the vitality of the continent and bring the feeling of freedom and identity nearer to himself and his compatriots.

lines 2–8 The strength and hope which Bamako inspired in participants at the conference are illustrated by images suggesting nourishment and growth. The 'truth' (i.e. words of wisdom spoken at the conference) dropping on the shining surface of leaves suggests the freshness and vitality brought by rain. This idea of new life and strength is reinforced in the next few lines by the picture of a young tree with strong roots, warmed by the soil, nurtured by the waters of the Niger, shaded by the huge trees of the Congo forest, and fanned by a breeze which has a touch of tenderness characteristic of Africans. The pan-African sentiment of this poem is well conveyed by references here to diverse areas of the continent.

lines 19–22 dry and *vivified* are used as adjectives: i.e. 'the tears shed over the centuries . . .' are now dry, and 'the nourishing juice . . .' and 'the aroma . . .' have now been further vivified, or strengthened.

lines 23–24 Kilimanjaro is Africa's highest mountain spanning the Kenyan/Tanzanian border. Here it is used as a metaphor for a heroic race of new Africans, who are at last freed from the shackles of domination and living in peace.

lines 25–31 The *living arteries of Africa* are the internal, traditional qualities of the black race which nourish the growth of the Africa of future generations. Bamako is here seen as a symbol of the future results (*fruit*) of the hope and friendship which the present conference has inspired across the continent. Note the emphasis throughout this poem on words denoting life, hope, and growth: together they constitute its cheerful and optimistic tone.

Questions

Explain fully the meaning of each of the following phrases: 'important fires of goodness' (line 12); 'the blue sky of peace' (line 24); 'the elegance of the palm and the black skin' (line 31).

In this poem celebrating Bamako, is there any evidence of nationalist anger?

27 Elavanyo concerto

This poem is a celebration of the courage of those who stand up tenaciously in defence of truth, here represented by the figure of the Italian scientist Galileo Galilei (1564–1642). On the basis of some experiments and observations he had carried out, Galileo disproved some well-established views held by the church and the general society in his day. For this he was put on trial (the Inquisition) by the Roman Catholic Church, the supreme authority in Europe at that time, and sentenced to life imprisonment. This poem is a tribute to the noble struggle which Galileo put up – alone against the formidable authorities of the time – in defence of scientific truth against ancient but powerful prejudices. In dedicating the poem to Angela Davis and Wole Soyinka – the one a black American radical spokeswoman and the other a progressive Nigerian writer, both of whom have suffered under the governments of their countries – Okai, like Mtshali in *The birth of Shaka*, is invoking the achievements of the past as an encouragement, a battle-cry, to present-day figures engaged in the same sort of struggle.

One notable achievement of Okai in this poem is in incorporating some of the techniques of the oral performance so effectively. First, there is a clamorous effect in the entire piece: this is a poem which has to be read aloud to be fully appreciated. As a student in Russia in the sixties, Okai was exposed to the practice of poets reading their works aloud; this is one major reason he has put into the poem so many patterns of sound (e.g. exclamations) that can only be brought out well by an open reading. Secondly, as a Ghanaian, Okai has listened very closely to the music of drums, and there is no doubt that the frequent duplications of sound which we get in this poem – alliteration, rhyme, and assonance – are in some ways a reflection of the repetitive patterns of sound in drum music. There is of course no regularity in this use of sound patterns; in fact, there is on the whole a certain disorderliness about them which may be Okai's way of celebrating Galileo's act in destabilising the system of belief in his day. Thirdly, there is considerable exaggeration in Okai's portrait of the courage shown by Galileo in his trial. Available records show that Galileo was in fact forced during the trial to renounce his view about the centrality of the sun; consequently, rather than put him to death, the Inquisition simply decided to sentence him to life imprisonment. But Okai – very much like the oral praise-singer – magnifies the courage of Galileo on that occasion so as to present as much a picture of heroism as possible. Finally, in his resort to the indigenous language (*Elavanyo*) Okai reveals an attachment to his African roots.

There is also a skilful use of modern techniques in this poem, especially in the adoption of the concerto framework. A concerto (the word, by the way, is Italian) is a musical performance composed to feature a solo instrument against a full orchestra, and is structured into several 'movements'. In this poem we see the predicament of Galileo played against the church authorities in the following sequence: the contest between Galileo's ideas and the conservative, authoritarian image of the authorities (lines 1–6); Galileo's trial, in which he is likened to a bull-fighter facing dangers in the ring (7–54); the period when Galileo sits waiting, in defeat and despair, for the seed of his ideas to take root (55–67); the renewal of the struggle between truth or knowledge and the oppressive forces of ignorance (68–87); the final stanza (88–100) celebrates the victory of the forces of knowledge and holds out hope for those who find themselves in a similar predicament to Galileo's. In *Elavanyo concerto* generally, Okai has tried to unite the resources of the oral culture and contemporary art in a celebration of the revolutionary spirit.

Title *Elavanyo* an Ewe word meaning 'Things will be all right.'

lines 1–2 Okai here reverses the order of lines so as to achieve a special effect: each word is meant to be read with the one immediately below it. The resulting rhymes carry with them the effect of irony and scorn, for it is Okai's aim to ridicule all forms of authority. *Cross*, the symbol of the Christian Church (which was prosecuting Galileo), is matched with *Dross*, which means trash or dirt. *Banner* probably stands for the American flag (sometimes called 'the star-spangled banner'); to equate it with a *hammer* is to imply that the American government destroys its citizens. *Swatistika* was the symbol of Nazi Germany under Hitler: *floodfire* signifies how he tried to engulf the whole world with destruction. *Sickle* is part of the emblem of Soviet authority, and *spittle* implies either that the Soviet system is worth nothing or that it belittles the dignity of its citizens.

lines 3—6 These lines summarise, with appropriate symbols, the essence of Galileo's conflict with the Church authorities. He supported the theory of an earlier scientist, Copernicus, that the sun is the body around which all the planets revolve – contrary to the generally held view that the sun moved around the earth. He also dropped two stones (of different weights) from the leaning tower of Pisa; the fact that they reached the ground at the same time helped him to challenge generally held views about the laws of motion. For these revolutionary views he was summoned to a grand trial (Inquisition) in Rome. The usual punishment was being burned at a stake. But this was commuted to a life imprisonment when Galileo withdrew his claims (line 6).

lines 7—14 These lines prepare us for Galileo's trial, by comparing his predicament to that of the famous Spanish bullfighter El Cordobes. But at least (Okai suggests in line 13) the bulls Cordobes fought were defenceless.

lines 15—19 The prejudices against which Galileo contended were severe and frightful ones. *Rot-ring of scorn*: in the court or arena (*ring*) where he was tried, Galileo was contending against the old, crumbling ideas (*rot*) of men who had nothing but scorn for him. A *bull* is also a papal decree banning any statement or publication.

line 23 *toddler* i.e. in terms of science, the world was still learning how to walk.

lines 27—54 These are imagined arguments between Galileo and his accusers at the trial. In essence he is charged with having lost his senses, and warned that he is wasting his time and making a nuisance of himself (lines 27—32). He replies that he does not care how isolated he becomes; he will not abandon his ideas under any circumstances; their theories are out of date, and the falsehoods which they support from their positions of divine authority are headed towards destruction; the seed of truth has been sown, and it will not be long before the fruit emerges for the benefit of everyone (33—54).

lines 41—48 God has been fooled by his ministers, who from their privileged positions have told lies which they pass off as truths. They have abused their positions very much as Judas Iscariot abused his. Like him they will soon be cast adrift to face the stubborn truth and be sunk in chaos.

lines 55—67 Galileo has lost. The poet here sympathises with him (notice the African exclamation of lament, *hei!*) as he sinks into dejection while the hard-headed enemies of truth sing triumphantly. The hero (*preying mantis*) has lost his dignity, and he wisely abandons his views in obedience to those peddlers of cheap lies who are looking for every chance to destroy his life.

Questions

Do you consider Okai's use of the techniques of sound (rhyme, alliteration, etc.) adequate or overdone? Support your answer with references to the text.

How effectively do you think Okai has portrayed the predicaments of Galileo here? Discuss specific passages.

28 Taga for Mbaye Dyob

Although they championed causes that were not popular in their times and suffered greatly for doing so, both Martin Luther King and Galileo Galilei were outstanding leaders whose ideas are today part of the cultural and scientific history of mankind. In this poem, however, Senghor has chosen to celebrate an unranked and unknown Senegalese soldier who died during the Second World War to give him an honour which Senghor thinks he richly deserves but would not normally be given. What Senghor is saying in this poem is essentially this: Dyob, I will glorify you. I know that both in background and in rank you were a very common man. But you showed a deep attachment and warmth to your colleagues. You served them faithfully and suffered so as to make their lives better. For all this, you will be celebrated throughout the length and breadth of Senegal with music and song.

The poem is one of a collection written by Senghor during the Second World War and published in 1948 under the title *Hosties Noires* (Black Hostages). In this collection Senghor is concerned with the plight of black (both African and American) soldiers enlisted to fight against Germany. Many Africans from the French colonies (like Senegal) were enrolled to fight on the side of France, and they went happily, believing they were fighting a just cause. But there was a great deal of discrimination against these black soldiers, and in *Hosties Noires* Senghor frequently condemns this practice of treating the blacks as if they were non-beings. In this poem, Senghor has deliberately chosen to celebrate a small man mainly to demonstrate that, though small, he has an identity of his own.

Senghor is very conscious here of the contradiction in his bestowing honour and glory on a little man who would not ordinarily be glorified. Consequently, the language of the poem reflects this sense of contrasts. Thus, in line 4, a stove which is *red* with fire only succeeds in making the soldiers cold; Dyob's ancestors have no distinguished place in *black* history (line 5), but he has earned himself a *white* honour which the poet determines to celebrate; he may have been mocked or underestimated by *griots* (who are mostly male), but the poet recommends that he be treated with warmth and respect by beautiful girls singing his praise.

High spirits are evident throughout in this poem; the poet will hoist Dyob's name 'to the high mast of the ship' bringing back his body, and ring it 'like a bell.' Notice also that the *tama* is a high-pitched Senegalese drum, which suggests that the poet wishes the poem to be given a high-spirited performance. The song of the maidens will match and mingle with the loud noise of the waves and the wind, and their high-pitched voices will be supported by the equally high-sounding *kora* (a traditional guitar).

Title *Taga* means praise.
line 3 *Dyobene* an affectionate way of calling *Dyob*. Literally it means, 'son of the Dyob clan or family'.
line 5 By identifying his ancestors and pointing out the times and significance of their careers, he would have supplied some of the missing links in the history of Africa.
line 6 Dyob was too gentle even to bear arms.
line 8 The *Senegal Rifles* were a Senegalese (colonial) regiment of the French army during the Second World War.

line 9 *white honour* distinction won in the white man's war. *White* may also mean 'shining,' 'glaring,' 'outstanding.'

line 16 A *griot* was traditionally a male praise-singer in a royal Mandinka household. But today griots (some of them women) are to be found as semiprofessional musicians performing for anyone who can pay them.

line 17 As Christ suffered for mankind, so is Dyob seen here to have suffered for his companions in the war. His death is one more act of suffering which shows his steadfast loyalty to them.

line 18 Though it is not openly declared, there is a bond (pact) of loyalty binding soldiers fighting on the same side.

line 20 Notice the PARADOX in this statement. A man's arm should grow tired from his shaking other people's hands. But the bond of loyalty and friendship between these soldiers is a source of strength to them, so that the death of Dyob removes one element from this strength and brings about weakness.

Questions

What do you think is Senghor's purpose in constantly calling the name of a man who is (a) dead, and (b) insignificant?

Identify all the colour references in this poem. Explain the relevance of at least four of them to the negritude of Senghor.

29 Katini's complaint

The story behind this painful song is essentially as follows. The musician Katini had been making xylophones (*timbila*) for their chief, Wani Zavala, when he received instructions from the chief's messenger, Bakubakwane, to finish the chief's hut before the rains came. So Katini went off to do that. While he was at it, he received a query from Kapitini, a newly appointed messenger – who was either throwing his weight around or bearing an old grudge – wanting to know why Katini had not finished the *timbila*. Not only that, Kapitini sent two of his henchmen, Malova and Dibuliani, early one morning to beat up Katini and his wife Mashewani while they were still sleeping. Mashewani died a few months afterwards, though some claimed the beating had little to do with it.

Notice the basic narrative structure of this complaint as contained in stanzas 2 to 4. Notice too the repetition of the whole of stanza 1 at the end. Although the experience is a painful one, it has nevertheless been made into a song and is therefore treated with the traditional poetic devices; indeed, the repetition here does give an added emotional impact to the complaint.

line 2 *cider* is beer locally brewed from cashew fruits. Katini is here charging Kapitini with being under the influence of alcohol.

line 6 Here the poet invokes the name of the chief as an oath that he is telling the truth.

line 10 *You* is for Kapitini. *Sjambok* is a short, stout whip made from rhinoceros or other leather.

lines 15 and 17 Chipaupau and Fainde were two fellow musicians and friends of Katini's.

Questions

Would you consider this complaint angry or sorrowful? Explain.

In what ways does Katini try to build a strong case against Kapitini?

30 Kodzo the imbecile

Halo poetry among the Ewe of Ghana is essentially a poetry of personal abuse, in which the poet attacks individuals against whom he has a grudge. Traditional Ewe society of course discouraged slander and reckless abuse, but the poets who practised *halo* were mostly excused on the grounds that their art contributed immensely to curbing social excesses. Nowadays, however, the art is no longer popular partly because the old village life is fast giving way to urban life and partly because such open abuse is discouraged by the law. Komi Ekpe was seventy-six years old when the modern poet Kofi Awoonor recorded this poem from him at the Ewe village of Tsiame, and was one of the few surviving practitioners of this old poetry.

Kodzo, the victim of this poem, had apparently been goaded by some women admirers and prominent men in Tsiame (e.g. Amegavi, line 21) into singing a *halo* against Ekpe. The latter here retaliates to prove to his opponent that as a *halo* poet he can give as good as he got! Kofi Awoonor says of this poem: 'The typical ingredients of the *halo* are employed: accumulated insults through the use of metaphors and similes, exaggeration, and imagery drawn from the animal world loaded in its pithiness. From line 23 on, abuse becomes the main characteristic forte of the poem. In performance, the rapidity and stress on emphasis with which aspects of this insults are repeated, add power and depth and "pain" to them' (see: *Guardians of the Sacred Word*, Nok Publishers, 1974).

line 1   The humming notes are used here partly as a melodic introduction and as a warning to Kodzo to stop playing with fire.

line 6   Ekpe had given the name 'Question' to his drum, apparently because of its duty in treating serious issues. The *Questioners* are thus the drum musicians accompanying Ekpe in his performances.

line 10   *winding* making foul air.

line 18   *I forgive him his debt* Though Ekpe pretends to treat this offence lightly, his very mention of it is a deliberate attempt to draw attention to it.

lines 19—20   *he poked ... ants grove* a metaphor for a man bringing trouble upon himself.

line 23   *his* i.e. Kodzo's.

line 24   *breathing spot* the soft, beating spot on the top of an infant's head. Ekpe implies there is a lump there which looks like a medicine house.

line 25   *ass* a colloquial American form for *arse*.

lines 28—29   This metaphor describes Kodzo as a thoroughly weak and ineffective man who has no control over his household.

line 34   That is, because the fetish will kill Kodzo and save him the torment of his wretched life.

line 36   *fatteningly* i.e. making them pregnant.

line 41   A *sun-inspector* is a man continually gazing at the sun.

Questions

Explain the metaphor 'the evil firewood he'd gathered' (lines 6–7).

There are two broad categories into which Ekpe's abuses on Kodzo fall: (a) his bodily features, and (b) his life-style or general habits. Group the details of Ekpe's insults under the appropriate categories.

31 Attack traders

Among the Igbo of southeastern Nigeria women frequently form song-and-dance groups. These regularly perform songs on a variety of festive occasions such as the taking of a chieftaincy title, marriage, the opening of a school, and others. Some of the songs are harmless and celebrative, but in others the women take the opportunity to draw attention to the misdemeanour of certain elements in the social and political life of the society. This is an old poetic tradition, but its continuing vitality can be seen in the treatment here of a very recent experience. In 1967 the Eastern Region of Nigeria seceded from the federation and named itself the Republic of Biafra; the resulting civil war lasted three years (1967–70). This song was collected from Mbaise by Professor Nwoga of the University of Nigeria, Nsukka shortly after the end of the war.

    'Attack' traders were young women from Biafra who traded across the fighting lines with Nigerians on the other side; they were called 'attack' for their boldness in dealing with enemy forces and territory. As the poem suggests, some of them carried this boldness into their households in their attitudes to their husbands.

    Part of the poetic effectiveness of this tradition lies in the sheer physical spectacle of the performance; the women are frequently decked out in colourful uniforms and dance their tunes in appropriately regulated movements which provide a moving accompaniment to the tunes. The other part of the poetry here lies in the pointed representation of the subjects of the satire: note the sharp contrast between the arrogance of the women (lines 8–13) and their total helplessness at the end of the war (lines 14–15) when 'Biafran money' became worthless currency.

> *line 6* In traditional society, women do not put their money in a leather purse but tie it in a convenient knot made in a strip of cloth worn around the waist as a girdle.
> *line 10* That is, as bride wealth.

Questions

In what ways may we explain the repetitive structure of lines in this poem?

What does this poem tell us, by implication, about what is expected of a married woman in Igbo society?

32 Lamba courts

The practice of one community composing songs to lampoon another community (or specific individuals in it) is a widespread one in traditional African satirical poetry. In *Lamba courts* we have such an example of one community satirising another – the Kelela mocking the adulterous habits of the Lamba. It should however be noted that the fact that one community sings lampoons against another does not always imply a relationship of hostility between them. In some cases, it is true, an earlier experience of warfare between two neighbouring communities may lead later to a tradition of mutual insults. But quite frequently also these pieces of satirical poetry may be the product of what anthropologists have called a 'joking relationship' between communities. Early in the history of their social development, these communities may have been joined together by certain links, (e.g. being separately founded by two brothers or friends) which confer upon them the liberty to talk to and about one another in any form of language without either party feeling offence.

The Kelela are in the northwestern part of Zambia, while the Lamba are in the copper belt (to the west) of that country.

line 7 *tribute-labour* When group A has established its supremacy or overlordship over group B through war or any other means, it generally demands that the members of group B pay certain tributes to it – whether in the form of money or of members of group B doing some manual labour for group A on specific projects or occasions – as an acknowledgement of that historical supremacy.

Questions

Does the appeal to 'Mothers' (line 1) make the case against the Lamba any more effective?

In what ways does the poet achieve the effect of exaggeration in this song?

33 The woes of independence

This is an example of *udje*, the poetry of social comment among the Urhobo of southwestern Nigeria. Most of this poetry set out to lampoon individuals between communities; in fact, this tradition was so well developed that the contest (between one community and another) in highly crafted lampoons was the high point of festivals held periodically in the central parts of Urhoboland. *Udje* is no longer practised as in the olden days, partly because the young men who composed the songs have been leaving the villages in large numbers to seek their livelihood in the big towns, and partly because the law of libel discourages reckless abuse of people. This particular poem is one of the less harmful ones from the tradition, being concerned with a subject of wider national interest; but the sharpness of the wit here is evidence of the poetic force of the tradition as a whole.

The subject of this poem is the value of independence to Nigerians. The poem makes the point that independence has brought about a decline rather than an improvement in the quality of living among Nigerians. With the departure of the colonial government, the society has been thrown into chaos: the economy has suffered a slump rather than a boom as was promised; politics has become a desperate tussle for power among rival parties; and persistent tax raids have driven the ordinary people into a perpetual feeling of insecurity.

Both in imagery and organisation this selection bears witness to the standards of poetic excellence achieved by the *udje* tradition. The opening chant by the leader of the group sets the appropriate tone for their performance. The first five lines introduce the note of regret which underscores the entire message of the poem. The rest of this introductory section gives credit to the festive circumstances in which the song is performed: the leader gives due recognition first to the communal deity, then to the audience, and finally invites the group to carry on the song. This graceful transition from leader to group shows a perfect sense of timing and coordination in a poetic tradition that has achieved a high level of excellence.

One noticeable element in this poem is the narrative, which has been used for the entire portion sung by the group. This device is used more frequently in the traditional poetry of protest and abuse than in praise poetry. The reason may be that protest entails a certain amount of complaint about injustice done to someone or to a community; to convince the audience that your case is good, you may need to tell a fairly detailed story. Here the story is told with full dramatic details of speech and action; in language and style there is a good deal of humour and exaggeration designed to expose political independence as a fabulous joke.

line 3   The line implies that, out of sheer ignorance, we have taken a step that is destroying us. A *pangolin* is an ant-eating animal with scales all over its body.

lines 4–11   In parts of Central Urhobo festivals were held every few years (mostly in December) to honour the local divinities (*djudju* or *juju*) like Ogude. During these festivals there would be contests in lampoon poetry between one community and another in the entire region. In line 4 the composers of this song brag about how sweet their songs generally are. Line 5 either implies that these songs also give a sharp and quick pain, or else continues the warning contained in the second line, that Nigeria should never repeat the sort of mistake it made in taking independence.

line 15   Benin is the capital of Nigeria's Bendel state in which the Urhobo are located.

line 16   *UAC* is the United Africa Company, a commercial venture established by the British during the colonial era.

lines 19–20   These were promises made by Nigerian politicians fighting for independence. Palm and rubber are the major cash crops in this part of Nigeria. Notice the tone of exaggeration in these statements.

line 22   The *referendum* was to determine what percentage of the Nigerian population were in favour of self-rule.

line 24   We have here a mixture of parties, figures and slogans, all of which featured prominently in the political life of Nigeria up to the 1960s. *Demo* is for the Midwest Democratic Front; *Power* was the slogan frequently used during and since the constitutional crisis that ravaged the Western Region from 1962 to 1966; *Zik* is for Dr. Nnamdi Azikiwe, a veteran

Nigerian political leader who helped win independence for the country and became first Governor-General and then President; *Okokoroko* is the cry of the cock, the symbol of the National Party of Nigeria and the Cameroons (later, National Party of Nigerian Citizens) of which Zik was leader.

line 25 This proverb describes the desperate tussle for power between rival politicians and groups.

line 29 *Kikighwo* is an IDEOPHONE (a word whose sound carries its own meaning) indicating a rush or stampede.

line 34 However long you keep away from a debt, you still have to pay it.

line 43 *One Nigeria* was a slogan advertised by the Federal Government during the civil war of 1967–70. The fact that the images used in this song come from several periods of Nigeria's history may indicate how long the song has been in vogue. It may also be that, like all true poetry, this song is using a confusion of images and periods as a metaphor for the confusion which it believes independence has brought to the lives of Nigerians.

Questions

In what ways do the proverbs used in this song contribute to the poetic quality of it?

Comment on the use of humour and exaggeration in this poem.

34 Armanda

In this poem, Jared Angira paints a satirical picture of a growing class of women in present-day society. They are well-educated, sophisticated, and even beautiful. They are so sophisticated they can afford to discard certain items of relaxation (e.g. chess and television) with which high society is often identified. And they leave the impression of being well-meaning, open-minded people. But this open-mindedness collapses at the sign of the least discomfort. For instance, Armanda hates all the detailed work involved in the kitchen. She falls in love with and marries a handicapped man (Ray), pretending to be truly in love with him and justifying the crutches with which Ray walks. But her real reason for marrying Ray is to get his wealth. She takes care to get all his money deposited in the bank in her name. When his health gets worse, and he becomes more and more a burden on Armanda's comforts, she finds a ready reason to leave him and take all the money away.

This poem is no doubt an attack on the false life-styles which Africans live when they try to copy European habits. The names which Angira gives his characters belong to nobody in particular. Even if he had anybody in mind, the danger of being taken to court for libel discourages him from being specific; unlike most traditional African poets in such a situation, he has chosen general names for characters who represent a general tendency in society today.

The satire in this poem is achieved by a steady use of SARCASM or tongue-in-cheek statements: Armanda is frequently called 'a well-meaning lass' when she is far from being so; 'true love' (line 17) and 'happiness' (line 23) are the opposites of the true state of the relationship between her and Ray; and so on. On

205

the whole there is a musical, sing-song movement to this poem – achieved through repetition of words and phrases – which is simply intended to mock Armanda's pretences.

line 2   *anthropology* is the study of man. The implication here is that Armanda is well equipped for an understanding of human nature. But she has only exploited this understanding for her own selfish purposes.

line 5   *Dunhill* is an expensive brand of cigarettes; *to the hills* implies she blew the smoke high in an ostentatious manner, but the internal rhyme between 'Dunhill' and 'the hills' is a kind of jingle intended to mock Armanda's habits.

line 7   *peahen* (female for peacock) here indicates the arrogance or ostentatiousness of Armanda.

line 10   *bridge* a kind of card game.

line 15   *turned the apple-cart* acted contrary to expectations.

line 19   *sent her on heat* gave her sexual excitement.

lines 24–25, 30–31   In these lines irony is achieved through sound and sense. The poet rhymes *hell* with *well* though the two ideas neutralise each other, as do the ideas of God (or heavens) and hell.

line 33   *orthopaedics* are doctors who take care of injured limbs.

line 45   This implies that Armanda kept away from Ray the pills recommended to ease his pain or prevent infection, i.e. she deliberately helped the deterioration of his health.

lines 48–57   By this educated assessment of the state of affairs between her and Ray, Armanda (a university graduate) tries to justify her abandonment of him.

Questions

In the latter part of the poem, the poet drops the epithet 'well-meaning' from the position of prominence that he has given it up to the fifth stanza. Why does he do this?

What is the purpose of the narrative structure to the poem?

35 Songs of abuse: (i) To Stanislaus the renegade

As the general title indicates, this is lampoon poetry such as is found in abundance in the oral tradition but which is rare in modern African poetry. Kofi Awoonor, who has collected many of such songs from his native Ewe tradition (see also no. 30) has here decided to pay homage to that tradition in a poem which echoes some of its qualities (not excluding sexual references).

The level of achievement in this poem can be seen from a comparison with Ekpe's abuse of Kodzo. The poetry of Awoonor's piece lies mainly in its direct and forceful expression of the poet's emotion – just as in Ekpe's. There is also evidence of a damming use of exaggeration, as in lines 7–8 and 15–16. The poem lacks the depth which the traditional form easily achieves in its use of proverbs. But it makes up for this in its fast changes of geographic setting which successfully represent the subject (Stanislaus) as an irrespressible vagabond, spreading evil across the world.

206

line 2 *punk* worthless person.
line 4 *split* escaped, vanished.
line 5 *cashmere* made of soft, expensive wool.
line 6 *Pueblo Indians* a tribe of American Indians.
line 7 *hippies* A group particularly widespread in America in the 1960s, known for their rebellion (through dress and behaviour) against organised society. Many young middle-class Americans 'dropped out' to become hippies; they would have been easy prey for a trickster like Stanislaus.
line 10 *ass* American for *arse*.
line 13 *hashish* Indian hemp.
line 15 *assegai* a Zulu spear.

Questions

What contrast do you think is intended between 'guns' and 'assegai'; 'swords' and 'machetes' in lines 14–16?

Does a poem to a character like Stanislaus gain or lose poetic flavour by being composed in ordinary language?

36 I am ignorant of the Good Word in the Clean Book

This selection has been put together from one section of Okot p'Bitek's *Song of Lawino* criticising the image of Christianity in a traditional African society. The whole book is made up of a series of complaints by a young Acholi woman, Lawino, against her husband Ocol, who has received Western education and is now scorning the traditional ways of his people. The complaints are directed against various aspects of modern life – education, religion, fashion and other social habits – that represent ways in which the youths of today are turning their backs on the world of their ancestors.

This particular poem deserves comparison with Echeruo's *Easter Penitence* (no. 40) as an attack on Christianity. In Echeruo's poem we see an educated man questioning certain concepts and symbols and the image that they present of divinity; inevitably, it is expressed in the complicated idioms (including a learned reference from the Bible) of the educated. In Okot's poem, however, the criticism has been put in the mouth of a woman who has no formal Western education; the language of the poem is therefore simple and straightforward, without any fanciful logic. Each poem pours some scorn or ridicule on its subject; but while Echeruo uses dry irony, in Okot we have down-to-earth humour. Echeruo's poem is motivated mainly by a conflict of ideas, Okot's by a conflict of cultures.

line 10 *Clean Book* This refers to the Bible, which is normally called the Holy Book. Lawino makes the mistake because she has not been educated enough to know the real name. But the error may be a deliberate jest. See also line 31.
line 15 *Jok* is the name of a divinity or spirit among the Acholi.
line 35 *padre* or father, the title of a Roman Catholic priest.
lines 38–81 This second portion of the poem is an attack on the way that some

missionaries exploit the local youths in African villages. They gather
them together to instruct them in Christian doctrine, and some of these
youths may eventually enter one of the lower orders of the Church. But
in the process they will have been made to perform some of the menial
domestic jobs for the missionary and his wife.

Questions

Comment on Okot's use of humour in this poem.

How would you describe Lawino – proud, rebellious, frivolous, self-confident,
ignorant? – or a combination of these? Defend your choice with references from
the poem.

37 Abolish laughter first, I say

This is one of the poems which Dennis Brutus wrote from a South African jail in
the mid 1950s. On the whole it is a very angry poem denouncing apartheid, but
there are also some subtle changes of mood which reveal the emotional pressures
on a confined man. In the first stanza the poet hears – or imagines he hears –
some laughter, and his immediate reaction is to condemn strongly the idea of
laughing in the midst of the present circumstances. In the second stanza the
laughter has died down, but its place has been taken by violent sounds made both
by man – 'jackboots' – and by nature – 'wolfwind'. In stanza three the poet still
hates the idea of laughter and views it with disgust, but is prepared to see in it
some positive uses: the breath from the laughter of the oppressors may succeed
in ventilating the anger of the oppressed, thus strengthening their will to resist –
in the same way that air blown on fire helps to forge a sword. In the last stanza the
poet fully welcomes laughter and would indeed want it preserved, because it
ensures that the flame of anger in his heart is kept alive while the oppressor is
burning out his own powers or energy.

The force of protest in this poem is conveyed by the use of words which
indicate violent or strong action: 'shattering', 'jackboots battering', 'rasp', etc.) as
well as the emphatic way in which Brutus drives home his point: 'I say, . . . this . . .
this . . . this . . ., Never!' The large number of words with prominently strong
consonants – abolish, gusts, drowned, gapes, apocalyptic, pleuras, cackle,
oppression's power, dust, etc. – also bears witness to the temper behind the
poetry.

line 1 *first* i.e. before we can deal effectively with the menace of apartheid.
lines 2–4 If we don't do that, we will only be deceiving ourselves by setting up a
clever but weak resistance (*halls of glass*) that cannot stand up to the force
of apartheid.
line 6 *multi-choired thunder* a loud noise composed of many kinds of sound.
line 7 Cries both loud and soft.
lines 8–9 While the apartheid police tear down the protection erected around
people's homes, howling winds rush through the cracks that they make.
line 10 The earth rages with warnings of future catastrophe. The Apocalypse is
the last book of the New Testament containing prophetic statements
about the end of the world.

Brutus paints their laughter in the image of a man suffering from tuberculosis.

line 16 We cannot afford to laugh along with them like obedient slaves. *Jim Crow* is the image of the submissive negro in America before the emancipation of slaves.

Questions

Both this poem and *Nightsong: Country* (no. 6) are concerned with aspects of Brutus' native South Africa. In what ways does the language of each poem reflect these aspects?

Would you say the poet has been economical or extravagant in his expression of emotion here?

38 Peasants

This is a very powerful poem denouncing the way in which the poor are treated by the leadership in various countries of Africa. They are left to live in unimaginably miserable and unhealthy conditions with their families, they are exploited by politicians but never rewarded, their support is courted but they are never treated with respect, the wealth of the nation is paraded and wasted before their eyes but they never get a share of it, and they are treated to all kinds of foreign theories that have no practical meaning for their lives. If care is not taken, they will explode in revolt.

The poem reveals an admirable depth of sympathy on the part of the poet. The statements are simple, direct and uncomplicated. The anger in the poet's voice is also subdued: although it is clear from the very beginning that he does not like the state of affairs he sees before him, the long list of grievances is read more in a tone of lament until the last line but one, when the poet seems to spit out his criticism more fiercely ('damn'). And yet we feel throughout a strong sense of an overhanging danger: the persistent repetition of 'the agony of . . .' signifies the tolling of a bell warning of a coming catastrophe or perhaps a clock ticking steadily towards a deadline.

line 6 *lugubrious* sad, mournful; *battered soul* dejected spirits.
line 7 *party cards* cards indicating membership in a political party.
line 9 *melliferous* honey-sweet; *mildewed* mouldy.
line 11 *tarmac* tarred road.
line 12 *projectile bellies* bellies protruded due to malnutrition.
line 16 *cavalcade* parade.

Questions

Explain the full significance of the words 'them' and 'their' as used in this context.

The poet addresses his warning to 'Africa.' What does that tell you about the difference in outlook between the modern African poet and his traditional counterpart?

39 Loser of everything

There were essentially two ways in which most pre-independence African poets reacted against the violation of the dignity of their race and helped in the fight to recover its freedom from the colonisers. One was through poetry that by the fierceness of its language was nothing short of a call to arms, a challenge to a physical fight for liberation. The other was by means of poems that painted the picture of an Africa so beautiful, so happy and harmonious in the relationship between man and nature that the European coloniser looked like an abominable villain coming to violate this state of affairs. David Diop wrote both forms of poetry. In this selection the contrast between the villainy of the European coloniser and the gentle harmony of Africa is so striking that, even though there is no open call to a fight, we can feel the subtle fire of revolt in his words.

line 1   *my hut*   The speaker of this poem is Africa personified. It was characteristic of this generation of poets to glorify what, from the point of view of modern technology, would be considered a mark of underdevelopment or backwardness. See, for example, *nakedness* in line 16.

line 8   *tom-tom*   a kind of drum. Notice the rhythmic effect of the repetition of this word over the next line.

line 11   The capital letter in *Silence* reflects the arrogance, the superior posture of the colonial presence, or else the heavy impact of its coming. The dots represent an ELLIPSIS: something left unsaid or an experience which leaves you lost for words.

line 13   *empty*   This adjective is used in a CONSECUTIVE way, i.e. the hut was empty *after*, not before, the coming of the colonisers. This device is common in poetry.

line 18   *Your*   i.e. the tom-tom's.

Questions

Discuss the poet's use of contrasts and their effectiveness.

What words and phrases in this poem bring out the villainy of the colonial presence?

40 Easter penitence

Some modern African poets direct their criticism not only at the social and political conditions in which they live but also at the ideas and concepts with which they have been educated. This revolt is due partly to the fact that the ideas are considered foreign and not necessarily better than the ones contained in the poet's indigenous traditions, and partly to the fact that the poets consider the logic in those ideas fundamentally weak.

Michael Echeruo has written some of the most demanding but brilliant poetry of ideas in Africa today. In this piece he is attacking the image of God as advertised in Christian worship. He is not necessarily opposed to the idea of God or the supernatural. Here he has simply used an aspect of Christian worship – the rites of Easter – as a symbol to demonstrate his rejection of the unnecessarily elaborate advertisement of faith in Christianity and the image of God that emerges from it: that of an aloof and unsympathetic father. In the first stanza he sees the sacrifices offered as an empty display; in the second stanza the rituals only cause him constipation; stanzas 4 and 5 refer to an event that took place after Christ's resurrection, portraying God as showing no feeling for poor, ignorant mortals; the sixth stanza returns to ridicule the language and the articles used in all this elaborate worship.

The tone of criticism used in this poem is one of IRONY. The ideas and symbols are introduced in the language of devotion ('O . . .!'), and the repetition of lines (e.g. 17 and 22) and phrase structure (3–4 and 7–8; 10 and 11; 20 and 21) echoes the system of repetition in prayer. But every once in a while this pretence at devotion is punctuated by a word (e.g. delirium, emptiness, heartburn) or image (see especially lines 19 and 20) that paints a negative picture. In line 24 Echeruo inverts the order of the language of devotion ('crucible O') as a final ridicule of the system; even though the name of God is invoked at the end of the poem, it is quite clear that the poet rejects the Christian image of Him.

lines 1–4 The idea of sacrifice is conveyed by fire (*furnace*) and the dish (*crucible*) in which offerings are burnt. The poet condemns as empty these rites performed away from general view (done in *darkness*) which only induce a loss of consciousness (*delirium, ecstasy*).

line 7 *fragrance* the smell of the burnt offering or incense.

li..es 13–17 In the Bible's New Testament, Luke XXIV 13–35 tells the story of how Christ, after his resurrection, encounters two men on their way to Emmaus and joins their discussion about the mysterious event. When they try to educate him on what had happened, he in turn undertakes to show them how all these events had been foretold in the past. His answer to them begins with the words, 'O fools . . .' *Raca* is a Hebrew word of abuse, and with it Echeruo implies that the Christ figure in that story adopted a rather superior, contemptuous attitude towards the travellers.

line 24 Latin, meaning 'have mercy'.

line 25 These are various symbols of worship found in the church: *oil* is for fuelling the lamps; *water* probably stands for holy water; *light* is apparently that of the burning lamps or candles. There is a note of contempt in the recital of the list.

Questions

Can you trace a connection between the symbols in lines 9–12 and the idea of Easter?

In view of the scornful tone of this poem, how can you explain the idea of penitence in the title?

41 Yes, Mandela, we shall be moved

This is a poem of defiance against oppression. The main focus is on apartheid South Africa; but certain images from black American protest (see lines 7 and 13) imply that Kgositsile includes in his attack oppression of the black man generally.

Nelson Mandela (b. 1918) is a leader of the African National Congress (ANC) which since its formation in 1959 has steadily opposed the South African apartheid system. Under this system, the ANC was banned and Mandela found himself forced to 'live the life of an outlaw'; in 1963 , he was sentenced to life imprisonment on charges of sabotage and conspiracy to overthrow the government. He has been imprisoned on Robben Island ever since, while his wife, Winifred Mandela, has been held under continual house arrest.

line 7   Rahsaan *Roland* Kirk was a black American jazz musician who played several horns (sometimes two or three at the same time) with a fierceness that portrayed the black man's anger and frustration with his social condition.

line 9   *island inferno* the maximum-security jail on Robben Island, off the coast of South Africa, is practically a hell (*inferno*) on earth.

line 10   Notice how the temper of the poet so overflows that he can no longer maintain his neat sequence of phrases: (*We emerge . . . We emerge*).

line 13   This line is from an American Negro spiritual song expressing hope in the future improvement of the black man's condition.

Questions

What stylistic technique does the poet use here to emphasise his protest? Identify the relevant phrases.

Which of these is the dominant sentiment in the poem: hate, or humanism? Illustrate your answer with reference to particular words and phrases.

42 When this carnival finally closes

This poem is a condemnation of autocratic African rulers and their sycophants. It is addressed to a drum musician, here used for representing those who fill the ruler's head with sweet words and so encourage his irresponsible acts of leadership. What the poet is telling the musician is essentially this: Today you may be recognised and applauded (see 'praises' line 3) as a great artist. But when your master's wild rule is over, you will be treated with just as much disgrace. A new ruler will emerge and new sycophants will be appointed to take your place. Your drums and even your abode will be burnt down, while your old master is cursed as he is being carried to his grave. In short, the poet is warning both autocrat and sycophant that they are building a world of illusion around themselves (see especially lines 6 and 14) and that their days are numbered.

line 1   *frothful* The wild and irresponsible rule of the autocrat is likened to a drunken festival (*froth* is the foam of drinks like beer). But *frothful* is also a type of PUN: it mimics the sound of another word – frightful – and this may be Mapanje's way of suggesting a reign of terror.

line 2   *these very officers* i.e. of the present government.

lines 5–6   *drums* (i.e. words of praise) charm the ears of the ruler. These drums and the ruler's portraits (*effigies*) contribute (as *accomplices*) to make up the world of illusion that these men have built around themselves.

line 8   *hero* is used as a SARCASM (i.e. saying one thing while meaning another) for 'villain'.
line 11   *at the wake* means either at the wake-keeping night or 'soon afterwards'.
line 12   *skins* i.e. of drums.
line 13   *clans* Mapanje here implies that at the death of the present ruler, other ethnic groups than his own will come into control: a clever hint at the element of ethnic rivalry in African politics. *Undertakers* are people who arrange burials.

Questions

What mockery do you detect in the statement about the 'bamboo hut' (line 7)?

What do you feel is the dominant tone of the poem: anger, or contempt? Give reasons for your answer.

43 How can I sing?

This poem examines the responsibility of the poet to his society, and in the process takes a very critical look at social and political conditions in present-day Africa. What Ofeimun is saying here is essentially this. Poetry (the 'song' referred to in line 11) should celebrate life and those who create the right conditions for it. But there is too much filth and corruption around (stanza 1); rather than correct this ugly situation, our leaders – whose duty it is to show us the way and make us feel happy to be alive – are trying by all sorts of cruel measures to cover up or to suppress it (stanza 2); they gag and blindfold the poet by their awkward measures, making it difficult for him to find his way and move purposefully (stanza 3). How can the poet write poetry under these conditions? However, he cannot afford to minimise the seriousness of these bitter experiences and the pain that they cause: in my poetry I shall portray my beloved country in language that revolts against these disgusting things I see before me.

    The overriding mood of this poem is anger, and this can be seen in the frequent use of strong language: 'putrefying carcasses', 'mind-ripping scorpion-tails', 'stuff cobwebs', 'spit rheum' etc. The questions also reveal a certain amount of impatience. There are no less than nine adjectives in this fairly short poem, virtually all of which have a negative meaning: they illustrate the loaded feelings of the poet.

line 2   *putrefying* rotting.
line 3   *pulling* attracting.
lines 5–8   *flywhisk* A whip (usually made from horsetail or cow-tail) that is used in beating away flies. These lines are no doubt a reference to the suppression of writers by intolerant African leaders. When these writers try to expose the ugly conditions in society, the leaders suppress them by taking them secretly (*in the dark*) to jail and using all sorts of cruel measures (*scorpion-tails*) to ruin their minds. In this way the leaders are acting like people using flywhisks to beat off the flies that are drawing attention to a rotting mess.
lines 12–14   These leaders frequently issue orders or laws which are meant to

prevent the writers from speaking out or seeing their way ahead in their work. *Rheum* is a slimy discharge from the eyes, nose, or even mouth. The *blank sense of direction* implies that the laws reveal the leaders don't know where they are going.

line 15 *portals* gates.
line 16 *desultory* without plan or purpose.
line 17 *blunt my feelers* be less sensitive than I usually am.
line 21 *litanies* strings of statements.
line 22 *morbid landscapes* sickening sights.
line 23 That is, my country that I love so much.

Questions

Discuss the poet's use of imagery in his attack.

In spite of the poet's negative feelings, are there any words in the poem that reveal a positive commitment to his society?

44 Pedestrian, to passing Benz-man

Although he has written far more poetry than most of the established Kenyan and other East African writers, Ojuka has not been taken very seriously because his writing is considered rather 'popular', i.e. not very sophisticated. But his more recent poetry is really quite sensitive, as in this poem portraying the grievances of the poor against the rich.

Since the attainment of independence by most African countries, which has shifted political and economic power from the white colonisers to native African leaders, there has been a noticeable widening of the gap between the haves and the have-nots among the African citizens. Ojuka's poem is an example of the dissatisfaction of the average African against this ugly social situation. The Mercedes Benz is frequently seen as a symbol of the oppressive wealth of the rich.

Like Brutus, Ojuka here uses the sonnet-form (fourteen lines) loosely, i.e. without using rhyme or making any conscious effort to organise the poem into two balanced parts. Perhaps this is because the situation he is portraying lacks beauty and promises social chaos. The language of the poem is simple, mainly because it is spoken by an ordinary man. The last line of the poem is an example of SARCASM, i.e. saying one thing and meaning another. 'A few years' is really not 'too long a time', but the speaker is accusing the rich man of having moved so far in status that he has forgotten where he once belonged.

line 8 *diesel* A petroleum product used for fuelling some car engines.
line 13 *parasite* i.e. the white colonisers who exploited the wealth of Africa.

Questions

Do you consider the poem angry or sorrowful? In your answer, point out specific words and phrases.

In what ways does Ojuka portray the differences between rich and poor?

45 I anoint my flesh (Tenth day of fast)

In 1967 Wole Soyinka was detained under maximum security by the Federal Military Government of Nigeria, apparently on charges that he was secretly collaborating with the authorities of the secessionist government of Biafra with which the Federal Government was at war. Soyinka denied the charges, and in protest against the military authorities' treatment of him he went into a long hunger strike in the prison. This poem, taken from the volume *A Shuttle in the Crypt* which includes his prison poems, stoutly proclaims his righteousness and reflects the defiance of a spirit that refuses to surrender to the forces of repression.

The poet here assumes the image of a man undergoing a purification rite, determined to demonstrate the purity of his mind and body and daring the forces of evil. We are led carefully through the processes of this ritual ceremony and get an insight into the significance of each act; the repetition of the phrase 'I anoint' at the beginning of each process emphasises the ritual character of the entire experience. However, the atmosphere is one of confrontation between two spiritual forces (aptly introduced in the first stanza by the conflict between 'light' and 'dark') and there is no doubt that the poet sees the system that has confined him as an evil enemy.

lines 2–3 The imagery here is complex. Solitude (i.e. the poet's solitary confinement) has made his body lean and in the process has purified or blessed (*hallowed*) his thought. The poet's anointment of his flesh is a symbolic act of purification as effective as that of solitude making his body lean. *Lean oil* is an example of TRANSFERRED EPITHET, because it is the body, not the oil, that is lean.

line 4 *you* i.e. the enemy.

line 10 *void* i.e. the lonely, empty room in which the poet has been confined.

lines 14–15 A powerful image. In the confrontation between the righteous poet and his evil enemy, the *hate* of the latter has been burnt out (*spent*) and the triumphant poet now sprinkles the ashes on his heart that still blazes with righteousness, as the final act of his purifying ritual.

Questions

Would you characterise this poem as public or as private protest? Defend your choice.

Explain lines 10–12 of the poem.

46 The sky

This poem addresses itself to a remote aspect of the natural environment, and in doing so illustrates a certain amount of social concern. The poet admires the order, harmony, and absolute lack of danger among the stars, in contrast to the chaotic conditions on earth. The poem is also admirable for its quiet, almost philosophical tone.

Questions

In what ways does the poet make a distant scene a little more familiar?

Discuss in detail the critical statements made by the poem.

47 The train

This poem has been translated from the original Sesotho version written by B. M. Khaketla. Although it was written in the same way as the poems described as 'modern' in this anthology, it is much closer to the indigenous tradition than some other poems here discussed, such as *To Stanislaus the renegade* (no. 35) or *I am ignorant . . .* (no. 36), and is intended as a recreation of the oral tradition in print.

The poem reflects one way in which the tradition looks at modern technology. The poet does not deny the structural beauty of the train, but for the most part he sees the train in a somewhat negative light. The phrase 'thing of the White man' probably marks the train off as a foreign element. The rest of the poem portrays the train in its fierceness (lines 2–3), its effect on the environment (lines 4–19), and its impact on people (lines 20–26). However, in spite of this image, the poet has no choice but to take the train for travelling long distances to his homeland in the interior (lines 29–32).

The effectiveness of this poem lies mainly in the PERSONIFICATION of the train: by giving it life sometimes as a person (e.g. lines 4–5), sometimes as an animal (i.e. lines 2 and 27), and crediting it with feelings, the poet shows the train as an active body and so allows us to appreciate it in a variety of ways (notice the vividness of the long descriptive titles). We should observe also that the poet projects his own feelings onto the train: in fact, it is possible that he has chosen to describe the train in fairly negative terms because of an unhappy experience he once had of it (lines 23–26). This practice of internalising the outside world is perhaps a characteristic of all good poetry.

line 1 *Tjhutjhumakgala* an IDEOPHONE reflecting the chug-chug sound of the engine of the moving train.

line 2 *bovine* an ox-like creature.

line 5 *Madman* because 'the train runs as if demented' (D. P. Kunene, *Heroic Poetry of the Basuto*). The *grass hat* is a METAPHOR for the train's funnel.

line 6 *fog* a heavy mist.

line 11 *Bringer of sorrow* The train carries away loved ones. 'Mostly the reference is to young men who leave their rural homes to work in the cities, when girls are left with none to marry them, and the old people with none to care for them' (D. P. Kunene, which includes Khaketla's poem). See also lines 22–26.

line 22 *Black* here describes the colour of the engine, as *Dark-brown* (line 27) describes the colour of the coaches.

lines 31–32 These are locations in Lesotho.

Questions

Discuss in detail the use of personification in this poem.

216

The poet describes the train in mostly exaggerated words and phrases. Identify these and show how they reflect the attitude of the poet to the train.

48 The baboon

This poem comes from the same tradition of Yoruba hunters' celebrative poetry – *ijala* – that gave us the *Salute to Fabunmi* (no. 21). However, while the latter poem celebrates the achievements of a man in a particular career, the present poem gives us a portrait of the physical features and characteristics of an aspect of the natural environment.

The closeness to detail of such naturalist poetry is very striking. The poet observes carefully the colour of skin, the length of fingers, the peculiar shapes of the jaws and chest, the look of the eyes in different contexts, but above all the baboon's gluttonous habits. This vividness of detail is enhanced by various stylistic qualities. One of these is the generous use of imagery – like the long fingers of the baboon being seen as whips (line 6), or the spots on his body being compared to smallpox scars (line 8), or his broad chest being thought to look 'as if it has a wooden bar in it' (line 19). Another stylistic device used here, the IDEOPHONE, is very much a feature of indigenous African speech. It is basically a descriptive sound, giving us a vivid dramatic idea of the looks, movement or behaviour of an object or person: like 'Opomu' (line 2) which mimics the cry of the baboon, and 'Ladoogi' (line 18) which captures the long, drooping protrusion of the baboon's jaws. There is also some humour here: the audience are likely to laugh at the sharp reference to Dahomeians (line 14), or the comparison of the baboon to a bride (line 15), or to the insatiable hunger of the animal (lines 21–25).

One more factor which makes this kind of poetry attractive in the oral tradition is its *performance* character, which brings it closer both to the performer and his audience. In lines 5 and 11 the performer addresses himself directly to his subject as a way of establishing some contact between the two of them. And at the end of the chant the performer and his group break into a song (the audience often join in this, since many of them know it) pinpointing some of the most striking features of the baboon that the chant has emphasised.

line 1   *Laare* an attributive name that points out the baboon's distinction in running (Yoruba: *are*).

line 8   The *cap* apparently refers to the distinct texture and shade of hair on the baboon's head. *Drummer* Baboons frequently drum on their chests.

lines 10–11   A reference to the crouching and kneeling posture of the hunter as he prepares to shoot at the baboon.

lines 12–13   Such abbreviated stories are often used in *ijala* as a way of lending more vividness to a detail – in this case, the insatiable hunger for meat on the part of the baboon. For a similar example see lines 21–25.

line 20   'This is a joke, its point being that, were the baboon a human being, no consideration of persons would affect his sphere of operation' (see: S.A. Babalola, *The Content and Form of Yoruba Ijala*, Oxford University Press, 1966).

lines 21–25   The numbers referred to are for the corn cobs devoured by the baboon.

lines 26–27   There is a great deal of SARCASM here which will cause laughter among the audience. Although the poet portrays the baboon as a strong, bold animal, he does not seem to think much of his physical features, as we may conclude from the descriptions in lines 5, 6, 8, 14, 18, 19, and 28. Here in lines 26–27, as indeed in line 17, the poet is quietly mocking the baboon by making him and his mother believe he is the most beautiful animal in the forest. However, for fear of incurring the anger of the animal, the poet speaks with his tongue in his cheek.

line 29 Since this poem comes from the same poetic tradition – the hunters poetry, *ijala* – as no. 21, there are some common epithets shared by poets singing on a variety of subjects. Here, in describing the boldness of the baboon, the poet uses the same epithet as the earlier poet has used in describing Fabunmi, i.e. the tendency to stare hard at a man without blinking (The Yoruba in both cases is *atoroojuwoni*).

Questions

Identify and discuss five attributes in this poem which most clearly indicate that the poem was composed by a hunter (and not, say, a farmer or a blacksmith).

'The success of Yoruba naturalist poetry rests largely on the way it portrays wild life with attributes and features taken from human society.' Do you think this is a correct assessment of *The baboon*?

49 Ibadan

This is one of the best known poems of J. P. Clark. Using simple but very evocative language and imagery, the poet paints a powerful picture of a Nigerian city. Ibadan is an administrative capital (now the capital of Oyo State) in western Nigeria, as well as the site of the nation's oldest university, the University of Ibadan.

In this poem Clark tries to capture the mixed character of the city: the combination of cleanliness and dirt, of excellence and squalor, of natural beauty on the one hand and man-made recklessness on the other. The great strength of the poem lies in its economy and conciseness: in these very few words we not only see the full picture of a varied landscape but indeed feel the force of the poet's comment on the failure of modern town planning.

lines 2–3 running splash compresses two vivid impressions. *Running* indicates distance, and in it the poet tends to suggest the size of the city: Ibadan is one of the largest towns in black Africa. *Splash* on the other hand indicates the disorderly way in which the city has developed. *Rust* primarily refers to the old corrugated tin roofs of houses: anyone standing on one of the hills of Ibadan can see the wide spread of these across the city. *Gold* on the other hand is a metaphor for the expensive modern buildings of the city – some of which are skyscrapers. On another level, the coexistence between rust and gold may be seen as a reflection of the survival of old glory (Ibadan has a distinguished past as a centre of Yoruba warfare in the nineteenth century) side by side with modern excellence (as a site of a world-renowned university and a centre of very prosperous commercial activity in Nigeria). *Flung and scattered*, however, emphasises the impression of disorder and planlessness which the city leaves on the poet.

lines 4–5 *Seven* may not be the actual number of hills on which the city stands but has been used more for metaphorical purposes. Ancient Rome is said to have been founded on seven hills; by using the same number for Ibadan, Clark (who was himself educated at the University of Ibadan) sees the city in the light of the same greatness and glory that characterised Rome. *China* ware is a highly valued commodity, and here it stands as a metaphor emphasising the image of excellence (the university) and prosperity (the commercial life) in the city of Ibadan; but *broken* reinforces the picture of disorder which we have seen above. It may be that in the image of *the sun* the poet wishes to reflect the brilliance of the tropical landscape; but the idea of *broken china* indicates his regret that a precious thing has been carelessly treated.

Questions

How does the arrangement of words or lines in this poem illustrate the impression which Clark has of Ibadan?

What do you think is the poet's attitude to Ibadan: does he dislike it? does he feel attached to it? or is he indifferent? Support your answer with adequate references.

50 Daybreak

Dawn, or the early morning light, has been a favourite subject of poetry in many societies and for many generations. This simple poem captures the beauty and vitality that is usually connected with the break of day. Dawn is PERSONIFIED in this poem throughout for either of two reasons: one, the poet may be following the tradition of European poetry (ancient and modern) which conceives of dawn as a beautiful goddess (Aurora); two, the poet may be independently convinced that the beauty and order which we associate with early morning life must be the work of a powerful figure. The repeated address 'O Dawn' and the frequent questions show a combination of wonder at and admiration of this figure.

line 10 This is a rather sensitive way of showing a connection between the environment and the sensations of the people who live in it. Notice also the note of African nationalism in the idea.

line 15 *askari* (Swahili) a uniformed policeman or soldier.

line 21 *familiar* is sometimes used in poetry in the sense of 'belonging to the family'. In this context, *familiar noises* would be the noises of the children.

Questions

Why does the poet speak of dawn as a painter (line 2)?

Unlike the other stanzas, stanza four is not framed as a question. Do you observe any difference in tone or mood between that stanza and the earlier three?

51 The sweet brew at Chitakale

Much of the attraction of recent East African poetry is that it focuses attention on the lives and concerns of common people. Although this is evident also in West African poetry, the concern for the masses has been part of the intellectual life of East Africa longer than of the West, largely because East African politicians and intellectuals embraced socialist ideas somewhat sooner than their West African counterparts. You may have seen some of this concern in Albert Ojuka's *Pedestrian, to passing Benz-man* (no. 44).

This delightful poem by Mapanje portrays a prominent feature of social life in the small town or the 'township', the section of a city inhabited mostly by the less privileged African population. The scene is a little bar where a woman serves *thobwa*, a sweet drink usually brewed from millet. Notice that the steady pace of movement of the stanzas (three lines constantly) reflects the equally steady pace of customership at the bar. The dash at the end of line 12 indicates that the poet cannot complete his observation because of the sudden departure of the bus.

Questions

Why is the language of this poem so simple?

Can you identify at least four phrases in the poem that portray the excitement and enjoyment which the poet has observed at the bar?

52 Sunset

This poem, by the radical South African poet Mtshali, uses an aspect of the natural environment as a comment on the system in which he lives. Like Dennis Brutus, Mtshali is resentful of the denial of his freedom and his land by the apartheid regime. But like many of the youths of his generation – who have chosen to defy the bullets of the oppressor – he writes in a language that is combative and, as in this poem, bemoans a system in which natural goodness has been destroyed.

The poem presents a harsh and unromantic view of the setting sun. The harshness can be seen in the words chosen for describing the experience of the poor sun in its descent across the sky into the horizon – spun, tossed, whirled, clattered, popped, etc. – and especially in the use of harsh-sounding consonants (*t, c, b, p, sp*). The experience of the sun in this poem is used as a METAPHOR for the destruction of nature and natural sentiments by the impersonal and insensitive machine of the apartheid regime. Much of this impersonality and lack of feeling can be seen in the objects in whose terms the sun is portrayed: coin, slot, neon-lights, parking meter. The poem seems to end in a fierce warning to the apartheid system: time is running out!

Questions

What effect does the poet achieve by repeatedly representing the sun with the neuter pronoun 'it'?

Does this portrait of the sun in any way reveal the nature of apartheid as a repressive or manipulative system? Examine the poet's choice of words for your answer.

53 Autumn burns me

There is a certain tradition in European poetry whereby the poet describes his own feelings and moods as a reflection or product of the atmosphere or season within which he is writing. Spring, when the flowers appear on the trees, is a season that inspires feelings of joy and love in the poet. Summer is the season of heat and excitement, inspiring a feeling for action and adventure. In autumn, the leaves first change their (mostly green) colours into beautiful shades of yellow, but that is only because they are fading and are about to die and fall; here the poet writes in a rather sad and regretful tone. Then, in winter, the entire environment is frozen and chilly, and all vegetation suffers a temporary death; the poet becomes truly mournful and writes like one shedding tears. The nineteenth-century English critic John Ruskin, obviously not impressed by this kind of practice among creative artists, coined the phrase PATHETIC FALLACY — that is, 'lying about feeling' — for it, because he did not believe there is any direct connection between our feelings and the surrounding weather.

Peters is equally unwilling to be tied down by this habit. He starts this poem by acknowledging that he is at first tempted to be sad in the traditional fashion and look forward to the worst; but, in the second stanza, his instinct tells him that nature is still very much alive and he encourages the feeling by remembering cheerful times; in stanza three, the image of trees losing their leaves strikes up the feeling of loneliness and shame; but from the fourth stanza to the end we can feel the poet's determination to wrest some cheerfulness and even hope out of an atmosphere of silence, decay and impending death.

The stanzas are of uniform length, and this may be an indication of the way the poet takes control of himself and refuses to go under. The repeated use of the phrase 'I will' emphasises his determination. Notice also the affirmation of 'love' in lines 26 and 27; for him to love amidst dying leaves (lines 27–28) shows his determination to oppose death with life. In the last line of the poem, the poet completely reverses the feeling with which the poem began: instead of being up-tight, or 'taut' with fear of impending death, he is now inclined to appreciate the marvels of autumn and to derive 'hope' from this.

lines 1–2 Autumn torments the poet with a traditional feeling. The feeling is called *primaeval*, i.e. ancient, because it has been known to worry poets since time immemorial.

line 4 By the end of summer we are pretty well tired of the heat.

lines 6–8 As a surgeon, Peters often borrows medical imagery.

line 10 *cascading* rushing.

line 11 *in transit fall* as the falling leaves drift past them.

line 12 *in languor of shame* as they droop with shame.

line 18 The poet hopes there will be enough fire, even in a streak of sunlight, to light up the dead leaves.

lines 21–22 *tasselled latticed tree-avenues of light* Imagine a path lined on both sides with trees whose branches meet in criss-crosses (*lattices*) and overhanging silky foliage (*tassels*), and the sunlight shining through this beautiful network. This is the sort of scene that Peters has in mind.

line 23   *tantrums* wild, uncontrolled behaviour.

line 25   *coiling stuff* We will not be far wrong if we render this as 'snake': the poet is so overjoyed with nature that he can touch anything in it. But perhaps he implies something like 'the essence of movement.'

Questions

Peters uses strong words to convey his feelings in this poem. Discuss some of these words.

The poet is so determined to celebrate autumn that, in the last few stanzas, he embraces nature with the senses of sight, sound, smell and touch. Indicate those points in the poem where he introduces these senses. How does he bring them all together?

54 An African thunderstorm

This is a lively picture of a thunderstorm: a turmoil in the elements followed by heavy rainfall. Two kinds of activities are visible in this scene. First, the tumultuous movement of the elements: notice that the poet proceeds carefully in the representation – first the hurried drift of clouds accompanying the rush of winds, then thunder and lightning, and finally the heavy rainfall (represented in *pelting march*, line 33). Second, there is the varied activity in the village through which the storm blows: children playing, women rushing in confusion.

There are also two different attitudes to the storm reflected in this poem. On the one hand the storm is pictured as an evil, destructive force: words like 'plague', 'madman', 'sinister', and 'blinding' paint a rather negative picture. On the other hand, the poet acknowledges the cheerful disorder of village life during the thunderstorm. The poem is also admirable for the way in which its movement reflects the movement of the storm: short lines (some containing only one word or two) followed by long lines suggest wildness and disorder in the atmosphere. The repetition of lines 14–15 in lines 25–26 helps to build up the feeling of turmoil and confusion following the wind. The similes (especially lines 9, 13 and 27) describe the danger and confusion quite fittingly, just as the ALLITERATION (e.g. lines 8, 14, 18, 19, etc.) help us to appreciate the force of the storm.

line 6   *Locusts* resemble drifting clouds as they move in large numbers. They are called a *plague* because they generally cause damage to a wide area of vegetation, like a disease which attacks a large population.

Questions

Attempt a detailed explanation of the images in lines 32 and 33.

Identify and discuss the words which the poet has chosen for portraying the forceful movement of the storm.

55 I think it rains

This is a unique view of the rain. There is no doubt that the poet aims partly to conjure up a lively picture of rainfall. The idea of loosening up dryness or 'parch', the action of rain on ashes (stanza two), the beating force of the water (stanza four), and the persistently straight lines of showers falling on the ground – all these are the result of a careful and sensitive observation of a heavy fall in the wet season. There is also a certain tone of excitement in the first lines of the first five stanzas that reflects the joy and vitality we feel at the fall of rain.

But in this poem Soyinka has used the picture of rainfall more as a symbol to reflect his own state of mind. In fact, it is quite possible that no actual rain is falling here, but that the poet has simply conjured in his mind a picture of rainfall from his previous experience of it. We see here the image of a man determined to overcome a feeling of depression, resolved to fight the forces that limit his freedom of thought and speech, bent on getting rid of the unhealthy sentiments within him and remaining a free spirit. The persistent force with which the rain falls, the excitement which it brings, and its success in opening up all kinds of rigid surfaces, serve here as an inspiration for the determination and spirit of the poet. One of the marks of modern African poetry is the way in which the poet uses aspects of nature or the human experience to reflect his own private sentiments. This poem is another good example in this section of that tendency.

lines 1–4 The action of rain in loosening the dried thatches on the roofs of mud-houses and making them heavy with water is here transferred to the human mouth, as a symbol reflecting the poet's search for freedom of speech.

lines 5–8 When the rain falls on ashes, it raises a grey cloud which is soon forced back to the earth by the rain, and now forms with the water a grey *ring* (in the sense of an area of play or activity). This continuing play between the ashes and the rain is used as a symbol for the continued *circling* (i.e. activity) of the spirit of the poet. It is likely that the poet uses *ashes* as a symbol for burnt or wasted energies which are here reactivated with the coming of the rain.

line 10 *closures* restrictions.

line 12 A poetic way of saying 'pure sadness'.

lines 14–15 If you run a shower of water on a feather, you will notice that the water disorganises its orderly appearance into matted (*skeined*) tangles, creating openings (*transparencies*) through which you can see clearly. This is what the poet imagines the rain doing on his desires. *Wings* implies that these desires are flighty or frivolous; by pulling them apart the rain is doing the good job of exposing them.

lines 15–16 The whole idea contained here is an example of PARADOX. The rain's action in punishing the poet's evil wishes (*dark longings*) is seen in terms of burning (*searing*). This fierce act on the part of water is described as a *cruel baptism*. The idea is a paradox because the rain is doing good by causing pain. Incidentally, when two opposing ideas are contained in a phrase – with one word negative (*cruel*) and the other positive (*baptism*) – we call the phrase an OXYMORON.

lines 17–20 Though they are experienced in the act of falling (*yielding*) gracefully from the sky, these shafts of rain water are nevertheless firm in the straightness of their lines. The union (*conjugation*) between their water and the sources (*earth*) of the poet's feelings helps to loosen (*bare*) the hardness (*rocks*) within him.

Questions

What does the phrase 'from afar' (line 19) tell us of the relationship between the rain and the poet?

The stanzas of this poem are all of equal length. How does this pattern reflect the impulse within the poet?

56 The stone speaks

Huge rocks and rocky hills are very much a feature of the environment in the Inyanga Highlands, Zimbabwe, where Zimunya grew up. Four prominent qualities of these monumental stones are presented in this poem. First, the voice is brisk, firm, and authoritative, reflecting the solidity and stability of rocks deep-rooted in the earth. Second, the use of PARADOXES ('young and youth-less' etc.) reflects a certain amount of mystery about inanimate objects which nevertheless reveal so much about themselves. Third, we do get the feeling of antiquity about these stones going a long way back in the history of the earth – further even than the ancient civilisations of the past. And fourth, there is the quality of grandeur: in considering itself older than the great figures and civilisations of the past (both native and foreign), the stone demands to be accorded greater respect and recognition than them all.

line 9   The *river* here is the great Zambezi; *ruins* are the ancient walls of Zimbabwe, which have deteriorated over time.

line 10   *Mwenemutapa* was the title of a line of kings who ruled for a long time in Zimbabwe's past history. Cecil Rhodes was the Englishman who effectively colonised Rhodesia (named after him) by his misuse of the treaty granting him mining concessions there.

line 11   *Chaminuka* is one of the ancestors of the Shona of Zimbabwe whose spirit is frequently invoked by them in prayer.

line 13   The word *moment* has two senses here. It sometimes means importance, weightiness, or significance (as in the adjective: momentous). The brisk, heavy sound of that word, especially at the end of the poem, is apparently intended to emphasise the authority and importance of the stone in the life of Zimbabwe. The word *moment* is also used in the sense of a particular point in time. It is thus part of the structure of paradoxes in this poem that, whereas we are being invited to see the stone as a timeless presence, we are also being forcefully arrested by the image of it at one particular point in time.

Questions

Explain the PARADOXES in the first four lines of the poem.

Explain the relationship between line 5 and the title of the poem.

57 On truth

This reflective poem is clearly intended to teach morality. It is interesting how, despite the high seriousness of his subject, the poet makes use of objects that are close to the lives of the common people: the thread and shuttle from the traditional weaving industry of the Kanuri (who inhabit the northeastern part of Nigeria), the lice which afflict the bodies of mostly poor people, and so on. Another important feature of this poem is the reference to God. Although they resisted Islam for a long time during their history, the Kanuri are today mostly Islamised, and this religion forms much of the basis of their reflections on various aspects of life. The point about God here is simply this. God knows and can do everything, including those things that seem complicated or impossible. We should not compete with Him in this, but should pursue the path of truth which is painful (line 4) but direct and clear (line 11) and has a cleansing effect (line 3).

line 3 *biliousness* an illness accompanied by indigestion, drowsiness and a sour taste in the mouth.

Questions

Comment on the use of contrasts in this poem.

How effective is the comparison with 'darkness at sunset' in line 12?

58 The well

This poem is another proof of the fact that, contrary to the view of some anthropologists, traditional African philosophical poetry can engage in some abstract reflection and is not always geared towards practical needs. Here we have a rather deep connection made between biology and psychology. The fluid content in the human head is analysed in terms of the various attitudes and temperaments which men harbour within them: sweetness or pleasantness 'sugared water', a balanced disposition 'salty water', lack of spirit 'tasteless water', and evil disposition 'bitter water'. Notice that the fifth water is not blood, but only red like blood. The poet is aware that there is blood in the head, but his interest in this discussion is more a metaphysical one: redness may symbolise any number of things, but the comparison with blood seems to indicate a more forceful way of describing the violent, warlike temper in us which traditional society holds quite highly.

Questions

Why does the poet refer to the head as a 'well'?

In view of the fact that water is *fluid* – not rigid or solid – what do you think the poet is saying about the nature of human temperament?

59 On companionship

The Swahili live mostly in the areas of Kenya, Tanzania and Somalia that lie to the coasts of the Indian Ocean, and speak a dialect of the Bantu language that is heavily influenced by Arabic. Their contact with the Arabs goes back to the Middle Ages, and for this reason the Islamic religion has become deeply entrenched in their lives and their thinking. This early contact with Arabic culture has also influenced their oral traditions. For many generations their oral poetry has been reduced to writing, and these texts reveal various traits of style and structure which are characteristic of Arabic verse. Some of them are not easily conveyed in translation, such as rhymed endings and the division of each line into two structurally balanced parts.

But even in this translation we can see something of the dignified movement of each line and the elaborateness of the imagery. The poem starts off as a sermon on the need for women to be married. But as it progresses it uses so many ANALOGIES or associations to prove its point that it becomes a general discussion of the beauty and dignity of companionship, beautifully illustrated with images from the familiar life of the people: the trees of the east African coast (lines 6–7), the thorn as a symbol of the risks facing the poor (line 9), and types of clothing that reflect class differences in the society (line 12).

line 5   *Cleave unto* Hold fast to.
line 6   That is, they have not been as lucky as you (in securing a companion).
lines 6–7   These are varieties of tropical trees found in Kenya. The dum-palm is obviously not a highly valued type of palm, but the other trees mentioned here are (from the context) highly rated. The borassus is a type of tropical palm with large fan-shaped leaves. The teak has solid wood, especially good for making furniture and for building. The solanum is a shrub with medicinal qualities.
line 11   *across the shroud* in death. A shroud is the cloth used for wrapping a corpse.

Questions

What qualities of oral poetry are evident in this poem?

Trace carefully the connection here between marriage and companionship in general.

60 Life's variety

One of the observable marks of oral poetry is the exuberant use of details, which the performer piles one on top of the other as a way of impressing his audience about how much he knows. As in the Swahili poem just examined, this Yoruba poem moves along by linking one area of existence to another by association: the aim is to demonstrate that life is made up of advantages and disadvantages, which together constitute its wealth and variety. Everyone should be happy with what they get from this variety.

A few other features of oral poetry should be noted here. The variety in lines 5–7 is achieved in a spiral sort of way, in which one detail is repeated only to lead up to the next – an interesting twist to the device of repetition. In lines 8–9 we have a different form of repetition, this time employed to achieve contrast, and a sense of opposites. The same effect is seen in lines 10–11, where it is aided by the difference in sound between 'Ifa' and 'Ofa': not only do the initial vowels differ in sound, but in the original Yoruba the final *a* in Ifa is voiced high, while the final *a* in Ofa is voiced low. This poem is a good instance in which the resources of the oral art are used for the expression of some of man's deepest philosophical concerns.

line 9   Owa is the title of the traditional ruler of the Ijesha, a Yoruba subgroup.
line 10   Ifa is the Yoruba traditional body of knowledge, which contains answers
          to a wide variety of issues ranging from health and wealth to morality
          and abstract universal mysteries (see no. 61). *Ofa* is a town in the northern
          part of Yorubaland.

Questions

Can you detect a slight touch of humour 'between the lines' of this poem?

Half of this poem is expressed in rhetorical questions, demanding no answer, and the other half in plain statements. How effective is this pattern in handling the topic of the poem?

61 The lion refused to perform sacrifice

Orunmila is one of the major divinities of the Yoruba, but he is better known by his other name, Ifa, whereby he is the guardian of all forms of wisdom available to the Yoruba through a system of divination. The process of *ifa* divination is complex, but it is essentially as follows. A client brings a problem or an enquiry to a diviner (*babalawo*), who chooses an *ese* (or parable) from a specific category which relates to the issue brought by the client. This *ese* (like *ese* generally) tells a story which relates to an experience similar to the one brought for consultation by the client; the consultation ends by the *babalawo* telling the client (in accordance with the *ese* narrated to him) what sacrifice to perform in respect of his problem.

In this sense, *ifa* divination is a system of using poetic narratives to probe the most important issues relating to life. This particular poem is an *ese* which deals with the element of chance or luck in natural affairs. This element is represented in Yoruba mythology by the trickster god Esu, and stands essentially as a warning that, however great we may think we are (as the behaviour of the lion in the story demonstrates), our fortunes are not within our control but are dependent on the whims and caprices of some hidden forces which have to be consulted before we can succeed.

There are no musical instruments played in the process of consultation. But there is usually a certain intensity in the whole atmosphere surrounding this complex search for the right answers. The intensity and excitement can be seen perhaps in the pace of this story. The excitement propels the instincts of the diviner and provides a certain rhythm to his statements: to some extent this explains the repetitive pattern that we find in the *ese* (compare for instance lines 1–3 and 34–36; 32 and 33; 37 and 38; 40 and 41). It may be noted that in the recitation of texts of the *ese* the ideas and some basic phrases do not change; but the quality of performance of any *ese* depends very much (as all oral art does) on the skill of the *babalawo* and the circumstances of the recital (e.g. the personality of the client).

line 1   This is a salute to the trickster god Esu, whose ways are never direct.

line 11 In Yoruba mythology, the figures of Esu and Ifa (Orunmila) are often closely related; some sources even claim that it was from Esu that Orunmila got the art of divination.

lines 34–42 It is not always easy to punctuate speeches in the oral narrative, because quite often the narrator – as we shall see in the extract from *The White Bagre* (no. 69) – assumes several voices. If these lines are spoken by the lion, it would be a reflection of his total submission at this point.

Questions

Give an interpretation of the last three lines of this poem.

How successful is the characterisation of the lion in the story?

62 An evening libretto

A libretto is the text of a musical performance such as an opera. The idea of 'a large hall' (line 3) certainly suggests that the poet wishes us to see the sentiment contained in this poem as a reflection of a performance. But this is a performance that never materialises because the audience finds there is no place to sit. The poet thinks his conscience – the room inside him, so to speak – is clear; but when he opens himself up to others, they show him that his conscience is not clear after all. On one level Angira is warning us against deceiving ourselves; on a deeper level the poem is saying that we are not the best judge of ourselves, that one's character is best defined in relation to other people. The simplicity of the language of this poem underlines the honesty of the sentiments expressed.

Questions

What is the relation between 'evening' (in the title) and the feeling in this poem?

There is some evidence of rhyme in the first stanza, but none at all in the rest of the poem. In what way is this change a reflection of the difference in mood between that stanza and the others?

63 Their behaviour

Though Dennis Brutus is known generally for his resistance to apartheid, he has frequently moved, in his poetry, beyond the limits of South African life to an examination of the human condition in general. For this he has often been denounced, especially by African critics, as an idealist wasting his attention on abstract matters when the situation in South Africa calls for constant and total condemnation. But he has been hailed by others as a humanist who recognises that the situation in his country is only part of a larger human problem. Written while Brutus was under house-arrest, this is one of those poems in which he tries to take an objective look at the morality of the apartheid system: for him it is simply a reflection, on a larger scale, of a basic human love of power. Notice, however, that despite his objectivity there is an underlying tone of condemnation in this poem: the emphasis on 'guilt' and the rather strong language of lines 8–12 betrays a deep-seated resentment against the system.

line 16 *deshabille* loose-fitting dress, carelessly worn.

Questions

Why has the poet bracketed the question in line 6? Is it because he wants to give particular emphasis to it, or because he thinks it is a truth which he is ashamed to admit?

Comment on Brutus' use of personal pronouns like 'their' and 'ours' in this poem.

64 Streamside exchange

This poem brings out two features that are characteristic of the poetry of J.P. Clark. One is the deliberate simplicity of his language especially in the shorter poems (compare *Ibadan*, no. 49); Clark clearly demonstrates that the most important and most complex issues in human life can be discussed in simple language. The second feature is the imagery of his poems. Clark comes from the delta region of Nigeria, and he frequently makes use of images which reflect the peculiarities of the riverside environment – such as 'river bird' and 'tide' here. This poem comes from his collection entitled *A Reed in the Tide* (a reed is a grass growing in the water-bed – the same kind of grass on which the river bird of this poem is sitting) in which such imagery frequently occurs.

The message of this poem may be simple but it is certainly very haunting. There is some excitement and anxiety in the child's request, whereas the reply of the bird is restrained and heavy. The message of the bird is that life is a passing thing and we have no way of knowing what it holds in store for us. A dialogue between a child and a bird looks at first like the kind of joyous stuff of which folk literature is made; but the bird in this particular poem carries a rather sad and fatalistic message.

line 3 As the bird perches on the grass, its weight bends the grass over in the form of a hook.
line 11 *tide* reflects the ebb and flow of the waves of a river or the sea; *market* suggests a transfer of goods from one hand to the other. Together these images emphasise the idea of *exchange* in the title as well as of unsteadiness in the fortunes of men.

Questions

Why does the poet give the first stanza to a child – what is so child-like about that stanza?

Discuss the structure of each stanza and how it reflects the mood within the stanza.

65 With purity hath nothing been won

Taban lo Liyong is a very sensitive poet who, in a great deal of his poetry, tries to reflect on large questions like the human condition, the relation of literature to culture, and (as in this poem) the morality of culture. He has travelled widely; perhaps it is this large contact with the world that has given him a deep awareness of the depressing condition of his own African continent, of the injustice by which the white races have constantly exploited the other races, and consequently an element of cynicism towards human nature in general.

This poem, a reflection on the relationship between good and evil, comes from a collection by Liyong titled *Another Nigger Dead*. Liyong, who studied at Howard University, Washington, D.C. (a mostly black city), knows very well the implications of the word 'nigger'. Racist Americans have been known to say, when a black man dies, 'Oh, nothing much — just another nigger dead', as if it doesn't matter. When people (or nations) continue to make progress in spite of such evil dispositions, some people are tempted to conclude that evil, or impurity, pays and that good, or 'purity', does not and is indeed an impediment to real achievement.

That is the main logic of this poem. But Liyong does not hesitate to contradict himself and so lead us to believe that he should not be taken seriously. For instance, 'christ died through the impure' (line 3) is either a condemnation of the 'impure' action of killing Christ or a justification of an act through which He died for the salvation of mankind. Also, line 8 may imply that, but for her impure intentions, Eve would not have enjoyed the apple in Paradise; and yet that impure act has been the cause of evil in the world.

Such double play on intentions or meanings is Liyong's cynical way of trivialising human affairs. Other ways are evident. One is the use of the small letter throughout, a technique made popular by the American poet e.e. cummings (who constantly spelt his name in small letters) and used throughout *Another Nigger Dead*: even the names of God and Christ are not spared. Also, although Liyong puts the poem in serious Biblical language — with the use of words like 'hath' and 'thyself' and images of angels and the soul — the poem goes mostly against the teachings of the Bible. However, quite apart from the disturbing moral issues which the poem raises, this sensitive play on our imagination is one major achievement of the piece as poetry.

line 2 The greatness of Greece was achieved through the subjugation of other nations around and beyond it.

line 4 Japan is alleged to have achieved her technological success by stealing the secrets of machines made in Europe and America and copying them.

line 5 *Beast* implies not only the enormous size of America in area and population but also the danger that American technology (bombs, etc.) poses to the survival of mankind. That technology has been achieved through the inhuman exploitation of blacks and other races.

line 6 *purity* here may mean virginity, which prevents a woman from carrying creation (a child) in her womb.

lines 10—12 truck deal. If the poet's heart loves impurity, how can it rise above the evil earth and hell and be compared to angels in heaven? We can see the deliberate contradiction or PARADOX here – part of the poet's technique of trivialisation.

Questions

What do you think are the two contradictory meanings of line 13?

This poem has been written in the sonnet convention of fourteen lines. Is there any contradiction between this respected convention and the subject of the poem?

66 Look at this globe

This poem shows once again – as J. P. Clark's *Streamside exchange* does – how poetry can use relatively simple language to tackle complex or intense questions. In this poem, the poet would obviously like ('I should rejoice') to see himself as a cheerful person with a brilliant and vibrant heart. But a comparison of his heart with the light enclosed within a bulb or globe makes him wonder if that pleasure or cheerfulness is justified. Although it is enclosed, the light of the lamp shines through the globe in all its brilliance and arrests our attention; on the contrary, his dark flesh does not permit his heart to reflect its brilliance and cheerfulness.

The twelve lines of the poem are evenly divided between the excitement of the first six and the regretfulness of the latter six. In the first six lines, the jubilant poet reaches out and invites others (the subject of 'Look' is 'you') to share his happy discovery. In the latter six, he withdraws into himself with the subject 'I'.

Questions

Does the word 'ebony' (line 10), which means black, have a positive or a negative sense in this poem? Explain your interpretation.

What is the meaning of the word 'beat' (line 12) in this context?

67 Drum appeal

In several communities of tropical Africa – examples abound in Ghana, Nigeria, Cameroun, Zaïre, etc. – there is a very old and highly-specialised tradition of drum-playing. There are many kinds of drums, but the one that has commanded the greatest attention is the 'talking drum', which comes in different sizes (depending on the community) and is usually beaten with a stick. The peculiar quality of this drum is that the tones can be controlled so that they come close to those of human speech. In this way it is possible to play certain statements and transmit messages which can be understood by those familiar with such a language. It should be understood, however, that it takes a considerable amount of time (years, in fact) to fully master the art of playing such a drum. Besides, the notes which can be sounded on it are rather limited; so that a full statement or a message can only be played in a highly coded arrangement. It is this tightness of structure, and the intensity of expression which it gives rise to, that form the poetic basis of drum messages.

In this piece the drum poet is appealing to the protecting divinities of his community, who must be consulted before any major undertaking, to help him become a successful drummer. He begins his appeal with a proverbial statement: proverbs in African speech are usually a mark of wisdom and philosophical depth, and in drum poetry they are an indispensable means of achieving that economy of expression characteristic of a coded system. What the drummer is saying in his proverbial statement to the river god Tano is essentially this: Although there are many things which have been with us since time immemorial, we recognise you as the oldest of all creation, and that is why we consult you before we do anything serious.

The repeated statements in this piece have the emphatic tone of prayer. But they also follow the structure of drumming: phrases are struck several times (see especially lines 16–18) both to emphasise their message and to heighten the musical tone of the sounds.

lines 7–8 *Tano* is the name of an Ashanti river god. His name is frequently invoked in Ashanti oaths and prayers. *Kokon* and *Birefia* are his subordinates or subsidiaries, through whom the drummer is passing his appeal.

line 15 *Ta* is short for Tano; *Kofi* is another one of his subordinates or guards.

line 16 *Firampon* is another title for the god. In many traditional African communities, spirits and protective divinities are treated as dead ancestors; *condolences* are frequently addressed to them for having been deprived (by death) of the joy of living.

Questions

Discuss the various ways in which the drummer tries to win the favour of the god Tano.

'Drum poetry is frequently marked by a combination of brevity and fullness of expression.' Comment on this statement with reference to the above poem.

68 Rain-making litany

The words of a piece of prayer may sound very commonplace to someone who has not watched the act of praying, particularly in a traditional ritual ceremony such as we have in this poem. There is a total commitment of body and spirit in the recitation of the words, which lifts the whole performance away from the level of an ordinary statement or request. The persistent repetition of words and phrases is also based on a very intense belief in the power of words: the idea is that there is so much force in the frequent calling of the object that the object will ultimately be drawn to the caller. The responses (on the right) also enhance the power of the words.

Although he obsessively concentrates on certain key words, the chanter's mind is nevertheless able to make some subtle connections between ideas. Thus in lines 5–14, the idea of ripening suggests an image of cheerfulness which is echoed by the idea of rejoicing and singing. Also, in lines 15–17 the idea of flowing torrents reflects a hope for a similar abundance in the granaries. This device of one idea suggesting another, and both being linked in the same or in adjacent lines, is called ASSOCIATION, a technique which frequently occurs in oral poetry.

Questions

Poetry frequently reflects the social or economic life of a community. What kind of community is portrayed here?

From the response to the chanter's lines, what do you consider the two major wishes of this prayer?

69 The White Bagre [*opening lines*]

This piece of poetry is part of an initiation ceremony (among the LoDagaa of Northern Ghana) known as the Bagre. When a citizen is afflicted with disease or any other problem in life, he performs this ceremony during which he learns — through submission to the spiritual powers of divinity, the ancestors, and other forces — the secrets that will help him to overcome his affliction and lead a life of wisdom. There are two stages to the initiation into Bagre. The 'White' ceremony is done by those who are coming into Bagre for the first time; the 'Black' ceremony is done at a later stage only by those who have first done the White. Each of these ceremonies is accompanied by an extensive text which simultaneously traces the origins of the ritual and outlines the steps that present-day performers are supposed to follow.

The background is essentially as follows. The brothers — the original ancestors of the LoDagaa and 'children of God' — were once troubled by some (unspecified) problem. To be able to find the solution to it, they made approaches ('the elder' of course taking the lead in all this) to God and to some 'beings of the wild.' Since communication was not yet well developed at this early stage in creation, the brothers were able to learn only through a long series of trial and error, first how to identify the problem and then how to tackle it (by taboos and other means).

The Bagre ceremony is essentially an appeal to supernatural forces: that is why it begins here by invoking the gods, ancestors, etc. But the form of it is an interesting combination of several elements. First there is the *narrative voice*. In this the intermediary (known as the 'elder,' who takes the initiates through the ceremony) recounts the experiences of the original men who underwent the same kind of experiences: the dramatic force of this text reflects the officiant's effort to capture the excitement experienced by those confused and groping first men. Then there is what we may call the *statutory voice* of the intermediary: here we get the feeling that he is following certain processes that have been recommended by tradition in a particular situation (see, for instance, lines 5–6). And finally there is the *imperative voice*: many parts of the Bagre text sound very much like instructions being given to the present-day initiates on what to do and what to avoid, very much in line with the procedure followed by their ancestors. Because of this mixture of elements, we find frequently a confusion of the first, second and third person pronouns reflecting the shift in the contexts (past, present, or perennial) within which the ritual is conceived.

The recitation of the Bagre text here reflects the general atmosphere of divination in many a traditional African society. Consequently we get some insight into the ritual objects with which the ceremony is conducted (e.g. 'leather bottles', line 5) and the symbolic language (e.g. 'bowstring', line 34, representing hunting) which marks this highly serious business. The short lines of the recitation are accompanied by the beating of two sticks on a bowl or the shaking of a rattle – which increases the feeling of excitement or agitation in this oral performance. If, as suggested in the Introduction, poetry is the product of an intensity of emotion and seriousness of purpose, surely this is poetry of a high order.

line 4   spirits of the bush.

line 5   As Jacky Goody explains in *The Myth of the Bagre* (Oxford University Press, 1972): 'The leather bottle is a small container made from hide, in which senior members of the society keep the cowries which they use for divination.'

lines 7–10   These are various troubles afflicting mankind. The four mentioned here are employed symbolically to represent trouble in general.

line 13   *guinea-corn* was originally used as payment for divination. Nowadays it is cowries or coins.

line 15   Notice that the intermediary here occupies the position of a 'diviner'. The initiates for whom he is performing the Bagre ceremony are clients to him very much as the 'elder brother' of this story was to the 'diviner'. This mixture of the past and the present is echoed throughout the language of *The White Bagre*.

lines 18–40   *Sticks* are thrown in LoDagaa divination very much as cowries or seeds are used in other communities. The formation into which the throw falls indicates which 'deity' is to be consulted. As we can see here, the 'elder brother' and his diviner try all combinations until they get the right answer.

lines 49–50   Notice the touch of humour in these lines, which enhances the dramatic quality of the recitation.

lines 55–66   This is the first stage of the Bagre ceremony: the purification (by water) of the initiates and the announcement of the foods they should not eat during the period of the ceremony (one month). Here we can see the 'elder' or intermediary of today imposing his knowledge of the Bagre procedures on the ignorant 'elder' in the story: if the latter was such an ignorant or groping figure, how did he know about this necessary step in the ceremony?

line 95   Notice the dramatic touch here: the reciter now speaks in his own voice as a narrator-performer, drawing the attention of his audience to an arresting event.

line 106   'This is the Bagre deity, who comes in front of a man, that is comes with the truth. It is only a coward or a liar who sneaks up from behind' (Goody).

lines 107–8   That is, indicating good fortune.

line 136 *it* could mean either Bagre (which, as is implied in lines 138–40, is a burdensome ceremony), or trouble, or even death.

lines 138–40 Here we can see something of the statutory voice of this text, as mentioned above.

Questions

Identify those passages where repetition occurs most frequently in this text. What effect do they leave on the whole recitation?

In what phrases or passages do we feel the sense of futility and frustration in the efforts of the 'elder'?

70 To Ogun

As we saw in the *Salute to Fabunmi* (no. 21), Ogun is the patron divinity of Yoruba hunters. In this piece – another example of *ijala* poetry – a hunter evokes the formidable power of the god for his own success: he prays for 'good luck' as a hunter (line 8), and cites as his testimonial the fact that he gives service to good people (line 50).

One striking element in this chant is the euphemistic tone as well as the feeling of awe with which the performer refers to Ogun. Ogun is notable for his fierce temper and his bloodthirsty record in his dealings with human beings; he is certainly a god to be cultivated with caution, as our poet here recognises. The bloody temper of Ogun is revealed by the brutal way in which he deals with people who refused to acknowledge his hunting skills (lines 40–42). In traditional society, what Ogun did is not necessarily understood as cruelty: the fiercer a man is, the greater is the respect he enjoys in the society, as we saw in *Ali, Lion of the World*, (no. 17). Nevertheless, this chanter does not wish to tangle at all with the god; he craves neither the friendship nor the hostility of the god, simply his blessing. The frequent repetition of this prayer (lines 6–28) reveals not only the intensity of feeling that goes into the chant but also the tremendous awe which the chanter feels before the god. This poem is essentially an appeal that some of that fierce and unfailing energy for which Ogun is known should work to the advantage of the hunter-poet.

A few peculiarities of oral poetry are noticeable in this chant. One of these is the pace of delivery. In the *Salute to Fabunmi* we mentioned that *ijala* poetry is normally chanted at a fast pace. Under the circumstances there is a frequent challenge to the performer to demonstrate his speed at the job: in line 39 here the performer has demonstrated his skill by chanting in one line attributes to Ogun that he did previously in three lines (2–4). Another notable quality here is the tendency towards introducing or alluding to mythical events in highly abbreviated references: for instance, line 5 is chanted simply as a proverb, but behind it lies a memorable incident in the heroic career of Ogun (compare *Shaka*, no. 23).

line 3 *Ejemu* was a chieftaincy title conferred on Ogun by the king of Iwonran in western Nigeria.

line 5 'The allusion is to one of the episodes of Ogun's life. One day, arriving at the gates of a town that he had never visited before, Ogun sought from the gate-keeper permission to enter. To his surprise the gate-keeper refused to let him in. Thereupon, Ogun walked back a few steps and then did a record high-jump, landing himself astride the neck of the gatekeeper and pressing down on his neck tormentingly. The great height to which Ogun jumped on this occasion is here likened to the great height to which butterflies fly when they come upon a civet-cat's excrement' (see S. A. Babalola, *The Content and Form of Yoruba Ijala*).

lines 9–26 The references here are to the circumcision of boys and girls and the sacrifice of various animals to the gods. These acts are normally carried out with a knife made of metal, of which Ogun is the god.

lines 33–37 Just as the Ashanti drum poet appeals to the god Tano through his subsidiary divinities (no. 67), the *ijala* poet here makes his appeal to Ogun by extending honour and recognition to one of Ogun's 'sons'.

line 34 *Ilagbede* is another name for Ire, the town with which Ogun is mostly associated.

line 36 *He* is Ogun.

line 50 That is, to well-intentioned citizens.

Questions

Discuss the image of Ogun as it emerges from this chant.

What effect do the pieces of narrative or ALLUSIONS to events have on the poet's portraiture of Ogun?

71 A plea for mercy

This poem, from Brew's collection *Shadows of Laughter*, appears in a section where the poet deals with religious matters. It presents the image of prodigal sons who, after being away so long, have returned home to be reconciled with a tradition that they had apparently turned their backs on. They now kneel before the shrine of their ancestors and beg for forgiveness and reacceptance.

The poem endeavours to portray the dilemma of the modern African who goes away in pursuit of European culture and ideals only to find that he has lost contact with his tradition. What the suppliants in this poem are saying to their ancestral God ('Master') is essentially this. We know we have been away too long and have come home too late (lines 3–13). Nevertheless, we are still 'sons of the land' (lines 2 and 14) and deserve to be heard. While other things in nature show nothing but pride (lines 18–12), we submit ourselves humbly before you with praise in our hearts (line 16), repentance on our lips (line 17), and poverty in our looks (line 22); in spite of these efforts, there is still no sign that we have been heeded or accepted (line 15).

The tone of the poem is subdued. Perhaps the absence of repetition demonstrates the lack of a feeling of excitement.

line 5 Shepherds and cowherds usually play the flute or other musical instrument to occupy themselves while their herds are grazing or resting. (Compare *Where has my love blown his horn?*, no. 1).

236

line 9   *shadows* i.e. of evening or night.
line 21   *Volta* the biggest river in Ghana.
line 23   *Master* Some commentators think that this word suggests the colonial African's respect for the European, and that the divinity being appealed to in this poem is the Christian God; the suppliants are therefore praying forgiveness (*mercy*) for their pagan ways and asking that God should accept them into the Christian faith.

Questions

What is the point of the emphasis on the idea 'sons of the land'?

In what way do the suppliants here show that they have not lost all familiarity with their culture?

72 Dear God

This poem appears in Brutus' collection entitled *Stubborn Hope*. The poems in this volume were written after Brutus emigrated from South Africa and settled as a political refugee first in England and later in the United States of America (where he now lives). The poems describe various environments and places to which Brutus has had a chance to travel (including China). They also reflect a certain freedom of spirit which it was difficult to feel under the painful restrictions that he had experienced in South Africa.

In these poems Brutus has had an opportunity to reaffirm his faith in human nature and in freedom. But he has equally discovered that South Africa is not the only place where freedom is denied and where man shows his inhumanity to man. His immediate instinct would be to revolt against these painful conditions in his new abode outside South Africa. In this poem we can feel the intense restlessness and helplessness of a man whose instincts naturally revolt against injustice but who is forbidden, by the peculiar terms under which he is living, to do anything about it. There is a total absence of those techniques by which Brutus normally asserts his commitment to beauty and order – alliteration, rhyme, sonnet form, etc. – because the poet is confronted with a situation to which he dare not apply his normal responses.

lines 2–5 *here* refers to the United States, and *the evil* is obviously racial discrimination.
lines 12–14 That is, in South Africa.
line 16 *conformable* agreeable.

Questions

The language of this poem is mostly simple and direct. What does this tell us about the mood of the poet?

Discuss the phrases here which most vividly reveal the poet's impatience and irritation.

73 Afa (before Chukwu at dusk)

This poem comes from the only collection of the late Pol Ndu, titled *Songs for Seers*. Devoted mostly to poems dealing with the Nigerian Civil War (1967–70), the collection was clearly meant for those who have sufficient wisdom to see, in the troubles of the day, the lessons for the future.

Ndu here places himself in the position of a priest doing a divination (*afa*). The procedure in divination is for the priest to throw his articles (seeds of the kola-nut, or cowries, or other objects) either on the floor where he sits or on a wooden tray meant for the purpose. The formation into which these articles fall represents a particular message, which the priest then begins to decipher. The poetry of divination is often difficult to understand because the priest is trying hard to untie the complex symbols which the articles have sketched on the floor (compare *The White Bagre*, no. 69). In this piece the poet-priest, throwing down his articles, makes an appeal to the supreme deity (lines 1–11); the articles arrange themselves in symbolic patterns which represent Igwekala's response to the question posed to him (12–18); the poet-priest then proceeds to interpret the meaning of those symbols (19–27). In the divination here the priest is enquiring about the future of the Nigerian Civil War.

line 1   *Igwekala*, another name for the supreme God (*Chukwu*) of the Igbo of eastern Nigeria. It means, literally, 'the sky is greater than the earth', and has its origins in the contest between these two elements in traditional Igbo mythology.

lines 3–9   The Nigerian Civil War began effectively in late summer (July/August) 1967. The divination is here set at the early stages of the war (apparently during the August break when the rains have temporarily ceased). By now the farmers, having completed their harvesting, have hung up their hoes (line 6) and are burning their farms (*smoky fields*, line 8) to prepare them for the next planting season. In summer, the sunlight also tends to last longer on the horizon (lines 4–5) than at other times of the year.

line 11   What prevents you from showing us a sign?

lines 12–18   This is the symbolic pattern formed by the articles cast on the floor. In more direct terms, the meaning here is that soldiers from the four corners of the country will converge at a point (Eastern Nigeria, which seceded and declared itself Biafra, March 1967); the conflagration (*spark*) that results will fill the land with heaps (*furrows*) of corpses and bloodshed (*fluid*), giving rise to conflicts that will continue for a long time to come.

lines 19–27   The diviner's reading of the message, or his counter-response to Igwekala whose message, though he does not speak, is infinitely loud and clear (line 19). It is an extremely difficult passage because it tries to capture the complex symbolic language in which diviners normally conduct their proceedings. In general the passage indicates that unborn generations of brave young men (*unhatched glory*) will be involved in the damage (*mutilation*) started by a war that is fought by modern machinery (*grease and oil*) and weapons (*shells*); although these future generations have no share in the original guilt (*stainless*), they will put a stamp (*hallmark*) on the history of the country forever.

line 27   *here*   Notice the poetic touch in the repetition of the word with which the whole poem began.

Questions

Explain fully the images contained in the following lines: 4–5 and 8–9.

The first six lines of the poem are rhymed and there is a certain tenderness to them; but as the poem progresses the mood changes drastically. How do you explain the change?

74 Heavensgate: (i) the passage

This selection represents the first movement of the first part ('Heavensgate') of a long sequence of poems that make up Christopher Okigbo's *Labyrinths*. In these poems we can see a poet struggling very hard to reconcile the various cultural backgrounds (native African and Indo-European) that have influenced him, so that he could better understand himself and discover the truly individual voice with which he could express the concerns of his society. He begins this journey of self-examination at 'Heavensgate': here images of a traditional ritual worship mingle with those of Christian service to portray a man steeped in devotion, one who fully acknowledges the powers of nature and divinity around him.

There is a fundamental similarity between this poem and the Ashanti *Drum appeal* (no. 67): both poems show the artist appealing to the superior powers in his search for his own artistic voice, and in both poems the symbols reveal a deep and intense seriousness of purpose. But what makes Okigbo's poem particularly difficult is that it reflects the complex mixture of cultural influences which the poet has undergone. The poem begins with an appeal to the water-divinity of Okigbo's village, but soon the symbols reveal a conflict of traditional and Christian images. The images are mixed up one with the other, and there is a certain incoherence in the expressions which reflects the internal struggle that the poet is undergoing to reconcile the two cultures.

In this search for the self through a reconciliation of cultural influences, Okigbo reminds us of the Anglo-American poet T. S. Eliot, whose long sequence entitled *The Wasteland* contains a mixture of symbols which reflect a long history of influences in Indo-European culture. Okigbo's poem here, like Eliot's, is composed of multiple symbols which are logically associated with one another. In the Ashanti *Drum appeal* there is a feeling of total submission; in Okigbo's poem we see instead a confused search for a footing.

line 1   *Idoto* a river-goddess in Ojoto, the village in eastern Nigeria where Okigbo was born.

line 3   *watery presence* a METAPHOR reflecting Idoto's essence as a water-spirit.

line 4   *prodigal* Okigbo returns to reconcile with his culture after a long period of studying and embracing foreign cultures. In this he is like the Biblical prodigal son who, having wasted his inheritance in foreign lands, returns home to seek forgiveness of his father. This sense of the prodigal is one that many African intellectuals feel (compare no. 71 above).

line 5   *oilbean* a kind of tropical tree.

line 6   *Lost* implies either that Okigbo has forgotten (as a result of long absence), or is trying to figure out, the message contained in the image of Idoto.

line 10   *Heavensgate* In one of his sonnets (Sonnet 29), Shakespeare has the image of an outcast singing 'at heaven's gate' hymns that are hardly heeded. Okigbo may have borrowed this learned reference for his portrait of the prodigal pleading desperately before the divine presence of the goddess Idoto.

line 13   Having paid his homage to Idoto, Okigbo now enters into an intense spiritual journey. The rest of this poem is made up of a mixture of images – from both traditional ritual and Christian worship – which go through the mind of the poet as he searches through himself. They may in fact be taken as the response of Idoto to the poet's appeal, sent through the mind of the poet who is now in a state of spiritual possession and experiencing a vision.

lines 13–17   The spiritual journey begins at the very beginning of the world, when there is absolute darkness and the elements are in chaos. The repeated use of *foreshadow* and *dreamed* emphasises the atmosphere of a vision and a tone of prophesy.

lines 18–27   The poet here catches the first glimpse of himself as a future 'singer' or poet, in the image of a garrulous, tell-tale bird (*wagtail*). In his poetry he will be concerned with social crisis (*tangled-wood*), will lament (*mourn*) the abandonment of tradition (here represented by *mother* Idoto in the *spray* or water), and will treat mythological subjects such as the fight between the rain and the sun. *Orangery* is an orange grove, apparently part of the environment around the shrine of Idoto at Ojoto.

lines 29–35   The vision shifts to a scene of ritual at a *crossroads*: in many traditional African communities, sacrifices to the gods are often left at a point where roads meet. The worshippers in this scene are dressed in black and march in a long file. This crossroads is situated behind a Christian church (here represented by a tower housing a bell for summoning worshippers).

lines 36–45   Okigbo, whose parents were devout Catholics, here summons his mother *Anna* – seen here holding the knobs of the oblong-panelled doors of the church – to hear his appeal from the meeting-point (*hinges*) of the crossroads. This sets the scene for a reconciliation of tradition and Christianity. The nearness of crossroads and church is emphasised by the combination of symbols of the traditional rural landscape (*cornfields* and *wind*) and the Christian church (*pipe organs* and *leather*-bound books). This nearness gives rise to a mixture of images from the two environments. The lovely music played by the wind moving through the stalks of corn in the cornfields is compared with the lovely wind music that sounds through the long pipes of the church organ.

lines 40–41   The images here further emphasise the union of Christianity and the traditional environment. Inside the leather-bound hymn book, from which the organ player takes his songs, we see the image of orange leaves which over a long period of time have bleached the pages of the book. This indelible mark left by the leaves in the book seems to be Okigbo's way of saying that the message of Christianity has been influenced by natural or traditional wisdom since time immemorial.

Questions

What impact do the repeated phrases have on the poem?

Discuss the words and phrases here which reflect (a) the conflict experienced or perceived by the poet, and (b) the loneliness surrounding this experience.

75 Young Africa's plea

This poem was written, according to Osadebay, between 1930 and 1950. The period was a crucial one in Africa's history, because many African politicians and intellectuals were agitating strongly for the liberation of their continent from colonial rule. One argument very frequently used by these agitators was that the European presence in Africa was detrimental to our traditional culture, and that Africans should be left to pursue their indigenous way of life and their destiny. And yet many Africans were beginning to acquire European education and to practise the foreign culture side by side with the indigenous one. Under these circumstances, the educated Africans were faced with a dilemma: What do we do with this new situation? Should we abandon the one culture and follow the other, or do we rather take the best we can from either culture and let things sort themselves out?

Osadebay here represents those Africans faced with such a dilemma and pleads that things be allowed to take their natural course; he and his colleagues have the will-power to go through the new experience and emerge better men. Africa is called 'young' in the title because, by this time, Africans had not had a long contact with the white man's culture; colonialism was still a recent experience in most of the continent, and people like Osadebay were indeed the earlier generation of Africans experiencing the clash between European culture and theirs. Living under forced control, they considered themselves to be in a somewhat helpless position and could only plead that their natural talents be allowed to develop freely and not forced into a pre-determined path of growth. This search for freedom is, of course, a legitimate sentiment of youth.

Most of Osadebay's poems are cast into various patterns of end-rhymes and various rhythmic structures. Indeed, if we look closely we can see much evidence of conscious workmanship in this poem. For instance, the first fifteen lines are patterned on a sequence of three-line statements; there is use of contrasts in lines 7–8 and 13–14; and there is obviously a deliberate balance between the first group of 'Let . . .' lines (7–9) and the second group (16–18). On the whole, however, the poem is written in considerably FREE VERSE, using no rhyme scheme until the final two lines. Perhaps this free movement reflects not only the freedom that the poet asks for but also the honesty of his sentiments.

> line 2 *curio* an object that arouses curiosity by its strangeness or oddness, like an antique carving from an unfamiliar community or country.
> line 5 *beats* surpasses.

Questions

Explain the full significance of lines 7–8, especially with reference to 'work' and 'play' as characterised by the respective races.

What do you think is Osadebay's attitude to the white man in this poem? Examine his use of words throughout the poem very carefully for your answer.

76 Prayer to masks

One fundamental belief that is common to practically all black African communities is the fact that, although they have lost their physical existence, the dead are still very much a part of our lives. Their spirits live effectively with us and we can communicate with them in a variety of ways. One way is to keep ancestor shrines in an inner room in the house; every morning when we wake up we address our greetings and prayers to these shrines, tell them our wishes, and periodically offer sacrifices of food, animal blood and palm-wine for them to eat and drink. On certain festive occasions – such as the burial rites for a dead man or even rites for the taking of a chieftaincy title – masquerades are paraded in display and dance, wearing appropriate ancestral masks and representing the spirits either of the dead man or of ancestors within the family being celebrated. The masquerades speak in falsetto voices, giving and answering greetings, saluting members of the family concerned with the rites and other spectators. In these various ways Africans acknowledge the continuing presence of the dead among them.

Such is the background to this poem, written by Senghor after World War II and published in the collection *Chants d'Ombre*. As always, Senghor's concern in this prayer is with Africa: its culture and its destiny. At the end of the war the world looked depleted of energy and hopeless. A new order had to be created if the world was to survive; as Senghor saw it, this order entailed that Africa and Europe should provide mutual support to save each other. Although Africa suffered domination and prejudice at the hands of Europe, Senghor believed that African culture contained the ingredients for creating a new world order that would provide a hopeful future for both races.

line 3   *of the four points* rectangular; *blows* blows air, breathes.

line 5   *Lion-headed Ancestor* The mask is in the shape of a lion's head. The lion may also be his family's *totem*, i.e. the animal symbol chosen by the family as representing the qualities (e.g. courage, dignity) with which it can be identified.

line 6   *this place* the family shrine. In many African communities it is men who worship at these shrines. Such a place, which preserves the eternal qualities of the family, has no room for frivolity.

line 8   A mask represents the essential qualities of an ancestor, not his physical features. In this form the ancestor has been *unmasked*, i.e. freed of the outer covering of a skin marked by scars and the lines of old age.

line 11   Although by this time many African nations belonged to the colonial empires governed by Britain, France, Spain and other European powers, Senghor is casting his mind further back to the great African empires of the past such as Mali, Ghana, Songhai, Zimbabwe, etc. whose values are gradually being eroded by European culture. Senghor has constantly portrayed Africa in his poetry with the symbol of a woman (see, for instance, *Relentlessly she drives me*, no. 15); so, logically, the Africa of the empires is a *princess*.

line 12   The long-standing commercial, colonial and other contacts between Africa and Europe are here likened to the umbilical cord joining a mother to the navel of her child. Although Senghor here simply intended to imply that the destinies of Africa and Europe have become inseparable, some African critics of his poetry and thought have often cited this poem (especially the parent-child image) to show that Senghor considers African culture subordinate to European culture.

line 13 *unchanging eyes* The eyes of a mask are motionless. Senghor may also be using the image to represent the timeless, perpetual values of African culture.

lines 13–14 Senghor here implies the colonial domination of Africa by Europe, which has forced Africans to fight and die in European wars like World War I and II.

line 18 *dawn* the reawakening of the world.

Question

Is the image of Africa that emerges from this poem a positive or a negative one? In your answer, make references to particular phrases and ideas in the poem.

77 Coward, crawl back!

All the fierceness and daring spirit of the traditional warrior is reflected in this war song from the Acholi of Uganda. The song is meant to discourage any division of opinion in a situation where the people have resolved to go to war and are actually on the march. Whoever questions the value or motive of the fighting is only 'arguing stupidly' and should never have been born; the best thing for such a 'coward' to do is 'crawl back' into his mother's womb.

We should appreciate that though the song is short, it is meant to be chanted many times to the rhythm of the stamping feet of men on the march. The musical quality of the song can be felt in the repetition of the opening line at the end.

Questions

Why do the warriors refer to themselves as 'sons of the brave' and not just as brave men?

At one point the song assumes a plural subject ('we'), at another it projects a singular personality ('my'). What is the significance of each to the spirit of the song?

78 The army is going to war

The Kipsigis live in the western Rift Valley region in southwestern Kenya. They are a cattle-raising people, and among them – as among many traditional peoples in eastern Africa – cattle raiding was one occupation in which men tested and proved their manhood. This song is meant to be sung by young Kipsigis warriors as they prepare to carry out a cattle raid against any one of the neighbouring communities, some of whom are mentioned here: Mangorori (line 11), Kipsiyabe (24), Masai (36), Jaluo (48), and Mayo (56).

Each line here shows the lead-singer's prompting, and the choral response '*oo wo ho*' from the other warriors. As in the Acholi song, we can feel the forcefulness of the humming and the stamping feet of the raiders. The lead singer's prompting is necessarily short, so as to leave room for the choral response that will complete the line within the structure of beats allowed for it. Notice the climax of the song in line 53. In such a song, clearly, war is upheld as a beautiful experience.

> *line 14 Arap* means 'son of'.
> *line 52 Kipranye* a local river.
> *line 55* A reference to the rocky landscape that is part of the Rift Valley.

Questions

How would this chant be affected if the choral response was taken out of it?

What does this song gain by the references to crouching warriors (lines 27–31) and to the colour of cattle (38–41)?

79 Sunjata summons his generals

Sunjata Keita is easily the best-known of the legendary warlords and rulers of the Western Sudan. A thirteenth-century leader of the Mandinka (Mandingo) ethnic group, he is reputed to have founded the empire of Mali by conquering many other neighbouring groups and bringing them under Mandinka control. His most notable victory in this regard was against the Sousou (Susu) led by their formidable chieftain Sumanguru (Soumaoro), who had first overrun the Mandinka (of Mali) and subjected them to his tyrannical rule. The war between Sunjata and Sumanguru was long and fierce, especially so because the two men were reputed to be well supported by magic and sorcery; Sunjata finally overcame Sumanguru, mainly because he found out the source of Sumanguru's magical powers and proceeded to destroy him at that source. This extract shows Sunjata summoning various allies in his preparation for the war to recapture the nation of Mali from Sumanguru. The emphasis here is on the heroes' zeal for war and their eagerness to prove themselves worthy of their valour and their reputation (see especially Tira Makhang's boastful display'.

   Stories about Sunjata and other heroic figures are told by professional musician-singers known across the Western Sudan under the name *griot* or *djeli*. In the olden days these artists were attached to royal households as court historians, among other related duties. They had to remember and record, in their songs, the names, titles, and attributes of members of the royal line as well as of important events and personalities in the community. With the decline of traditional culture, however, the griot is now a freelance (sometimes impoverished) performer singing his songs and his tales before all kinds of audiences, to the accompaniment of (mostly) a traditional harp (*kora*). His ancient role as a chronicler has, however, not completely disappeared. Among his audience – as he tells his tales in his community – there may be members of one or two of the old families reputed to have fought on Sunjata's side in those early days; the griot will stop to sing the full praises of the ancient hero just to make his descendant there in the audience feel proud of his ancestry. To a large extent this explains the large space given to the praise-names of the characters mentioned in this episode.

This version of the Sunjata story was told by Bamba Suso, reputedly one of the best griots from the Gambia whose work has been widely recorded. He has been particularly known for his concern for historical detail, which accounts for the elaborate references given to the respective characters and families in this tale.

This selection reflects some of the major features of the griot's narrative art. The first is the use of a repetitive structure that helps him control his details in the narration. By this method a regular stock of details, or a standard pattern of events, is used in various situations that are roughly similar; thus the narrator does not have to rack his brains too severely for fresh details between various episodes of the story. In this selection, for instance, the standard pattern in the summoning of the commanders is roughly as follows: (a) Sunjata calls for his commanders; (b) one appears with 1,444 bowmen to his side; (c) Sunjata is dissatisfied that a particular commander, Tira Makhang, has not appeared yet, and calls for more; later (d) the last commander is offended that Sunjata prefers Tira Makhang to him, thus forcing Sunjata to say why. This is the pattern followed throughout.

The second feature is the role of the griot's accompanist. Most professional griots are attended by at least one instrumentalist, one of whose duties is to help the leader out when he forgets a detail or to prompt him to elaborate or curtail certain details in his narration. Amadu Jebate performs such a duty here, thus giving this piece of poetry the proper flavour of a live performance. The third feature is the idiom of the narrative. The heroes of these tales are usually portrayed in superhuman terms; they are born under extraordinary circumstances, are equipped with magical powers and consequently do things that are beyond the reach of ordinary human beings. The griots are invariably convinced that the days of strong men have passed; crediting the heroes with extraordinary personalities is one way of giving their tales a unique appeal as well as ensuring that the great deeds of the past live vividly in our memories.

lines 3–4 Since the days of Sunjata, the Mandinka have spread far and wide across the Western Sudan. The Eastern Mandinka live in Mali (the original homeland) and Guinea, while the Western Mandinka are found in places like Senegal and Gambia.

line 6 Griots delight in using many names and titles in referring to a character. These are often (a) the character's own praise title, (b) the title of one or some of his relatives or ancestors, (c) nicknames. In many cases the meanings of these words are lost (having passed through so many generations). The character here is Kama Fofana.

lines 15–19 The character here is Makhang (i.e. king or chief) Kamara.

lines 25–29 Sankarang Madiba Konte, also known (among many other names) as Faa Ganda, was the father of Sunjata's mother.

lines 47–51 Griots love showmanship, and some of the names and details that appear in their tales are more often meant to impress the audience about their skill in manipulating their material, than as factual representations of history.

lines 52–62 Digressions of this kind are frequent in griots' narratives. Their main purpose is to explain aspects of history and culture that will help the audience appreciate the tale better.

lines 63–66 Gordon Innes explains these lines thus: 'Susu Sumanguru's father was a seven-headed [spirit] who lived in a hill. Sumanguru was invulnerable and invincible so long as his father remained alive, and his father could be killed only by an arrow tipped with the spur of a white cock. As is related later in this version. Sunjata's sister managed to trick Sumanguru into revealing the secret of his invulnerability, and having learned the secret, she returned and informed Sunjata, who thereupon arranged for an arrow to be prepared with a cock's spur tip. This was handed over to Sankarang Madiba Konte, and with it he killed Sumanguru's father, the [spirit] who lived in the hill. As soon as his father was dead, Sumanguru was easily overcome by Sunjata' (see G. Innes, *Sunjata: Three Mandinka Versions*, School of Oriental and African Studies, London, 1974).

lines 67–79 This section is printed deeper in the page because, while the rest of this poem is recited in a normal speech voice, in this portion the griot raises his voice in a spirited chant. Here Bamba Suso invokes the names of bygone Mandinka warriors – Sunjata (lines 67, 75) and the nineteenth-century leader Sheikh Umar (line 79) – in his lament that the great days, when men accomplished heroic feats and their griots enjoyed much respect, have gone for good.

line 80 Apparently Amadu Jebate feels his master is spending too much time on this digression and should get on with the facts of the story! But such a digression is particularly useful in helping the performer refresh his mind before going on.

lines 84–91 The character here is Faa Koli, known under several other names. He is Sumanguru's nephew, but defected from the tyrant because the latter had taken his wife away from him. Faa Koli now comes and joins Sunjata.

line 91 Bure (*Bureng*) is an area in north-east Guinea known for its gold deposits. The red eye stands for fierceness.

lines 98–99 That is, Tira Makhang has dependable stamina.

lines 100–130 More social history for the audience's benefit. Again, it is Amadu who decides that the digression is enough. This is clearly a carefully orchestrated performance.

line 146 Here Amadu calls for clarification so as to put the appearance of these generals in their proper perspective in terms of the sequence of action in the story.

Questions

Does the military life have a positive or a negative image in this poem? Use references from the poem to support your view.

How much influence does the interest of the audience have in this performance?

80 The fall of Kaabu

This tale refers to a much later period in the history of the Mandinka people – specifically, to the history of Kaabu, a confederation of states formed by Sunjata's followers who had moved westwards. Gordon Innes tells us about the subject of this particular poem: 'In this text Amadu Jebate describes the fall of Kaabu, which happened in the reign of Janke Waali, its last ruler. Kaabu appears to have been a confederation of states, under the supreme authority of the ruler of the state of Puropana, who had his capital at Kansala in north-east Guinea-Bissau. According to oral tradition, Kaabu endured for over six hundred years, and its founding is generally ascribed by the griots to one of Sunjata's generals, Tira Makhang, who moved west after Sunjata's victory over Sumanguru in the thirteenth century. Some areas of Kaabu had substantial Fula minorities and even the Mandinka griots themselves admit that the Mandinka rulers of Kaabu often treated their Fula subjects in a rapacious and heartless manner. Incensed at this treatment, some of the Fula subjects revolted about 1867, under the leadership of a hunter named Molo Ege who lived in the state of Jimara. They managed to secure the support of the Fula of Futa Jalon, under their leader, the Almani of Timbo, and after several years' campaigning this combined Fula force struck at Kansala, the heart of Kaabu. When his capital was on the point of falling to the attacking Fula, Janke Waali touched off the powder magazine, blowing himself and his wife to pieces.'

Amadu Jebate is not the same as the instrumentalist in no. 77, although he was closely associated with Bamba Suso and even lived with Bamba's son Baakoyo in the Gambian village of Serrekunda. He has not acquired a very wide reputation, 'probably because he is a man of retiring disposition, very modest in his bearing, and totally lacking in the showmanship and self-advertisement which some other griots display' (Innes). His performance here is certainly better controlled than Bamba's, with none of those elaborate digressions on history and society which we saw in Bamba's piece. But he has a striking sense of vivid and moving description. The attitude revealed here is also significant. The heroism of Janke Waali (supported, as usual, by magic and sorcery) is prominent, but we do not lose sight of the horrors of war, especially in lines 4–12. It may be that Amadu has to some extent been influenced by the modern society's resentment of violence and war. But this particular war was one in which the Mandinka lost to an invading Fula army; in reporting such a war, a Mandinka griot such as Amadu is just as likely to be critical of the experience as he is to commend the heroic spirit that goes into the fighting.

lines 13–21 In the olden days, the griot used to accompany the king to war, so as to (a) sing about the king's glories and those of his ancestors and so encourage the king (before the battle began) to live up to his name and his ancestry, and (b) record his victory or otherwise after the battle, for the benefit of future generations. The griot here apparently understood Janke Waali to mean (line 14) that he should leave, and didn't want to be denied the chance of observing and recording the events for the future.

lines 22–25 The prince and princess are meant to ensure the continuity of the royal blood. Notice also the effort that the griot Amadu Jebate makes in this account (as Bamba Suso in the previous account, no. 79) to stress the prominence of griots in earlier Mandinka society.

lines 26–33 The *jinn* is a spirit. It is this supernatural element that makes the heroes of these tales the sort of extraordinary characters that they are.

line 36 with added embellishments The griot usually had to be careful how he addressed his lord. This griot has obviously seen that Janke Waali is about to die, but does not want to say so directly. Amadu Jebate shows in this scene his sensitive understanding of human situations.

lines 38–39 Another guarded comment on the king's impending death. A *kooring* is

247

a man of royal blood, a prince. In the heroic society which these tales describe, the aristocratic youths chose to prove their manhood in warfare. Early death was therefore a frequent possibility: their bones were white, but not their hair (because they died young), and these young men were killed day after day.

lines 43–48 At this point one of the warriors from Futa Jalon saw a princess (no doubt Kumancho Saane, see below) and shouted *samo! samo!* (Elephant! Elephant!). According to Mandinka culture, if a soldier encountered a royal person alone in battle and shouted those words, it meant he was asking for the royal person's surrender. Notice the humour in this little scene.

line 49 The slave implies that the crowd of bodies is so thick there is no room even for hand-to-hand fighting.

line 52 That is, the gun. *Crazy* here either describes the wild destructive force of the weapon, or else reflects the Mandinka griot's sympathy with the fate of a Mandinka leader.

lines 58–59 Kumancho Saane was a Mandinka princess, a descendant of Tira Makhang (see line 117 in no. 79). It had been foretold to the Almani of Timbo that he would get a son from Kumancho, and that this son would rule Timbo after him. This may have been a strong incentive to the Almani's joining the Fula in the war against Janke Waali.

line 60 *kaatimo* charm, magic or poison.

lines 73–74 The Almani was of course a Muslim ruler, touched by religious qualms. Here is a fine touch of characterisation on the part of Amadu Jebate.

line 75 In Mandinka heroic tales, great warriors are often shown to have died an extraordinary death, being turned into objects like a stone, a bird, or a tree. In some versions of the Sunjata story, Sumanguru is said to have turned into a bird called a 'Senegalese coucal', in others into a stone at the foot of a mountain.

line 80 Griots, like most oral artists who deal with historical subjects, often try to convince the cynical audiences of today that the stories they tell are not fiction, but solid truth.

Questions

Discuss the poet's use of vivid dramatic touches in the tale.

In what ways does this Mandinka griot show his sympathy for the Mandinka cause in the war?

81 Take up arms and liberate yourselves
[an extract]

This song (titled *Tora gidi uzvitonge* in the original Shona version) was one of many used by members of the Zimbabwe African National Liberation Army (ZANLA) for enlisting recruits inside (then) Rhodesia for guerrilla war against forced white rule. It bears a close comparison with the Acholi war song (no. 77). Both songs show an equal sense of urgency, daring, and enthusiasm for facing danger. But whereas the Acholi song shows more a raw lust for battle (unwilling to entertain any questions or rationale), the Zimbabwe song reveals a greater sense of history (in invoking past heroes) and a larger sense of national commitment. This may be because, though this is oral poetry very much in the traditional sense, the liberation song was composed by enlightened men (fighting under the leadership of Robert Mugabe) who were not simply shedding enemy blood to prove their manhood. Perhaps it is also relevant to point out that, though we can feel the power of the warriors' determination even in this English translation, the original Shona version resounds even more thunderously than this one in its use of strong consonants.

line 1 *Nehanda* (sometimes referred to as Nehanda Nyagasikan). A spiritualist among the Shona, she is said to have been the first woman freedom fighter executed by the white people in the first armed resistance to colonial rule in the nineteenth century; she is thus regarded as the principal inspiration to the liberation war.

line 10 Herbert *Chitepo* was chairman of the war council ('Dare') of the Zimbabwe African National Union, the revolutionary party headed by Robert Mugabe. Chitepo was killed in Lusaka, Zambia in a land-mine explosion believed to have been engineered by colonialist agents.

Questions

What would you consider the basic musical element in this song?

Can you identify those words in the song that give a quality of *personal* warmth and commitment to the struggle?

82 The casualties

In March 1967 the former Eastern Region of Nigeria seceded from the federation and declared itself the Republic of Biafra, and in July the Federal Government declared a war that was meant to reunite the country. This war was fought essentially on two fronts. On the one hand each side tried to win as much support as possible from the outside world, so both sides sent out a good deal of conflicting propaganda through the media as well as through envoys to foreign countries. On the other hand there was intensive fighting on land, sea and air which claimed many lives and left many wounded. Now, there are less visible tragedies of the war than the more obvious physical damage done by the fighting, and these are what Clark has chosen to emphasise in this poem: for instance, the envoys spreading propaganda from one country to another are unknowingly spreading the evil of the war across an innocent world; at home, the conflict of propaganda is making Nigerians more distrustful and intolerant of one another; some people acquire the property and positions abandoned by others and thereafter live in endless fear that 'the owners may return'; and so on.

Written while the civil war was still raging, this poem reveals a humane and patriotic spirit lamenting the tragedy of a nation. It proceeds carefully by first granting the more obvious effects of the war: notice the repetitive structure of the first section which emphasises the relative insignificance of the more physical side of things. From the second section onwards the poet then enumerates – sometimes satirically (e.g. lines 21 and 38–39) – the less obvious but equally tragic aspects of the Nigerian crisis. The tone of the poem is mostly grave, and on the whole the language is simple so that it reflects a fundamental concern over a tragedy that affected all and sundry. The message of the poem, simply put, is this: in a civil war, everyone is a loser in one way or another.

line 4 Many of them have suffered such serious wounds that, despite medical treatment, they are dying little by little.

lines 6–8 That is, it is a painful thing to put out your hand to feel for someone or something, unaware it is no longer there. These lines vividly capture the sense of loss that war brings.

lines 9–11 On both sides of the war people were constantly arrested by government authorities on charges of collaborating with 'the enemy', and thrown into prison. Although the prison cell is a terrible place to be in, it could be seen as a safe refuge (*haven*) from the conflict and is certainly nothing like the total (*absolute*) exclusion from life that death (*the grave*) causes.

lines 15–17 Some people escape a bomb explosion (*shattered shell*) and run into what they consider a well-protected enclosure (*fortress*). But soon this place too is bombarded, and they are trapped within its falling walls.

line 20 *emissaries of rift* messengers of discord. This refers to envoys sent by both sides of the war to foreign countries to spread propaganda and seek military and diplomatic support.

line 21 *smug* arrogant but narrow-minded. The *smoke-rooms* refer to high class bars and restaurants that the envoys visit frequently (*haunt*).

line 22 *funeral piles* piles of dead bodies.

line 24 *wandering minstrels* A minstrel is a singer who performs from place to place – by extension, a poet or writer. Among the envoys sent abroad by the warring sides were writers like Chinua Achebe (to whom this poem is addressed) for Biafra, and Clark himself for Nigeria. In admitting that people like him are also casualties of the civil war, Clark is being perfectly honest. Notice the (*sm*) ALLITERATION in *smug* and *smoke*: it echoes satirically the comfortable circumstances of these envoys.

lines 25–27 The METAPHOR of *drums* provides a transition from the activities outside Nigeria to the effects inside. The end of line 27 fades out (...) to indicate the endlessly rolling sounds of the drums and thus the countless effects of the propaganda.

line 28 Notice the alliteration here: the harsh sounds of the *c* reflect the noisy conflict in propaganda between the two sides.

line 29 *niche* corner, position, e.g. in government or business.

line 30 This short line sharply captures a general sense of tragedy.

line 33 In the midst of all this propaganda, people can no longer recognise the real issues. Alternatively, the propaganda has made each side view the other as enemies so that it is no longer possible for anyone from either side to recognise a friendly face in the other.

line 38 *Taxes* were imposed by both sides in the war to raise money for the fighting.

lines 41–43 *kwashiorkor* is a disease, arising from poor feeding, which causes the body to become lean and pale and the stomach to be swollen; it is a common feature in places affected by war. A *camp-follower* is someone accompanying soldiers to war, usually assigned to carry a bagful of provisions, etc. – a metaphor that reflects the swollen stomach of a kwashiorkor patient.

Questions

In what sense do 'the drums overwhelm the guns' (line 27) in this war?

What are the various devices in this poem that give it a poetic effect?

83 The people went to war

For about fifteen years the people of Angola carried on a guerrilla warfare against the oppressive colonial control of their land by Portugal; in 1975 they won their independence. This poem, by a militant Angolan nationalist who was imprisoned by the Portuguese government for nearly the entire period of the war, records vividly the painful effect of the war on the average Angolan village. There is a haunting feeling in the picture of a village which has lost all its young men to the war. The portrait of loneliness is very strong here, but the poem ends in a note of defiance, and with confidence in the chances of victory for the forces of liberation.

lines 2–3 The image of *blackness* here portrays the misery in which this lonely woman lives.
line 15 There are no young men left to mend the thatched roofs.
line 20 Even the birds no longer fly.

Questions

In what ways does the poet paint a vivid picture of the village?

'Kaianga' may not come back, but 'the people' will. What does the poet imply by this subtle distinction?

84 Vietnam

For many years (from 1961 to 1975) the United States carried on a war in South Vietnam on the excuse that it was helping the government there to resist the take-over of the country by the Vietcong – the communist North Vietnamese. The war was particularly long because the Americans neither quite mastered the territory there nor could cope with the hide-and-seek, guerrilla tactics of the enemy. In the course of the fighting a lot of very destructive weapons were used which cost the Vietnamese many lives. In 1975 the Americans, worn out by an endless war which was not only wasting the youth of their country (who were constantly conscripted to the war) but was also ruining the national economy, were forced to flee from South Vietnam.

There is a predominance in the image of rice fields and flowing rivers in

251

this poem. In Vietnam, rice is cultivated mostly by women working all day long, with babies strapped to their backs, on fields watered by rivers. Many of these women were killed in the exchange of gunfire between the Americans and the Vietcong, but many were also cruelly massacred by troops from either side on the grounds that they were collaborating with the other. The poem vividly captures the cold-blooded horror in the killing of these Vietnamese women and their children, but it also portrays their undying spirit in a struggle they are convinced will last a long time. The endlessness of the struggle is well reflected in the symbol of rivers 'flowing on' and of seeds being sown in blood (to germinate into future struggle). The difficulty of the poem is due mainly to the fact that the poet is trying to reflect not only the complex nature of the Vietnamese situation (which neither the Americans nor the rest of the world really understood) but also the mysteries of the religious thinking (attitude to death, etc.) of this Oriental people.

line 3 *ashen* means white as the ash-tree (poplar). The whiteness here is the paleness which comes with death.

lines 5–7 Death had caused them to sit peacefully, like carvings.

line 8 The river rose (*heaved*) and levelled (*eased*) as it flowed over dead bodies; but the image also suggests a breathing process which indicates the continuity of life – in this case, the continuity of struggle.

line 13 That is, the river could not be stopped in its flow.

lines 15–16 A *booby trap* is a harmless looking object (e.g. a small tin) left lying on the ground; but it is actually a bomb and will explode as soon as it is picked up. It is used, frequently in guerrilla-type warfare, to destroy a careless soldier or civilian.

lines 19–20 The idea of a dead person sighing (as if alive) is a PARADOX, but it is an image intended to reflect the undying spirit of the Vietnamese.

lines 21–30 These women, working quietly in the rice fields, were often treated cruelly by the soldiers. They were hit with the gun, were asked to show the soldiers where the enemy had gone, and accused of betraying their defenders. The *dull* thud is the sound of the gun as it hits the head and makes the victim unconscious; the *metal fist* is the iron barrel of the gun used in hitting the victim's head. Line 24 implies that the questioners (*interrogators*) were not Vietnamese soldiers (raised on the rice cultivated by their parents) but Americans.

lines 31–32 The poet here laments the plight of the women trying to make a living from rice fields watered by river, only to suffer in vain.

lines 33–42 To *winnow* grain (such as rice) means to blow away the chaff and dirt (i.e. the *dross*) from it. In this passage we can see the poet using images of cultivation as METAPHORS. The dross here may be taken as the dead bodies of the women, now drifting down the river; the seed that is sown in blood is both the rice seedling and the spirit of the dead women being nurtured in violence (*blood*). Out of this will arise other Vietnamese children, well-armed – a *sheath* is the case that covers a sword – for future struggle.

line 43 This is a metaphorical way of saying that the country of the Vietnamese was teeming with people.

lines 44–51 These lines forcefully capture the quiet but determined spirit of the Vietnamese in the struggle. They may seem to have been overwhelmed by a terrible disaster; but they know it was destined to happen, and they line 55 are patiently waiting until they can triumph against it.

line 55 That is, to be recorded by historians.

lines 56–58 These lines refer to the young American soldiers sent by their government to fight in Vietnam.

lines 64–71 The spirit (*seed*) of resistance would be carried across the length and breadth of the Vietnamese nation by the corpses flowing down the river to their resting place (*House of Bone*). The idea of the seed being *sealed in the marrow* suggests that the spirit of resistance is well preserved and will remain a permanent feature of Vietnamese life. *Insane twitch* suggests quick, sharp movements, and emphasises (as lines 19–20 above) that there is continuing life in these Vietnamese even though they seem to be dead.

Questions

Discuss the words and phrases in this poem that convey vividly the physical horror of the Vietnam war.

Comment fully on the poet's use of the imagery of cultivation to portray life and death in wartime Vietnam.

85 Evacuation

Pol Ndu was in Biafra during the Nigerian civil war and here recreates some of the horror of that war. The poem describes a bombing raid by federal planes, which causes general panic as the resulting fire engulfs both people and dwellings. The panic of the moment is effectively captured by the very short lines of the poem, which leave a feeling of speed and breathlessness.

lines 14–15 Groups of people covered with fire and smoke, running about without knowing where they are going.

lines 16–18 Sulphur, which is a highly inflammable substance, is one of the materials used in making bombs. These people, caught in fire from the bombing, are therefore carrying with them sulphur which will cause more burning wherever they enter. *Tents* were set up during the war for refugees who had lost their homes in the course of the war.

line 19 The flag of the secessionist Republic of Biafra carried the symbol of the rising *sun*, signifying the determination of the new nation to rise in glory. This line tries to capture the spirit of that symbol: the tents will blaze not with fire (from the *sulphur*) but with the glory of the rising sun.

Questions

What effect do we get in the repeated structure of lines 7–11?

Does the poet aim to affect us with shock or with pity? Refer to words and phrases from the poem to support your view.

86 A militant's poem

Colonial rule is particularly objectionable because of the sorrow and the loss of dignity that it brings. The heartless colonial police suddenly swoop down on a young man suspected of planning a revolt; they throw him in chains, disgracing his manhood and leaving his wife or his mother in tears. The moment that the young man is able to escape and get hold of a gun, he is filled with an uncontrolled spirit of vengeance and feels he now has in his hands the power to right all the wrongs done to his people, especially his family. His is essentially a fight to recover a lost dignity. Although this poem – written by a Mozambican nationalist who worked actively for the liberation forces – recognises that guerrilla warfare has a larger national goal, its appeal lies in seeing the war of liberation through the eyes of the average aggrieved family.

Questions

Why does the poet take time to emphasise that his gun is made of iron (line 2)?

In what ways does the poet reveal his anger and determination?

87 Camp 1940

This poem is from the same volume (*Hosties Noires*) as the poem *Taga for Mbaye Dyob* treated earlier (no. 28). Here, however, Senghor concentrates both on the effect of the war on social life in France and and especially on the plight of prisoners of war (African and French) captured in France by the Germans. The real focus in this poem is on the discrimination suffered by the African soldiers. The poem begins and ends with a portrait of the damage done to the cheerful, happy life of French citizens in Paris. There is poetic music in this repetition, but the picture is really intended to set the tone for the contrast, which is emphasised in most of the poem, between the relative comfort of the white French prisoners and the harsh circumstances of the black prisoners.

At this time there was some debate among black intellectuals who were championing the cause of freedom of African nations from colonial rule. Some of them argued that Africans had no business fighting a war for the white man who was holding them in bondage. Others, like Senghor, argued on the other hand that the war against Hitler was a just war in defence of the freedom of mankind and Africans, despite the colonial situation, were right to fight in it. Senghor himself was one of these black soldiers. He became unhappy when he saw how shabbily they were treated in comparison with their white French colleagues, and in many poems he condemned the discrimination. But he stressed that these Africans were serving France not out of compulsion but out of a nobility of spirit. Here Senghor combines a lament over the prejudice suffered by the black soldiers with a portrait of noble-minded men serving with a sense of duty as well as pride in their black race.

In this poem, then, an African poet portrays the Second World War not in terms of the physical horror of the fighting – as Kariara does in *Vietnam* (no. 84) – but of the racial and political issues surrounding the participation of Africans in it. As usual, Senghor projects the glory of African culture through images of the

African landscape, with special emphasis on the village. Here, too, the frequent use of repetition evokes a musical feeling which helps to cool the racial sentiments encouraged by the war situation.

lines 1–5 German forces entered France in June 1940. This passage vividly portrays a country deserted by its fleeing youth and thrown into agony. The *garden* here, like the *fresh country of wines and songs* (line 4), may refer to the beauty and gaiety of France generally; but *garden* perhaps specifically stands for the famous Luxembourg Gardens of Paris, a park lined with flowers where young lovers could be seen every evening having a happy time. The *stormy evening* is a metaphor for the speed with which the Germans swept across France and captured Paris in late 1940.

lines 6–9 The village here is not literally situated in Africa. The image of an African village simply helps the poet to see the conditions in the prisoner-of-war camp from the position of the black soldiers in it. The camp is *crucified on two pestilent ditches* in the sense that the situation there is seriously affected by two disturbing factors which create a gulf (*ditch*) separating the black from the white prisoners: one is racial *hatred*, and the other is *hunger* which comes from the fact that the black prisoners were poorly fed (as illustrated in lines 10–11). Life in the camp is therefore full of dullness (*torpor*), but underneath this is the threat of a *deadly* clash between the two races. *Summer* here is a METAPHOR for the heat of anger felt by the uncomfortable Africans. Notice that, as in his earlier poems here, Sengor uses his metaphors in a tightly controlled manner.

line 8 The *barbed wire* which surrounds the prisoner-of-war camp is seen as cold (*frozen*, as ice) and unfriendly.

line 9 The implication here is that the four German soldiers manning the machine guns that protect the camp are particularly hostile to the Africans.

lines 10–11 Notice the PARADOX here between the noble spirits of the African soldiers and the degrading conditions in which they are made to live.

line 12 The capital letter in *They* is the poet's way of portraying the superior position and arrogance of the white French prisoners.

lines 13–14 In this very complex imagery, the poet seems to suggest that, with the coming of evening there is a chance that the anger (*blood*) which has been boiling (*sobbing*) in the black prisoners' hearts will settle, and they can now spend the night in relaxed sleep. Instead, they are made to watch over their white colleagues. There are racial undertones in line 14, but from here to line 28 the poet implies that the black soldiers performed their duties with loyalty and dignity.

line 15 *fleas* and *lice* are metaphors for nuisance.

lines 16–17 The African soldiers put their white colleagues to sleep by telling them stories and singing them songs, just as is done in the evening in Africa. But they (because of the war situation) have to do all this very quietly – without the background rhythm of drums and clapping hands.

lines 18–19 The black soldiers will know *that* music again only after the war (*tomorrow* stands for the future) – back in Africa, where they are free to sleep even in the afternoon and dream of impossible things. Line 19 is one of those romantic scenes of Africa that Senghor frequently paints.

Cavalcade is a parade or display, and *white* suggests a moonlit night (as in poems no. 14 and 15).

lines 20–24 The poet continues to surround the suffering black soldiers with romantic memories of the African culture and environment. The stars' *face* (line 22) is the sky. In lines 23–24 everything is so peaceful and tender in the night that both the grounds of the camp and the guards (*sentries*) are likely to let the African soldiers escape.

line 25 *Fatigue* here is a military term for a common duty (other than fighting) assigned to a soldier.

line 27 A *mess-tin* is a tin in which a soldier collects his food at a war camp.

line 28 Though it is now (i.e. during World War II) under colonial rule, the black race is destined to be free. This fact already confers freedom on the black soldiers, and they need not therefore seek any freedom by escaping from the camp.

Questions

The plight of the black soldiers is here enclosed within a portrait (lines 1–5 and 29–31) of the tragic situation in France. What does this tell us of Senghor's feeling about the soldiers' role in this situation?

Does this poem show Senghor as a man of peace? Support your answer with references to the text.

88 If death were not there

Rather than lament death as an irreparable loss, this poet thinks rather that it should be seen for the blessings it brings to many people. When a man dies, his property naturally passes on to relatives who may otherwise have had no other way of acquiring such things. This poem is more than a light-hearted statement about death: death, it seems to imply, is only part of a natural process – as one man passes away, someone else moves in to take his place.

line 13 In many traditional African communities, a dead man's wife (wives) passes (pass) on to his close relative, e.g. brother. If the dead man has no brother, his eldest son could inherit those wives; in some cases, in fact, a man's mother passes on to him nominally as his 'wife', if he is the eldest son of his dead father.

Questions

How do the questions contribute to the effectiveness of this poem?

Why do you suppose the poet puts emphasis on material wealth?

89 Mother! Mother!

Unlike the Acholi song, this is a *dirge* (lament) over a dead mother. Sung by a woman from Cape Coast, Ghana, it reveals a deep sense of loss and helplessness at the passing away of someone whose care and wisdom were deeply valued in life. The lament is remarkable particularly for the way in which it grows in intensity from the earlier to the latter part: towards the end the feeling of helplessness grows stronger and the mourner more frantic in her statements.

The poetry of mourning among the Akan-speaking people of Ghana appears to be a refined art. Here the link between the living and the dead, between one generation and another is fully recognised. The mourner, as we can see in this poem, not only takes care to mention her ancestors and their attributes (lines 10, 14, 17–19, etc.), but acknowledges a steady line of contact between the living and the dead (lines 10, and 21–22). The result is that in many Akan dirges there is a combination of a deep feeling of sorrow and a sense of an unbroken line of family relations.

line 2   *Aba Yaa!* a cry of lament, like 'Alas!'

line 14 *hails* calls (on you). The *Parrot that eats palm nuts* is the praise attribute of the ancestor, whose extraordinary power is further referred to in lines 17–18. The *Ancestral Chamber* is a special room in the house earmarked for the purpose of communicating with the ancestors. In some communities a shrine is actually set up in such a room, to which sacrifices are made and prayers offered from time to time (see the commentary on Senghor's *Prayer to masks*, no. 76).

line 19 *Grandsire* grandfather.

Questions

In what ways does this mourner reveal her sense of loss?

What effect does the reference to personal names have on this lament?

90 Zanu's death

As in the Akan dirge, there is here a deep sense of sorrow at the loss of someone very close. But, unlike the last dirge which was sung by a woman and which reveals a sense of utter helplessness, there is in this one a certain mature acceptance of death as an inevitable tragedy.

Amega Dunyo was about eighty-two years old when the Ghanaian (Ewe) poet Kofi Awoonor recorded this poem from him. Although he sang abuse songs (*halo*) like his friend, townsman and fellow poet Ekpe (see no. 30), Dunyo's main strength seems to have been in singing dirges: these were concerned with death generally, but he concentrated on lamenting the passing away of a relative and fellow poet named Zanu (also called *Ekuadzi* on line 8). These songs were chanted against a background of a chorus and the *adzima* drums which the poet had himself invented. Apart from the heaviness of sentiment in them, the songs are often dressed in metaphysical language, like the reference to death here as a farmer uprooting plants in life's field.

line 1 That is, he and his group are about to perform.

lines 3–4 A proverbial question, meaning: who is there that can resist the hand of death?

line 7 Life is essentially a journey in search of good fortune.

line 11 Death has visited our family.

lines 14–17 What is the use painting a beautiful picture of life after death, as the Christians do: will that reduce my sorrow?

line 18 Zanu is gone for good. In many traditional African communities, the state of dying is frequently represented as an act of being ferried across a river separating the land of the living from the land of death. This image is also found in ancient Greek mythology.

line 19 Compare line 2.

line 20 Dunyo accepts death fully.

lines 21–27 In these lines we see vividly stated the belief that no one ever comes back from the land of the dead. If it were possible, says Dunyo (line 26), he would gladly await the return of Zanu; instead, Death has shut the door firmly against his wishes (line 27).

Questions

Comment fully on the poet's belief in death as a final and inevitable tragedy.

Discuss the references in this poem that reveal it as a public performance.

91 Widow's lament

Although this Igbo dirge reveals the same sense of loss as the Akan and Ewe ones just considered, it is slightly different in attitude from either of them. While there is uncontrolled agitation in the Akan and a certain philosophical accommodation in the Ewe, there is in this poem a practical assessment of the loss entailed. Perhaps this is not surprising in a poem originating from the culture of the hardworking and commercially minded Igbo. In any case, this fact does not minimise the sense of sorrow in this poem. On the contrary, rather than waste her time in tearing her hair uncontrollably or reflecting in general terms on the tragedy of death, this widow shows a vivid awareness of how much in practical terms her husband meant to her and how deeply therefore he is being missed.

Unlike the Akan woman's lament, the length and pace of the statements here is evenly measured from beginning to end. The sentiment is expressed directly, not in metaphorical terms as in the Ewe lament. But the last instance of sorrow mentioned here (lines 15–16) has an imaginative effectiveness to it: the image of rain falling through the tattered roof to drench the woman is a symbolic way of ending this lament in a flood of tears.

lines 4–5 The *yam props* are sticks (cut from bamboo or other plants) for supporting and steadying the growing yam creepers.

lines 11–12 Among the Igbo, decisions on matters concerning the extended family are usually taken by men in meetings held periodically.

line 14 *Eke-ututu market* is the early-morning trading on Eke market day. On the four days of the traditional Igbo week, see note on line 30 of *The odo-*

masquerade (no. 18). Notice here how willingly the woman accepts, and relies on, the authority which tradition gives her husband over her.

Questions

What does the phrase 'in our early days' (line 10) tell us of the period of composition of this poem?

What do we call the kind of questions asked in this poem, and what is their effect?

92 The earth does not get fat

This Ngoni poem is an example of a well-known occurrence in African oral poetry — that there may be some difference between the theme of the poem and the context of its performance. The poem is undoubtedly about death, but it was originally intended for performance at wedding ceremonies; and nowadays it is sung in other situations like church meetings. The repetitive structure and the refrains of this song indeed give it as much a musical cheerfulness as a tone of affirmation and emphasis. However, the message of fatalism is clear; even if the poem is sung cheerfully, it may simply be that we are being warned to remember, even in our happiest moments, that death is the end to everybody — high and low, big and small. Notice the circular organisation of the poem: it ends (line 26) on the same note of affirmation on which it begins (line 2).

line 1   *The earth does not get fat* because, although people continue to be buried in it, it is never full. Among the Ngoni, wearing a head plume is a sign of seniority (age).

Questions

Comment on the effectiveness of the last four lines of this poem.

Discuss the use of contrasts in this poem.

93 Poet's lament on the death of his wife

This poem again treats death — especially of such a close companion as a wife — as an irreparable loss. The intensity of the mourner's emotion can easily be seen in the long list of terms in which he reckons the noise of his lament and the extent of his helplessness.

A more striking feature of this poem is its structure. As with the Swahili (see no. 59), Somali oral poetry reflects the strong influence of Arabic literary culture with which it has been in contact for several hundred years. Neither the rhymed endings of the original Somali version of this poem, nor the division of each line into two parts, has been retained in the English translation. But we can see some of the neatness and balance that characterises this tradition in the division of the poem into two virtually equal parts representing (a) comparative clauses, and (b) rhetorical questions. Line 8 indeed suggests that this is a poem carefully composed. The poet has had time to reflect on the ideas that he would use in the composition of the poem; with his stringed instrument in his hand, he now sits down and tunes the words to the patterns of movement and rhyme characteristic of the tradition. This is in sharp contrast to the loosely chanted lament of the Akan woman at the beginning of this section.

line 1 *yu'ub* a type of tree found in Somalia (the *gyrocarpus asiaticus*). To *geld* an animal is to cut off its male reproductive organs.

line 4 Causing the water to splash uncontrollably.

line 10 That is, those who were envious of the beauty of his wife or the happiness that she brought him.

Questions

Discuss the relevance of the metaphors in lines 11–14 to the plight of the mourner.

What two major characteristics of oral poetry are present in this lament?

94 But for death

This poem is an example of a lively Yoruba poetic tradition known as *ewi egungun*, i.e. the chant of the masquerade (*egungun*). Among the Yoruba, as among the Igbo (see notes on *The odo-masquerade*, no. 18 above), masquerades are featured on a variety of festive occasions like the taking of a chieftaincy title, the visit of a notable figure to the community, the funeral rites of a distinguished person, the dedication of a monument, and other such situations involving some form of celebration. Here again, as in the Ngoni poem discussed above (no. 92), we have a difference in spirit between the subject of an oral poem and the environment in which it is performed. The main business of masquerades on such occasions is to impress the audience by the attractiveness of their attire and their dance movements. The chanting of poetry or song is of secondary interest; in it they discuss a variety of issues, supplementing their physical attraction with the breadth of their wisdom. It is clear from this selection (especially the last three lines) that death is only one of the subjects treated in this masquerade performance.

It is, nonetheless, an interesting view of death: we see death here not only for the all-inclusiveness of its killing (as in the Ngoni poem) but also for the merciless force with which it claims its victims. Although the poem does not paint a happy picture, the liveliness of its performance is a fitting medium for the subject which it treats – the supreme power of death.

Oje is a performer, either the masquerade poet or any of his accompanying musicians.

line 1 These words are addressed to the drummer (named *Adisa* in line 5 below) accompanying the masquerade.

lines 2–3 These two lines refer to the masquerade poet himself – describing both his headwear and his peculiar music.

260

lines 17–20 These are the various kinds of spells or charms prepared by medicine-men.

line 23 *Papers* The reference is to a priest of the Christian Church or of Islam, the two literate religions known among the Yoruba.

line 26 *Ifa* See the commentary on *The lion did not perform sacrifice* (no. 58).

line 34 *Balaratu* is a corruption of an Islamic name for God.

line 36 The drummer (Adisa) is being asked to control his rhythm.

line 37 The masquerade poet now moves on to address someone else present at the occasion.

Questions

Discuss the *performance* qualities of this poem.

Do you think death is being praised or lamented in this poem? Make adequate references to the text.

95 Stop the death-cry

This poem is essentially indebted to the tradition of Ewe dirges which Kofi Awooner has recorded and studied; see, for example, *Zanu's death* (no. 90). But this poem gives us more of an insight into the proper context of dirge-singing than Dunyo's poem does. In the traditional setting, the body of the dead man is laid out in a chamber, where his close relatives and friends gather to weep and mourn over the loss. At an appointed time – on the evening of that day or a later day – an experienced performer (mourner), with or without a group, comes over and sings dirges and may continue this service until the dead man is finally lowered into the grave. Whether while lying in state in the chamber, or from the moment when he is buried, the dead man has effectively begun his journey across the river to the land of death. Having reached death's *home* (line 3), he now seeks formal admission into the company of ancestors.

For the dead man to be admitted into that company, however, the due preparations have to be made. The figure in this poem has obviously died unprepared, and this may have come about in a number of ways. He may have been killed, either by poison or by violence, before he had a chance to carry out some outstanding duties (like performing certain rites to his ancestors). It is also possible that he died from illness without doing the proper consultations. Among the Ewe, as Awooner explains in his commentary to one of Dunyo's dirges, a sick man must consult (through divination) 'the spirits, the gods and the ancestors about the meaning of an illness ... and its removal can only be achieved through a long process of cleansing and expiation; the herbs and roots that will achieve the physical healing are revealed by the gods themselves.' The dead man here has obviously not observed his traditional obligations properly. Consequently, he gets no sympathy from death's attendants (the dove and the crow); he comes back to see if he can do this, only to be distracted by the crying of the mourners.

The poem is beautiful for its dramatic use of the traditional mythology about death and for its well-controlled solemnity. The language also makes an

261

effort to reflect the tones of traditional speech (e.g. lines 1–2, and 9–10). The end of the poem captures the musical effect of a drum message.

lines 5–10 Addressed to death. The *debt* is apparently the sacrifices recommended by the diviner.

lines 13–15 The dead man's reply to the dove. Line 13 is a proverb by which he apologises for his dying so unprepared.

Questions

Try to explain the images of the dove and the crow here.

What does this poem tell us of the Ewe view of the relationship between the living and the dead?

96 Distanced

This piece comes from Echeruo's second volume of poems, *Distanced*, written during and after the Nigerian civil war. It was inspired largely by the death – in his early twenties – of the poet's younger brother during the war. The death of one so young and so dear is particularly painful. It leaves us with a sense of life unfulfilled, of a process not completed and left hanging in the air. That the dead man should be haunted by the same memories which haunt the living implies that he is not *quite* dead. There can be no more effective image than this of a life snatched away in its prime, and Echeruo has painted this image with a poetic technique for which he is particularly well known: a combination of economy of expression and intensity of thought.

This poem may be usefully compared with Awoonor's *Stop the death-cry* (no. 95) because they both deal with the plight of people who die before they are due. While Awoonor relies on traditional imagery and mythology to convey his picture, Echeruo leans heavily on European symbols – the 'tolling' bell, the 'hangman', etc. – to achieve an equally sharp effect. Between them these two poets give us a vivid picture of the dual character of African poetry today.

line 1 The way that this word is left hanging loosely – entirely on its own and grammatically unconnected with the rest of the poem – gives us a striking feeling of something suspended or unfulfilled. What is *tolling* is either (literally) the bell for the funeral service in the village church, or else (metaphorically) the memory of the dead man, which lingers on like the sound of a distant bell.

lines 2–3 Even if it were the hangman's bell, announcing the death (*doom*) of someone: that is, even if the bell was announcing the passing of someone being put to death for a crime he committed . . .

line 4 *Yet* still.

line 6 In older English literature the word *friend* was frequently used in the sense of 'relative'. It is possible that Echeruo has this meaning in mind.

line 7 *losers* i.e. those who have suffered the loss of one so dear.

Questions

What does the exclamation mark in line 6 tell us of the feeling of the poet to the idea contained in line 5?

In what ways has Echeruo conveyed the idea of distance contained in the title of this poem?

97 Gbassay – blades in regiment

Mukhtarr Mustapha is one of those modern African poets who demonstrate both a close attachment to their traditional culture and a deep concern for the situation in present-day Africa.

On a literal level, this poem echoes the language of initiation into manhood whereby some traditional African cults help young men, through certain fearful rites of physical torture, to overcome the fear of death. In one such cult which existed in the interior of Sierra Leone (the poet's country) during the fifties, young men were said to be tested with sharp razor blades and to utter fearful, manly cries of '*krrr, gbassay gbassay, krr gbassay*' as a way of fighting the pain. At the end of the ordeal the initiate could claim to have actually experienced death and survived its worst terrors: the last line of this poem may be taken to mean something like, 'Is that all there is to death?' Death no longer holds any fear.

On another level the poem represents a defiance of the terrors posed by present-day political leaders in Africa, who subject their opponents to all kinds of torment. By submitting himself readily to the limits of such a torment – torturing the body to the point of death – the victim is able to say to the oppressor at the end: is that all you can do?

On whatever level we read this poem, the message is still that death can be confronted and need not be seen as such a frightful experience; the poem is informed by the heroic spirit of traditional culture. The alliterations which the poet uses in a number of places (e.g. lines 1–2, 10, 14–15) have a touch of violence to them; and the frequent use of harsh consonants (*p, qu, b, d*) conveys quite forcefully the defiant spirit of the poet.

> *Title* *Blades in regiment* describes the line-up of sharp instruments used for torturing the cult member.
>
> *line 2* *quaint* strange or odd – apparently from the way the victim opens his eyes wide and fearlessly for the torturer.
>
> *line 3* *assagai* a long wooden spear used by Zulu warriors in the olden days.
>
> *line 4* *fibroid face* suggests a face that has swellings on a number of places where marks have previously been made. The picture we get is of someone who has been cut several times before with sharp instruments and does not mind submitting himself again to the same ordeal.
>
> *line 7* *rug needle* a thick, curved needle used for sewing carpets and bags.
>
> *line 9* *indigo* a purplish colour.
>
> *line 11* The image of a *tethered goat* puts this character in the proper light of a sacrificial victim.
>
> *line 12* *sanguine* bloody.

line 16   *hawks* are birds of prey, but the word is also used metaphorically for war-loving, aggressive people. It suggests that the poem may be addressed to the tyrannical leaders of the day.

line 18   *crater* deep ditch.

Questions

How is the effect of violence conveyed in this poem? Concentrate on specific words and phrases.

Several animals are mentioned in this poem. What feeling does this device leave in us?

98 What is death like?

This poem is a simple enquiry into the nature of death. Since no one (presumably) has ever died and come back to life, doubts about the nature of death, or what kind of condition awaits the dead after the event, will for ever remain in our minds. Whatever the case may be, the poem certainly does not show any obvious fear or frustration over the prospect of death.

Questions

What are the two different kinds of outlook on death that are revealed in this poem?

Compare this poem with the Acholi poem on death (no. 88).

99 Isatou died

The death of a little child, though painful enough, does not arouse as deep a sorrow as the death of a young man or woman, particularly because the child has not grown up enough to reveal certain qualities that may give his or her parents hopes for the future. So, although Isatou's parents bewail the loss of such a sweet little thing, they are at least consoled by the fact that she has left well before she could mean so much more to them. The short lines of this poem may be taken to reflect the brevity of the life that has passed away; but they are perhaps more likely to be intended to leave an impression of subdued sorrow on the part of the mourners.

lines 4–6   That is, before she was old enough to realise that her father and mother have suffered a loss, however small.

line 8   To God, that is.

line 13   *her* Isatou's.

lines 15–17   In some traditional African communities, professional or at least skilled mourners are sometimes invited to magnify the sense of sorrow at a funeral. The thought of how big a wedding Isatou would have had, had she lived, may be expressed in these mourners' lament.

264

line 19 *marble*, which is a shiny stone, describes the father's eyes as they are filled with tears.

lines 20–21 *spilt* the waste or loss which Isatou's death entails; *perfume* is a metaphor for her sweetness; *morning dew* suggests early youth.

Questions

There is a rhyme-pattern in the first nine lines of this poem, but it is soon abandoned. How does this device convey the message of the poem?

What is the economy of expression in this poem intended to reflect?

100 Post mortem

When a man dies, his body may be kept (if his relatives permit) in cold storage in a hospital mortuary; from here it is pulled out later on and dissected by a surgeon so as to ascertain the exact cause of the man's death. Even if the immediate cause of the death was a motor accident, it is the business of the doctor to establish whether the impact of the accident was enough to cause the death, or whether there was some other health problem that helped the accident to bring about the death. A body that has been stored in a mortuary is, inevitably, strikingly different from that of a man full of the bubble of life. This poem presents the reactions of the poet as he watches the chilling and depressing sight of a corpse pulled out of such storage and subjected to surgery.

The poet succeeds very well in conveying the horror and chill of the sight: notice the exclamation on line three. But his chief disappointment is in the way in which the imposing frame of a living man is so drastically reduced not only in size (line 6) but especially in image or prestige. Soyinka tries to convey this reduction in a number of ways. One, the entire poem is printed in small letters – no capitals, either at the beginning of each line or of a new sentence; two, the human body is put in the same class as 'beer' (line 2) as an object that can be conveniently tucked away in a refrigerator; three, there is a certain sneer here at the way parts of the body are toyed with by tools of surgery (scales, gloves, etc.). All these images clearly portray death as an unfortunate degradation of life. One other technique employed by Soyinka here is quite relevant: by sticking rigidly to the three-line pattern for each stanza, he apparently aims to reflect not only the frigid state of the corpse but also its effect in chilling us to a spot. In these various ways Soyinka conveys the loss of image, of cheer and warmth, that death brings about.

line 2 *bier* a case in which a corpse is placed; a coffin. The similarity in sound (yet wide difference in meaning) between *beer* and *bier* is called a PUN – a trick often used especially by poets and speakers to achieve an effect of ridicule or disdain.

line 3 In the phrase *submit their dues* Soyinka tries to reflect the reduction of the human body to a thing: pulling out a case containing a corpse is like pulling out a cash-box containing coins. *Harnessed* bound, tied.

line 5 *man-pike* i.e. the male organ.

line 6 *sub-soil grub* food substances under the soil. The dead man's organ is so shrunken (from the effect of the cold storage) that it is now not much bigger than an earthworm.

lines 7–9 The brain was taken out of the head and weighed, and the poet asks: was this intended to show, long after the man had died, that he may have known what he would die from? The positioning of *fore* and *after* is a deliberate PARADOX by which Soyinka rejects this unbecoming treatment of the human body. Compare the PUN in line 2.

lines 10–11 Either there is a deep wound on his body from an accident, or there is evidence on the skin of the disease that silenced the man (*stilled his tongue*).

lines 11–12 The gloved hands of the surgeon probe the body carefully, hoping to find the real cause of death and how to prevent such a tragedy in the future. Notice the contempt in the choice of image (especially *masked fingers*).

lines 13–15 Grey is a dull, cheerless colour, and aptly conveys Soyinka's feelings at seeing a body out of which all life and cheer has gone. This view of dullness is transferred to the platform (*slab*) on which the corpse is placed for surgery, the knife (*scalpel*) used in opening up the body, and even the state in which the body lies. *Love* here is used ironically – the cheerlessness of death is of course nothing to be loved; the poet is only urging that we accept it as an inevitable state of affairs.

Questions

How significant is the length of that last line of the poem to the feeling of the poet?

What would you consider to be the overall attitude of Soyinka to the image of death here: fear, distaste, or admiration? Support your view with appropriate references to the text.

Some general questions

NOTE: The numbers appearing in brackets after the following questions indicate the poems that contain a clue to an answer. Such poems are used only as examples; the reader may well prefer others.

1 How has African poetry in both the oral tradition and modern writing treated love as a relationship of deep value? (Nos. 4, 11)

2 Discuss any two poems which deal with either of the following topics: (a) love of family (Nos. 5, 9), or (b) disappointment in love. (Nos. 2, 12)

3 By an analysis of a poem, show how modern African poetry has used the theme of love to treat political issues. (Nos. 6 or 15)

4 Discuss any traditional poem of self-praise. (No. 16 or 18)

5 Exaggeration is said to be one of the major features of praise poetry. Discuss two poems, one traditional and one modern, which bear out this claim. (Nos. 21, 25)

6 Discuss two poems, one traditional and one modern, which show that praise poetry may be composed not for superior figures but for small

people who make honest efforts. (Nos. 19, 28)

7 Modern African praise poetry frequently contains an element of criticism. Discuss one such poem in detail. (No. 23 or 27)

8 Discuss the poetry of abuse in both oral and written African poetry, pointing out any possible influences. (Nos. 30, 35)

9 Discuss the criticism of social or political affairs in both traditional and modern African poetry. (Nos. 33, 37)

10 Analyse one poem which reveals an African reaction against foreign ideas or influences. (No. 36 or 40)

11 Discuss one traditional poem that combines an admiration of nature with a concern for livelihood. (No. 48)

12 To what extent does the poet, in both traditional and modern poetry, use aspects of the environment for projecting his own personal feelings? (Nos. 47, 55)

13 Discuss two environmental poems, one traditional and one modern, that comment negatively on the modern society. (Nos. 46, 49)

14 The traditional African philosopher is interested as much in independent reflection as in teaching proper conduct. Discuss two poems that bear out this point. (Nos. 57, 58)

15 Modern African philosophical poetry is influenced partly by traditional and partly by foreign attitudes. Analyse two poems to test this claim. (Nos. 62, 64)

16 Discuss any poem, traditional or modern, that deals with the artist's search for a voice of his own. (Nos. 67 or 74)

17 Divination poetry is basically an appeal to superior powers through the use of complex symbols. Discuss any poem, traditional or modern, which supports this claim. (Nos. 69 or 73)

18 Traditional African poetry frequently celebrates war as a true test of manhood or valour. Discuss one poem that illustrates this point. (No. 77 or 79)

19 Analyse one traditional and one modern poem so as to bring out their respective attitudes to 'the enemy'. (Nos. 78, 86)

20 Discuss two modern African poems that reflect two different attitudes to civil war. (Nos. 82, 85)

21 Analyse any modern African poem, in which the poet deals with a foreign war. (Nos. 84 or 87)

22 Discuss two poems, one traditional and one modern, that portray death as a painful loss. (Nos. 93, 96)

23 In African society, death does not always carry a negative image. Analyse any poem that supports this claim. (Nos. 88 or 97)

24 Traditional African thought accepts that there is a line of contact between the realms of the living and the dead. Discuss two poems, one traditional and one modern, which contain elements of this belief. (Nos. 89, 95)

25 If properly recorded, traditional African poetry frequently reveals significant evidence of the circumstances surrounding its performance. Illustrate this point with an analysis of one poem. (No. 79)

26 The dramatic beauty of traditional African poetry may be seen in the interaction between two performers. Analyse one poem that bears out this point. (No. 21 or 94)

27 Discuss any poem which brings out some of the major attitudes of negritude. (Nos. 15 or 76)

28 In assessing their relationship to European culture, African poets have adopted a variety of attitudes. Some have regretted that the experience of European culture has been a painful waste of time and have therefore rededicated themselves to their native land like prodigal sons. Others have felt that African and European cultures could work together towards building the modern African man. Discuss two poems which illustrate these two attitudes. (Nos. 7, 75)

29 Analyse two poems that reveal the poetic skill of any of the following: Dennis Brutus, Jack Mapanje, Léopold Sédar Senghor, Wole Soyinka.

30 Discuss one traditional and one modern African poem of your choice, showing what appeals to you in each of them.

PART FOUR
About the poets

We know next to nothing about the traditional poets whose works have been included in this anthology – except for Bamba Suso (no. 79) and Amadu Jebate (no. 80) of Gambia, and Amega Dunyo (no. 90) and Komi Ekpe (no. 30) of Ghana. Students and collectors of African oral poetry may be reminded that we cannot hope to understand that poetry fully until we can show as much interest in their composers and performers as we do in the writers of modern poetry.

ANGIRA, Jared. A Luo from Kenya, he studied Commerce at the University of Nairobi where he was editor of the literary magazine *Busara*. He also founded the Writers Association of Kenya. His published collections of poetry are: *Juices*, *Silent Voices*, and *Cascades*.

AWOONOR, Kofi. Formerly known as George Awooner-Williams, he was born in 1935 at Wheta, Ghana, in the Ewe country. He was educated at the Universities of Ghana and London and at the University of Texas at Austin. He has been director of the Ghana Film Corporation, editor of the Ghanaian literary journal *Okyeame* (which was devoted to the promotion of traditional African poetry), and taught literature at the State University of New York at Stony Brook. He is currently professor of literature at the University of Cape Coast, Ghana. His numerous books include *Rediscovery* (poems), *This Earth, My Brother* (a novel), *Night of my Blood* (poems), *Ride me, Memory* (poems), *Guardians of the Sacred Word* (traditional Ewe poetry), as well as *The Breast of the Earth* (a study of African literature and culture).

P'BITEK, Okot. He was born in 1931 of the Acholi clan in Uganda, where he had his secondary education. He later attended universities in the U.K., specialising in Education, Law, and Social Anthropology (the last of these subjects led him to research into the oral literature of his people). He was director of the National Theatre, Kampala, Uganda; taught literature at Makerere University and at the Universities of Nairobi and Ife. He died in 1982. Among his books are several volumes of poetry (*Song of Lawino*, *Song of Ocol*, and *Two Songs*); a collection of Acholi poetry (*Horn of My Love*); and a collection of Acholi folktales (*Hare and Hornbill*).

BREW, Kwesi. Born in 1928 at Cape Coast, Ghana, he was educated at the University of Ghana. He has also served his country as a diplomat for a long time, becoming ambassador to Mexico and to Senegal. Besides his collection of poems titled *Shadows of Laughter*, he has contributed poems to various literary magazines in East and West Africa, including the Ghanaian *Okyeame*.

BRUTUS, Dennis. He was born in 1924 in Salisbury, Rhodesia – now Harare, Zimbabwe, but moved with his coloured parents to South Africa in his childhood. There he was educated at Fort Hare and the University of the Witwatersrand. His protests against the apartheid regime led him first to house-arrest and then to eighteen months of hard labour at the penal colony of Robben Island. He finally emigrated in 1966 first to Britain and then to the United States, where he is currently a professor of literature at Northwestern University. His published collections of poetry include *Sirens, Knuckles and Boots*, *Letters to Martha*, *A Simple Lust* (which includes the earlier two), and *Stubborn Hope*.

CHEYNEY-COKER, Syl. Born in 1942 at Freetown, Sierra Leone, he was educated there and at universities in the United States. A poet of radical disposition, he has travelled widely in Africa, Europe, the United States, Russia, and Latin America. He has published two volumes of poetry – *Concerto for an Exile* and *The Graveyard Also Has Teeth* – and contributed poems to various periodicals. He currently teaches literature at the University of Maiduguri, Nigeria.

CLARK, John Pepper. Born in 1934 of Ijo and Urhobo parents at Kiagbodo, midwestern Nigeria, Clark read honours English at Ibadan University where he was one of the founding editors of *The Horn* (a student poetry magazine). After graduation he worked as a newspaper editor, studied briefly in the United States, then held research and teaching appointments at the universities of Ibadan and Lagos respectively. An early contributor to *Black Orpheus*, he has published volumes of poetry (*A Reed in the Tide*, *Casualties*, *State of the Nation*), drama (*Song of the Goat*, *The Masquerade*, *The Raft*, *Ozidi*), a memoir (*America, their America*), and a book of essays (*The Example of Shakespeare*), as well as a translation of a magnificent Ijo oral epic (*The Ozidi Saga*). He now runs a theatre enterprise in Lagos.

DADIÉ, Bernard. Born in 1916 at Assinie, Ivory Coast, he was educated in Dakar where he also worked at the *Institut Français* (now *Fondamental*) *de l'Afrique Noire*. He later returned to work as a civil servant in his country. He has published two volumes of poetry – *Afrique debout* and *La Ronde des Jours* – as well as novels and collections of African folklore.

DIOP, David Mandessi. He was born in 1927 at Bordeaux, France of a Senegalese father and a Camerounian mother. After a childhood and primary education in Senegal and Cameroun, he spent most of his life in France, where he contributed poetry regularly to the journal *Présence Africaine* and was part of the *négritude* movement. After World War II he returned to Senegal and taught for a time. Rather ill for most of his short life, he was killed with his wife in an air crash off Dakar in August 1960. His slim collection of poetry has been combined with some of his radical essays and reviews in a volume entitled *Hammer Blows and Other Writing*.

DUNYO, Amega. Born about 1892 in the Ewe country of Ghana, he is a descendent of a family of traditional poets. Both his grandfather and his father were famous poets. He founded a drum known as *adzima*, which is a combined drum of narrative and dirge. His major specialities are the *halo* (poetry of abuse) and the 'long song' dealing mostly with the topic of destiny and death. A good deal of his large repertory of songs is taken up with lamentations on the death of Zanu, his close friend and colleague in traditional poetry. He claims to have no *hadzivodu* (personal god of song) but to have inherited his poetic genius from his family: his success as a poet, he says, has been due to the gracious support of his household gods and his ancestors.

ECHERUO, Michael Joseph Chukwudalu. Born in Okigwi, eastern Nigeria in 1937, he had his secondary school education at Stella Maris College, Port Harcourt. He later read English literature at Ibadan University and Cornell University (U.S.A.), where he was elected to the distinguished fraternity of Phi Beta Kappa. He has been professor of English at the University of Nigeria, Nsukka and Ibadan University, and is currently Vice-Chancellor of Imo State University at Etiti. A man of quiet, philosophical disposition, he was founding President of the Nigerian Association for African and Comparative Literature. Besides numerous outstanding scholarly books on literature and culture, he has published two volumes of poetry under the titles *Mortality* and *Distanced*.

EKPE, Komi. Born about 1898, he started performing as a poet at twenty years old. He claims to have a *hadzivodu* (god of song) who protects him and ensures his excellence in song. His main speciality is the *halo* (poetry of abuse), and he has a reputation in the Ewe country of Ghana (where he was born) as a formidable lampoonist, so formidable that his songs have forced a victim or two to leave the village. He has performed through the length and breadth of the Ewe country and claims – although with very little support – to speak a large number of African and non-African languages. His drum of song is called *kwesiani*.

JACINTO, Antonio. Born in Luanda, Angola in 1932, he was very active in the liberation movement there and was consequently condemned to fourteen years' imprisonment by the Portuguese authorities. His collection of poems is entitled *Poemas*.

JEBATE, Amadu. Amadu was born in Casamance (in Senegal) in the 1920s and there received his earlier training as a *griot* (oral poet). He moved to the Gambia proper about 1955, where he attached himself further to older griots from whom he learned the historical traditions of the Mandinka ethnic group in the Senegambia. He has frequently performed with, and lives in the compound of, Baakoyo Suso, son of the griot Bamba Suso (see below) in Serrekunda, Gambia. He is a man of modest and retiring personality, due to which he has not sought (like most other griots) exposure in the radio and other media. He is particularly well informed on the oral traditions of the kingdom of Kaabu. In his performances he accompanies himself on the *kora*, a harp-lute of many strings.

KARIARA, Jonathan. Born in Kenya, formerly an editor with Oxford University Press in Nairobi, he now runs his own publishing enterprise. Many of his short stories and poems have appeared in the literary journal *Zuka* and elsewhere. He has also published a play, *The Green Bean Patch* as well as a critical anthology entitled *An Introduction to East African Poetry*.

KASSAM, Amin. Born in 1948 in Mombasa, Kenya, he was educated at the University of Nairobi where he was once assistant editor of the literary magazine *Busara*. He has published poems and short stories in *Busara* and other magazines, and some of these have been broadcast over the Voice of Kenya, Radio Uganda, and the British Broadcasting Corporation.

KGOSITSILE, Keorapetse. Born in Johannesburg, South Africa in 1940, he left that country in 1962 to live as an exile in the United States. There he studied at Lincoln University, the University of New Hampshire, Columbia University, and the New School for Social Research in New York. He has also held teaching and visiting positions in various American universities. Among his published collections of poetry are *For Melba*, *Spirits Unchained*, and *My Name is Afrika*.

LO LIYONG, Taban. A highly individualistic writer, he was born of Southern Sudanese and Ugandan parents and grew up mostly in Uganda. He had his university education in the United States (Howard University and the University of Iowa). Widely travelled, he has taught, among other places, at the Universities of Nairobi and of Papua/New Guinea. He has done considerable research in the oral literatures of the Luo and Masai, publishing two collections of oral literature and short stories (some influenced by the oral tradition) under the titles *Fixions* and *Eating Chiefs*. Among his collections of poetry are *Franz Fanon's Uneven Ribs* and *Another Nigger Dead*. He now works as a director of cultural affairs in Juba, Southern Sudan.

LWANGA, Susan. Born in Uganda, she has contributed poems to the East African publication *Pulsations*.

MALANGATANA, Valente. Born in 1936 in Marracuene, Mozambique, he has established a reputation as painter and poet. For his political activities he was sent to jail by the Portuguese colonial authorities. He has contributed poetry to the literary journal *Black Orpheus* and the anthology *Modern Poetry from Africa* (edited by Gerald Moore and Ulli Beier).

MAPANJE, Jack. He was born in Kadango, southern Malawi of Yao and Nyanja parents. He gained his first degree from the University of Malawi in Zomba; he also holds postgraduate degrees from the University of London. An acknowledged scholar in African oral literature, he has been editor of *Kalulu* (a Malawi-based journal of oral literature) and co-editor with Landeg White of the anthology *Oral Poetry from Africa* (Longman, 1983). He has published a volume of his own poems under the title *Of Chameleons and Gods*.

MTSHALI, Oswald Mbuyiseni. He was born in 1940 in Natal, South Africa. After his secondary education in Natal, he sought admission into the University of the Witwatersrand, but was denied by the apartheid authorities. He had to content himself with a messenger's job in Johannesburg, living in nearby Soweto. His only published volume of poems so far, *Sounds of a Cowhide Drum*, won him great acclaim as a poet but also the suspicion of the apartheid officials, who have subsequently placed him under house-arrest.

MUSTAPHA, Mukhtarr. He was born in 1943 in Freetown, Sierra Leone into a Muslim family of Wolof and Yoruba origins. Educated at an American university, he has travelled widely but has shown a strong attachment to his traditional culture. Among his works is a long dramatic poem entitled *Dalabani*.

NDU, Pol. Born in 1940 at Ihiala, eastern Nigeria, he read English at the University of Nigeria, Nsukka and (after the Nigerian Civil War) at the State University of New York at Buffalo. After teaching for two years at the University of Vermont in the United States, he returned to teach at Nsukka, but was killed in a tragic car crash the same year. As an undergraduate he was a talented and active contributor to the student verse produced at Nsukka partly under the influence of the poet Christopher Okigbo (see below). His poetry, which shows deep feeling for traditional forms, has appeared in several journals and anthologies as well as his only collected volume entitled *Songs for Seers*.

NETO, Agostinho. Born in 1922 at Içola e Bengo, Angola, he studied medicine in Lisbon and Coimbra, Portugal and returned to practise it in Angola. He joined a movement for the rediscovery of indigenous Angolan culture and in 1960 was elected President of the PMLA, a militant anti-colonial organisation. That year he was taken to jail in Portugal, but escaped two years later and, after a long guerrilla struggle, finally won independence for his country in 1975, becoming its first elected president. He died in 1980. He has published poetry in several Portuguese and Angolan publications and in a volume entitled *A Sagrada Esperanca (Sacred Hope)*.

NG'MARYO, Eric Sikujua. He is a Tanzanian poet who writes (like most Tanzanian poets today) as much in Kiswahili as in English. Many of his poems are represented in *Summons*, an anthology of Tanzanian poetry in English edited by Richard S. Mabala.

OFEIMUN, Odia. Born in 1946 of the Ishan ethnic group in the Bendel State of Nigeria, he read Political Science at Ibadan University, where he contributed verse to student magazines like *Opon Ifa*. He was a personal assistant to one of Nigeria's leading politicians, Chief Obafemi Awolowo, but has since returned to graduate studies at Ibadan. A man of strong radical feelings but pleasant disposition, he has so far published an excellent volume of poems under the title *The Poet Lied*.

OJUKA, Albert. He is a Kenyan journalist who has published his poems mostly in the *Sunday Nation*, a Nairobi-based national newspaper. He is also an active literary critic.

OKAI, Atukwei. Previously known as John Okai, he was born in 1941 of the Ga ethnic group in Ghana. After secondary school in Ghana, he took degrees in literature at the Gorky Institute in Moscow and the University of London. He has been lecturing at the University of Ghana, also serving for a short time as an executive in his country's administration. A most ebullient and cheerful personality, he enjoys reading his poems in public forums and travelling widely. His poetry, which has a strong rhetorical quality as well as deep attachment to the oral tradition, has appeared in numerous publications in and outside Africa. Of his published volumes of poems the best-known are *The Oath of the Fontonfrom* and *Lorgorligi Logarithms*.

OKIGBO, Christopher. Born in 1932 at Ojoto in eastern Nigeria, he was educated at Government College, Umuahia and read Classics at Ibadan University. After working as a secondary school teacher, a personal assistant to a federal minister, and librarian at the University of Nigeria, Nsukka, he took a job as West African representative for Cambridge University Press in Ibadan. During the Nigerian Civil War, he was killed fighting (1967) on the side of secessionist Biafra. In the few years that he spent at Nsukka, he provided some impetus to the development of student verse there, and was later — with J. P. Clark and Wole Soyinka — a prominent member of the Mbari cultural club at Ibadan and of the editorial board of the club's journal, *Black Orpheus*. Most of his published poems have been collected in a posthumous volume titled *Labyrinths*.

OSADEBAY, Dennis Chukwude. Born at Asaba on the western banks of the River Niger in Nigeria, he was educated at the Hope Waddell Institute, Calabar and later proceeded to study law in England. He has been very active in the political life of

Nigeria, contributing to the country's attainment of independence from Britain and later becoming the Premier of the Midwestern Region. Apart from writing his own poems, he has translated a few pieces of traditional poetry from his native Igbo to English. His collection of poems is entitled *Africa Sings*.

PETERS, Lenrie. Born in 1932 in Bathurst — now Banjul — Gambia, he was educated at the Prince of Wales School, Freetown, Sierra Leone and at Cambridge University. He studied and practised medicine for a long time in Britain before returning to practise in the Gambia. A man of varied talents, he has published a novel, *The Second Round*, some plays, and two volumes of poetry, *Satellites* and *Katchikali*.

RANAIVO, Flavien. Born in 1914 in the Imerina country of Madagascar, he went to school fairly late but took an early interest in the folk-song traditions of his people, especially that called the *hain-teny*. He has translated some of this into French and modelled his own poems after them. Among his published works are two highly acclaimed volumes of poetry, *L'Ombre et le Vent* and *Mes Chansons de Toujours*.

REBELO, Jorge. Born in 1940 in Lourenço Marques, Mozambique, he was educated at Coimbra University in Portugal. He has been an active member of the Liberation Movement (FRELIMO) that won his country's independence from Portugal. His poems have appeared in the anthology *When Bullets Begin to Flower*, and elsewhere.

RUBADIRI, David. Born in Malawi, he read English at Makerere University in Uganda and at Cambridge University, England. His deep involvement in the educational and political life of his country led to his detention in 1959 by the then colonial government. He later served as his country's ambassador to the United States, but has since been in voluntary exile. He has taught at Makerere, the University of Ife, and the University of Nairobi. Besides contributing poems to various periodicals and anthologies, he has published a novel titled *No Bride Price*.

SENGHOR, Léopold Sédar. Born in 1906 of the Serere tribe in Joal, Senegal, he had his secondary education in Dakar and his university education in Paris, becoming the first West African to graduate from the Sorbonne and teach in a French university. He served in the French army during the Second World War, becoming a prisoner-of-war in Germany for a time. He was later appointed a Deputy for Senegal in the French National Assembly, and led the group of African politicians who won independence for the French colonies in the continent. He was President of Senegal from 1960 to his retirement in 1980. A poet, philosopher, and man of letters, he was a prominent leader of the *négritude* movement which sought to uphold African culture and values against those of the hostile white world. Besides writing numerous critical and philosophical essays on aspects of African culture, he has published five volumes of poetry: *Chants d'Ombre*, *Hosties Noires*, *Chants pour Naett* (originally *Chants pour Signare*), *Ethiopiques*, and *Nocturnes*.

SOYINKA, Wole. Born in 1934 in Abeokuta, Nigeria, he was educated at the Universities of Ibadan and Leeds, where he took a degree in English. He has lectured at the University of Lagos, was Head of the Theatre Arts Department at Ibadan University, Visiting Fellow at Churchill College, Cambridge, and is currently Professor of Comparative Literature at the University of Ife. His deep concern for the social and political life of Nigeria has frequently brought him in conflict with the establishment, leading on two occasions to imprisonment. A distinguished dramatist, he has worked at the Royal Court Theatre in London and led his own theatre company in Nigeria (the 1960 Masks), producing as well as acting in his own and others' plays. He has published about fifteen plays and sketches, prominent among which are *A Dance of the Forests* and *Death and the King's Horseman*. Among his other writings are two novels, a memoir, a book of critical essays, and an autobiography of his childhood. His three books of poems are *Idanre*, *A Shuttle in the Crypt*, and *Ogun Abibiman*.

SUSO, Bamba. On both his mother's and his father's side, Bamba was descended from families which played distinguished roles in the military and political history of the Gambia. Born about the turn of the century, he lived mainly in the griots' village of Sotuma, but made frequent professional trips to the capital (Banjul) and other parts of Gambia. For most of his life he was closely acquainted – and sometimes connected in patronage – with many of the distinguished and wealthy families of the Gambia, some of whom were indeed his family kin; this ensured for him an authoritative knowledge of the facts of Gambia's oral history. He was also frequently featured on Radio Gambia, an exposure which ensured his widespread popularity as a griot. Many of his songs – about the historical figures of the Senegambia, including Sunjata and Janke Waali – have been recorded and released. Toward the end of his life he could no longer use his fingers effectively, so he left his playing of the harp-lute (*kora*) to one of Gambia's best harpists, Amadu Jebate (not the same as discussed above), while he simply chanted the tales. He died of a heart attack in 1974.

ZIMUNYA, Musaemura Bonas. He was born in Umtali and grew up in the Inyanga Highlands of Zimbabwe (the inspiration for much of his poetry). A lecturer at the University of Zimbabwe in Harare, he not only took part in the struggle that liberated his country (he had been thrown in jail by the white minority regime) but is also very much a part of the literary awakening there. Before publishing his own collection of poems, *Thought-tracks*, he had co-edited with M. Kadhani an anthology of Zimbabwean poetry under the title *And Now the Poets Speak*.

Index of first lines

Abolish laughter first, I say   89
All of this undulant earth   46
Armanda was a well-meaning lass   83
At that time, of the Fulas who had come with the Almani of Timbo   144
'Attack' traders were not good wives   79
Autumn burns me with/primaeval fire   104

Bamako!/Where the truth dropping on the leaf's sheen   69
Before you, mother Idoto,/naked I stand   132

Child's mother *oo wo ho*   137
Coward, crawl back into your mother's womb   137
Cross. Banner. Swastika. Sickle.   73

Dear God/get me out of here   130
Distance/explodes   153
Dlungwana, son of Ndaba!   64
Don't preserve my customs   133
Dry your tears, Africa!   46

Fortitude indeed we need   81
From the west/Clouds come hurrying with the wind   105

Give me the minstrel's seat that I may sit ...   112
Gods,/ancestors   123
Great Visitor, Son of Abdu   56

Here again, Igwekala   131
Hm hm hm. Beware   30
His baby cry/was of a cub   68

I am ignorant of the Good Word in the Clean Book   86
I am old and age-less   108
I anoint my flesh   96
I came with you as far as the village of grain-huts ...   51
I cannot blind myself   94
I painted my eyes with black antimony   40
I think it rains   107
I Who Am Praised thus held out in battle ...   55
I will cling to your garment like a wild grass seed: 49
Ibadan,/running splash of rust   102
If death were not there   159
In your absence   49
Into your arms I came   48
Isatou died   169

Kapitini, you make trouble   77

Laare./Opomu who teaches a dog how to hunt successfully   101

277

Let all of you stop the death-cry 166
Like the *yu'ub* wood bell tied to gelded camels that are running away 164
Look at this globe 118

Masks! Masks! 134
May the congregation here listen 58
Mbaye Dyob! I will speak your name and your honour 73
Morning smiles/In your eye 47
Mother/I have a gun of iron 154
Mother! Mother! 160
Mothers, I have been to many courts 80
My husband/Looks down upon me 86

Now I will chant a salute to my Ogun 127
Nyagumbe! Nyagumbe! 41

O crucible,/O furnace 92
O dawn/Where do you hide your paints at night 102
Offspring of Abilodesu, listen to my words 165
On the matting/bathed in the blackness 150
One thread of truth in a shuttle 111
Oolo of Iware Forest, why is it that we no longer see Fabunmi ... 62
Our Adzima drums have stepped out 161
Our ancestor Nehanda died with these words on her lips 147

Push a porcupine quill into/My quaint eyes 167

Relentlessly she drives me through the thickets of Time 52
River bird, river bird 117

See her caught in the throb of a drum 66
Six times the widow recalls the death of her husband 162
Sometimes I feel/The presence of space 115
Speak to me, child of my heart 43
Suddenly a stormy evening has laid waste the garden of lovers 155
Sunjata told his griot, 'You must summon my leading men,' 139

The agony: I say their agony! 90
The casualties are not only those who are dead 148
The earth does not get fat. It makes an end ... 162
The field was full of bruised babies 151
The moon has ascended between us 50
The old woman squats before a clay jar of *thobwa* 103
The path has crossed the river 121
The sky at night is like a big city 99
The sun spun like/a tossed coin 104
The sun used to laugh in my hut 91
The twisted wooden stump which crosses the road in a crooked way 113
Their guilt/is not so very different from ours 116
there are more functions to a freezing plant 170

278

There is a well   III
This is addressed to you, Stanislaus, wherever you are   85
Tjhutjhumakgala, beautiful thing of the White man   99
Today this place is full of noise and jollity   60
Tolling./Were it the hangman's only   167

Under Abraham's vacant eyes   67

We have come to your shrine to worship   129
We overcome this wind. *We overcome*   122
What is death like?   168
When I asked for him at Entoto, he was towards Akaki   39
When this frothful carnival finally closes, brother   94
Where has my love blown his horn?   39
Who is that making her steps clatter on the firm earth?   50
Why do we grumble because a tree is bent   112
With purity hath nothing been won   118

Yes, Mandela, we shall be moved   93
You man, lifted gently   95
You've been saying there's no one at Kholu's   61